A thoughtful, chatty book—reading it is like visiting, mead in hand and cross-legged on the forest floor, or sipping tea and nibbling dainties in an overstuffed chair, one fascinating person after another as they reflect, through their spiritual history, opinion, and advice, an exciting time in the evolution of modern Druidry and Celtic Neo-Paganism. Far from giving a single self-praising paean, the subject is pondered with care, scepticism, and occasional grumpiness from a multitude of viewpoints.
Mael Brigde, Daughters of the Flame, Brigit's Sparkling Flame

This book is a valuable resource for anyone interested in the history of modern Druidism. Hearing the stories of Druid leaders and artists from twenty years ago, shows us how much has been done, and how much more we still need to do! I will definitely be recommending this book for ADF's Dedicant coursework in the modern Paganism section!
Rev. Robert Lee (Skip) Ellison, Ár nDraíocht Féin (ADF) Archdruid Emeritus and author of *The Solitary Druid: Walking the Path of Wisdom and Spirit, Ogham: The Secret Language of the Druids, The Wheel of the Year at Muin Mound Grove, ADF*, and *The Fairy Races of the British Isles*.

Ellen Evert Hopman's interviews capture a moment in Druid history, in an array of influential voices from the time. Some of those voices have continued to define Druidry as it continues to evolve, some are less familiar to modern readers. For anyone interested in the evolution of modern Druidry, our recent history, and traditions, this is a must read.

Nimue Brown, author of *Druidry and the Ancestors* and *Druidry and Meditation*.

A Legacy of Druids is a fascinating selection of interviews with a variety of Druids in the late 20th century. Each gives the reader a different insight into opinions and viewpoints which have shaped modern Druidism and as such is essential reading for anyone either interested in Druidism as a religion or interested in Paganism as a modern cultural movement.

Morgan Daimler, author of *Where the Hawthorn Grows* and *Pagan Portals The Morrigan*

This extraordinary assembly of Druids reveals the paths leading to our native, spiritual heritage, without fear or favour. Deep and true!

Caitlín Matthews, author of *Celtic Visions*, past-presider of OBOD

This lovely book allows one to experience the true path of Druidry. The interviews present a picture that breaks away from the impersonal textbooks and gives an insight into the personal connection and dedication to the sacred path. A heart-warming connection to our global community.

Wally Dean Phillips, The Chosen Chief of the Secular Order of Druids

Ellen Evert Hopman brings us a magnificent tour-de-force of Druidic wisdom, knowledge and views from the elders of Druidry in this fascinating collection of interviews. Captured two decades ago, at a critical time in the formation of our everyday Druidic practices, we see the wide range of opinions, beliefs, political and religious views that provides the background to Modern Druidry as it exists today. In *A Legacy of Druids*, Ms. Hopman has answered all of our questions about where our modern tradition has come from and also gives us valuable guidance as we find our way amongst the well-trodden paths of some of our most well-known Druid leaders.

Gary & Ruth Colcombe, Celtic Myth Podshow

Ellen Evert Hopman brings her sharp, inquisitive focus to modern Druidry in this collection of in-depth interviews with some of the greatest contributors to the Druid movement in the late 20th century. *A Legacy of Druids* is a valuable contribution to the keeping of the Celtic branch of Neo-Pagan history.

Diana Rajchel, author of *Divorcing a Real Witch*

If you want to know what a wet Druid or a dry Druid are and how they are still relevant today, this is the book for you. By the way did I mention that it is fascinating, readable and a must have for any Druid's bookshelf?

Brendan Howlin, author of *The Handbook of Urban Druidry* and Druid tutor.

Ellen Evert Hopman has managed to devise a book comprising a collection of the Voice's of Modern Druidism, both past and present.

A Legacy of Druids, weaves together encapsulating, succinct views of Druidry, from historically, to practically and spiritually; from some of today's most renowned, authoritative names on the subject.

Including: Philip Carr-Gomm; Lady Olivia Robertson; John Matthews; Arthur Uther Pendragon; Dr. Ronald Hutton; and Isaac Bonewits; to name but a few, modern-day Druids sharing their knowledge and thoughts, both experiential and spiritual, via personal interview's conducted by Hopman.

Though the interviews are from a time gone by (1996), the kaleidoscope of information and viewpoints within give the book its organic flair. Hopman has adopted a very natural approach, in that all interviews have been kept pure, raw, and unedited, making the book an unusual though satisfying experience, as the reader feels immersed in the same sense as that of listening to a radio show or podcast.

Dorn Simon-Sinnott, Ireland

A Legacy
of Druids

Conversations with Druid leaders of Britain,
the USA and Canada, past and present

A Legacy
of Druids

Conversations with Druid leaders of Britain,
the USA and Canada, past and present

Ellen Evert Hopman

MOON

BOOKS

Winchester, UK
Washington, USA

First published by Moon Books, 2016
Moon Books is an imprint of John Hunt Publishing Ltd., Laurel House, Station Approach,
Alresford, Hants, SO24 9JH, UK
office1@jhpbooks.net
www.johnhuntpublishing.com
www.moon-books.net

For distributor details and how to order please visit the 'Ordering' section on our website.

ISBN: 978 1 78535 135 8
Library of Congress Control Number: 2015952166

A CIP catalogue record for this book is available from the British Library.

Design: Stuart Davies

Printed and bound by CPI Group (UK) Ltd, Croydon, CR0 4YY, UK

We operate a distinctive and ethical publishing philosophy in all
areas of our business, from our global network of authors to
production and worldwide distribution.

CONTENTS

This book is lovingly dedicated to Isaac Bonewits, Lady Olivia Robertson, Tim Sebastian, and all the other Druid teachers and mentors who have gone before us.
A special thanks to Ari Kinnehan, Nimue Brown, Veronica Hammond, Thomas Clough Daffern, Skip Ellison and Chris Funderberg for their support.

Preface by John Matthews

The Way of the Druid

It is apparent, reading more than one of the dozen or so books on Druids and Druidry, most of which have been published in the past ten years, that there is no single account of their history that can be regarded as one hundred percent accurate. Few scholars and researchers agree, and most offer very different views, which can be both conflicting and confusing.

The problem, then, is to identify what we can that might be called 'authentic', and to sort through the mass of impressionistic images that have constellated around Druidism in the past few decades since the 17th century – when Druidry was 're-discovered', and to a very large degree re-modeled, after a variety of styles and for a variety of reasons. Yet, what one finds, when one reads the extensive literature on Druidry, is that despite often poor or biased scholarship, there is an underlying thread of what can best be called 'spiritual truth', which somehow enables the subject matter to transcend everything that has yet been said or written about it.

Most of what we can claim, however marginally, to be 'true' of the history of Druidry comes from two sources: the accounts of Classical authors whom came into contact with the Celtic peoples from around 100 BC; and the insular writings of the Celts themselves. (As to whether Druids are truly Celtic is another matter, and is part of an ongoing discussion.) There is a third source, the evidence of archaeology, which adds a certain amount to the other two; but most of this is still so specialized that it is difficult to interpret and tells us virtually nothing about the actual beliefs of the Druids.

Both the primary sources mentioned above are, themselves,

problematic, the Classical because it was written largely by those with vested interests in giving the Celts a bad press (though that does not, of course, make it totally useless, one simply has to be careful).

The insular writings are problematic because they tend to have been corrupted by the Christian scribes who wrote them down (generally long after the event) and by 19th century translators (many of whose works have still to be replaced by more modern versions) who often imperfectly understood the manuscripts from which they were working. Thus there is a completely inconsistent use of the word 'wizard' in early Irish texts, where 'Druid' is actually intended, while many of the accounts of the later Druids are tainted with anti-Pagan propaganda.

What, therefore, is left, when one has stripped away all this detritus? More, I think than the 'romantic view' so often suggested by academic writers on the subject. Ultimately, all that one can say with any degree of certainty (and even here one has to be cautious) is that, from around 1300 BC, and possibly earlier, there were, in the lands that are generally considered 'Celtic' – that is all of Britain and Ireland, and parts of Gaul and Gallicia, a group of people who were perceived to be of great importance, and to some extent set apart from the mass of the population.

These people, who were called 'Drui' or 'Druids', a name which may possibly mean 'oak knowledge' or perhaps 'knowledge as old as the oaks', were of a priestly caste, not unlike the Brahmins of India. As priests, they performed the function of mediators between the people and their gods, as well as preserving the traditional beliefs and sacred history of the land. They also, almost certainly, acted as law-givers, as spiritual advisors, and as seers, whose task it was to check into the wishes of the gods and to report back to the people. As such they possess an aspect which one might, with due caution, call 'Shamanistic' – since many of the above definitions apply just as much to

Shamanic practitioners all over the ancient world.

Beyond this, I believe, it is difficult to go. There is an argument currently under way, which asks whether the Druids (and therefore Druidry) are a religion (in the modern understanding of the term) or a philosophy (in the Classical sense). Since none of the writings of the original Druids have survived (indeed they distrusted writing and committed all their knowledge to memory) we cannot really say. There is, however, a sense of what I would call 'spiritual philosophy', which continues to pervade the study of Druidry, both ancient and modern. It is, one might say, somehow right that we believe the Druids to have been of both a spiritual and a philosophical bent, and that the scattered relics of the Pagan religion that have come down to us (and of which Druidry is only a part) suggest (for example) a reasoned understanding of the natural world, and a sense of the underlying harmony of all created things, be they rocks, birds, fish, or people.

This may all be perceived as a 'romantic exercise' as several modern authorities have termed it, but it is something which is, I believe, inimical to Druidry, and a part of our consciousness in a way that is a product of racial memory (something else that many contemporary scholars would deny).

As I read the interviews contained in this book, I was amazed, as I have been before, by the huge variety of people involved in the neo-Druidic movement – if one can call it that. Thus we have American and Canadian Druids, and a whole range of British Druids representing most of the Orders. Almost all of the interviewees share a common heritage – a surprising number of them grew up in Catholic households – but all share in the heritage of Druidry; they love things Celtic, they see in the Druidic past a philosophy and a way of life which works in our own time just as well as it did for the ancient Celts. There are many points of disagreement, some doubt the veracity of the beliefs as practiced today. But under it all is a unity of spirit, which is what I personally find the most refreshing and exciting thing about the Druid path today.

I was especially struck by some words written by the young Canadian Druid named Cathbad, who wrote the following triad; 'Three elements to Druidry in the modern age: history, poetry, and mystery.' These three things do indeed characterize the tone of modern Druidry. Most of those who are practicing Druids are deeply concerned with the history of what they do. They are often poets themselves or love the Bardic mysteries, which are such an important aspect of Druidry. And they all appreciate the Mysteries that are at the heart of their beliefs. It is this threefold passion that continues to keep the spirit of Druidry alive in our age. These interviews are living testimony to a tradition that is as active today as it was two thousand years ago.

John Matthews
Oxford, 9 Dec., 1996

Introduction by Ellen Evert Hopman

Why this Book?

I have officially been a Druidess since 1984. That was the year when in casual conversation someone mentioned that there were still Druids walking the Earth and I immediately felt the resonance of the term like an alarm inside that had been waiting to go off. I was already an avid devotee of Irish dance, attending the regular Friday night *ceili* at the Irish Cultural Center in Philadelphia, Pennsylvania. I remember the first time I heard traditional Irish music on the radio as a kind of epiphany – something inside woke up to the rhythms of the jigs and the reels and I could never seem to get enough of them. It was a natural leap to the poetry of Yeats and A.E. and to the prose of Eleanor C. Merry and finally to the traditional stories and the *Táin Bó Cúailnge*.

People often ask me; 'Are you Irish?' To which my stock reply is; 'Only in my soul.'

I have felt so passionate about the political situation in

Northern Ireland that an Irish friend decided I must have been an Irish revolutionary in a past life. Yet I was born in Austria and spent half of my childhood in Spain, France, and Germany. I feel most connected to the ancient sacred stone sites of lands where I have visited but never lived – Ireland, Scotland and England, and I have even co-led tours to those places. The Druid path honors this connection to the ancestors and my passion is echoed by others following this tradition.

The Druid path honors the spirits of nature and I have been passionate in my defense of the natural world as well. I have done extensive political work and fundraising for environmental causes, my yearly donations going to organizations like The Nature Conservancy, and the Isle of Eigg Heritage Trust. Without the natural world no beings on Earth, animal or human, will have water to drink, air to breathe, or room to survive.

The Druid path also honors trees. I have spent decades writing about trees and educating the public about the medicinal, practical and spiritual value of these beings.

A Lakota grandmother gave me the medicine name Willow, yet I feel the strongest kinship with the oaks of Western Massachusetts. I am blessed to live in an oak forest and the trees have taught me much about stability and the ability to withstand the trials of life.

The Druid path encompasses the ancient traditional healing ways with prayer, meditation, herbs and water. I have been a professional herbalist since 1983, and a mental health counselor since 1990, lecturing and writing books on the subject, and training at least a score of students every year.

The Druid path is also a profoundly devotional path, honoring Goddesses and Gods as well as the spirits of the stones, plants, trees, birds, animals, and the honor of every human being. There is something within me that feels a profound need for the devotional path and in Druidism I have not been disappointed.

Intellectuality is a component of Druidism. The Druids of old were historians, lawyers, healers, poets, musicians, storytellers, philosophers, and political advisors. Since the age of five I have devoured at least a book a week, at times reading six or seven books at the same time. Most Druids I have met share this love of learning. Most recently this love of scholarship has spilled over to the internet where Druids across the globe participate in study groups focusing on Celtic culture, law and religion.

In 1996 I was the founder of the White Oak online discussion group that explored Celtic and Druidic ethics and Brehon Law. That group eventually became the Order of WhiteOak (*Ord na Darach Gile*) (www.whiteoakdruids.org) at Winter Solstice 1997 and I served as co-Chief with Craig Melia for five years. I am currently Arch Druid of Tribe of the Oak, an international Druidic teaching Grove (www.tribeoftheoak.com), along with co-Arch Druid Gwennic.

I also co-founded and was privileged to serve as the Vice-President of The Henge of Keltria, an American-based international Druid Order and the largest Celtic Neo-Pagan organization in the United States, for three terms. During that time I have met with and corresponded with Druids from England, Ireland, Scotland, Canada, Peru, France, Japan, Australia and Italy. Differences exist, but the devotion to the spirit of Druidry is the same, wherever I look.

In the book *People of the Earth* (Destiny Books, Rochester, VT 1996, now titled *Being a Pagan – Druids, Wiccans and Witches Today*) I interviewed Pagan leaders from across the United States, in an effort to create a forum where Pagans could give voice to their own opinions about their beliefs and practices. As Druidism slowly gained recognition, I saw that a forum was needed where Druids too could express themselves so that the public would come to know us more fully. At this time in history Druids are still a small sub-set of the current Neo-Pagan revival, with many different flavors and beliefs within each sect. OBOD (Order of Bards, Ovates and Druids) is attempting to be a

Universalist-style umbrella group, embracing all flavors, AODA (Ancient Order of Druids in America) is heavily Masonic and influenced by Romantic Revival British ideas, ADF (A Druid Fellowship) is Indo-European, The Henge of Keltria is Celtic, while the Order of WhiteOak and Tribe of the Oak are Celtic Reconstructionist, preferring to focus on the corpus of Irish material handed down to us from the 7th century. As you will see from the interviews that follow, there are also many smaller British Orders focused on worshipping at and preserving their local sacred sites. The one thing we all have in common is our reverence for nature and a passionate desire to protect our Mother Earth.

Some of these interviews were conducted in person, in England and in the U.S., and some were conducted by mail. Others were conducted over the internet, a practice that will surely become commonplace in the new century. There is a subtle difference in the way these various methods play out; at the top of each interview I list the method of information gathering for the interested reader.

As a single tree could never express the grandeur and power of a forest, many voices are required express the true essence of this ancient and ever new path. This book is dedicated to the hearts and souls of the Druids of today.

In the Peace of the Grove
Ellen Evert Hopman
New Moon, in the season of Imbolc, 2015

Foreword by Philip Carr-Gomm

The Legacy of Modern Druidry

To look backward for a while is to refresh the eye, to restore it...
Margaret Fairless Barber

Ellen Evert Hopman gathered the material for this book twenty
years ago. When I was invited to write the Foreword, I was
hesitant. Would anyone be interested in what some modern-day
Druids said or wrote two decades ago? But when I read the interviews Ellen has collected here, I realised that they articulate most
of the issues contemporary Druidry is still concerned with today,
and the insights they offer are as valid now as they were twenty
years ago. This in itself would be sufficient justification for publication, but in addition I found I could engage with the material
in another way. In reading the interviews, I had the benefit of
hindsight – twenty years on I could see what ambitions had been
realised, and whether any fears had proved justified. In addition,
I could imagine how a similar collection gathered today might

differ, and I could start to get some sense of what legacy modern Druidry might be leaving the world.

As the opening quote suggests when we look backward, we have the opportunity to refresh our perceptions, and this is what this collection offers – the potential to refresh our vision of what Druidry is, and what it can offer that is of lasting value.

Failed Predictions, Hopes and Fears

Let's begin with what this collection shows us about the contributors' hopes and fears. Every so often, someone calls for 'unity in the Druid movement' and this call can be found in these pages, and yet – or so it seems to me – this is a futile aspiration. Whether one draws analogies from the apparent inability of Celtic tribes to unite, or simply from observation of social and religious behaviour, it is quite clear that diversity is the dynamic that runs through modern Druidry, not the desire for uniformity, even of purpose. Calls for unity, or for gathering groups under an umbrella organisation, have never succeeded, as the history of the Council of British Druid Orders and various other initiatives, demonstrates. The fear, expressed by one of the interviewees, that this inability to achieve unity will harm the movement, has proved thankfully unfounded, and rather than attempting to 'unite everyone', it seems a far better policy to accept that this simply won't happen, and revel instead in Druidry's diversity, knowing that diversity is a key ingredient in a movement's ability to be sustainable.

Another fear expressed in this book has also proved unfounded. When the interviews were gathered, Celtic motifs had become popular, and concerns arose that a crass commercialism was exploiting a culture. As it turned out, the vulgar exploitation of these elements was simply a passing fad that continues only in a tired and reduced form in the overuse of images of Celtic knotwork. Instead, the popularity of Celtic inspiration has resulted in an enrichment in many fields, particularly in music and the arts.

Isaac Bonewits, who has proved such a seminal influence in modern Druidry, states in his interview:

> What I foresee is that within twenty years or so there will be public Pagan celebrations led primarily by Druids in most places, in every major and minor town in America. I see us doing publicly televised ritual on the Pagan holidays. I see us having a very strong impact on the environmental movement and vice versa. If anybody are the appropriate chaplains for the environmental movement it is going to be the Druids.

Twenty years on we can see that none of these predictions have materialized, and maybe that's a good thing. Druidry thrives as a sub-culture that has shown a steady growth, but not of the kind that would produce the numbers envisaged by Isaac, and as a result it has avoided many of the problems of mass movements. But the ideas central to Druid practice, acknowledging the need for a spirituality that reverences the Earth, and honouring the turning points on the Wheel of the Year, have gained a wider acceptance than any declared affiliation to Druidism. It is likely that Druidry will always represent a minority pursuit, and small, for Druids, really is beautiful. Even so, it can still act like leaven in the wider cultural milieu, producing an impact far beyond its apparent reach, and it has provided both inspiration and support to the environmental movement, as the popularity of John Michael Greer's *Archdruid Report* shows.

The Core Issues

If some of the hopes and fears expressed in these interviews have failed to materialise, what has been achieved, and what set of issues does this book bring to light? The first question that strikes me as I read through the chapters that follow, is: 'What keeps Druidry being a subject in its own right at all, when it has so many diverse manifestations?' The joke within the Druid community, 'Ask ten druids their opinion and you'll get eleven answers,' reflects this diversity, and rather than this representing a weakness in terms of philosophy or identity, I believe this reveals Druidry's strength. It is an approach that can bring together people with widely differing viewpoints, as this collection demonstrates.

Let's take the topic of how a Druid is to relate to the question of Celticism to illustrate this point. In these pages you will find divergent views – from the wounded anger of Kaledon Naddair, which holds to the now disproved theory that the term Celtic is a racial definition, to the approach of ADF, which sees the phenomenon as part of the great sweep of Indo-European culture; from the exclusivity of Celtic Reconstructionism to the inclusive universalism of groups like OBOD.

Those new to Druidry might find it surprising that there could be such a divergence of views on a topic that some believe represents a defining feature of Druidism, but at around the time the interviews were being compiled for this volume, the academic world of Celtic Studies was in turmoil. Malcolm Chapman's 1992 book *The Celts: The Construction of a Myth* had called into question the validity of the term Celtic, and the debate over the possibility that the term was so confused, so riddled with pitfalls once examined dispassionately, that it should be dropped entirely, continued for many years. Simon James's 1999 book *The Atlantic Celts: Ancient People or Modern Invention?* added fuel to the fire, and the existence of entire university departments was called into question. As one famous Celtic scholar from one of these institutions told me; 'We'll just have to continue fudging this issue if we are to survive.' They have survived, of course, but this re-evaluation of what we mean by the term Celtic is one of the major changes that has occurred in the twenty years since these interviews were compiled. Back then, many would have been unaware of the debate.

If the terms 'Celt' and 'Celtic' are hard to define, the word 'Druid' is problematic too, and one of the horrors or delights of this field of study comes from grappling with such questions. Are we dealing with a religion or a philosophy, an invention or an authentic spiritual movement? How those in the Druid community relate to these questions often seems to vary from one side of the Atlantic to the other. If I can risk making generalizations and exaggerating, to tease out some of the differing viewpoints expressed in this book, I would say that twenty years ago, many Americans probably believed that British Druids exerted no historical rigour, were duped by or deliberately ignored the provenance of Revival Druidry, and if English, engaged in cultural misappropriation. In contrast, those on the other side of the pond probably believed American Druids were unaware of the problematic nature of the term Celtic, and being separated from their ancestral homelands, romanticised Celticity. They failed to appreciate the value of Revival Druidry, and focused obsessively on the futile search for authenticity rather than on the pragmatic evolution of Druidry.

When Isaac Bonewits and others began writing about Druidry from the 1970s onwards, Revival Druidry was a sitting target. So much of the material being used by Druid groups in Britain seemed to be derived from material produced by a forger – Iolo Morganwg, a laudanum addict who had duped the world with his fantasies. The obvious approach seemed to be to ditch the entire corpus of Revival material, but what this ignored was the simple fact that more than two hundred years of practice makes a tradition, and tradition is hard to undo. Despite the attempts of Celtic Reconstructionism to create an authentic practice, British Druids stubbornly seemed to continue in their ways. In reality, great changes were afoot – a sort of triage and revision was occurring, with material being dropped or changed. In a parallel way to the revision of Wiccan history that was occurring at the same time, Druidry in Britain was coming to terms with its past.

Most Wiccans probably know now that their tradition was developed by Gardner and his friends in the 1950s, just as most Druids know that Iolo was a fraud. But many also believe that somehow these maverick characters tapped into information, and maybe even practices, that were either ancient or inspired, and whether or not this was the case, they take the pragmatic approach that 'it works' and that a tradition does not require a long time to gain traction.

I can think of three players in this process of historical revision that occurred in the years after these interviews were gathered: two from the United States and one from Britain. By 1999, Ronald Hutton, Professor of History at Bristol University, had already initiated the reappraisal of Wiccan history that resulted in his book *Triumph of the Moon*. In the opening years of the new century, Hutton turned his gaze towards Druidry, and in a research project that included a Mt Haemus paper for OBOD, and in two books, *The Druids: A History* (2007) and *Blood and Mistletoe: The History of the Druids in Britain* (2009) he reviewed the history of Druidry with precision and genius. Already, on the other side of the pond, Gordon Cooper, one of the founders of Celtic Reconstructionism had 'defected', and as archivist of OBOD, he busied himself reviewing all the OBOD course material with the eyes – as he put it memorably – of 'an authenticity Nazi'. He had been given this epithet in a message board spat. Hutton also scanned the entire OBOD course, again with a view to historical accuracy, and as a result of both these reviews, the material emerged enlarged and enhanced. While this process was going on behind the scenes, a third Druid, John Michael Greer, began leading the Ancient Order of Druids in America, and he openly championed Revival Druidry in his books and through his order.

All this has occurred in the twenty years since the interviews in this book were compiled, and it means that, in broad terms, as our understanding of the history of Druidry, and of the complexity of the meaning of the term Celtic, has deepened, the

14

tensions between Reconstructionist and Revival views no longer exist, or are no longer significant enough to feel relevant. Isaac Bonewits, and other contributors from American Druidry and the Reconstructionist movement found in this volume, had challenged British Druidry's complacency in relation to their history, and thanks to the exhaustive work of Ronald Hutton and others, this challenge was answered to the great benefit of Druidry worldwide, which now possesses a thorough and honest revision of its history. Twenty years ago there may have been the differences between the views of Druid history held on either side of the pond that I outlined in exaggerated terms earlier. Today these seem less likely.

Meanwhile, there are differences of opinion within the Druid community that are mentioned in this book, which still exist today. The two that stand out, for me, are between those who view Druidry as a religion, and those who don't, and between those who see Druidry as definitively Pagan, and those who don't.

We are back to terminology again – to what we mean by certain words, and if the terms Celtic and Druid are problematic, so too is the word religion, which to some offers food and drink, and to others seems like poison. Those who dislike the term religion prefer to see their Druidry as a spiritual or magical path, a philosophy, or even as a type of culture, which includes many dimensions including the spiritual and artistic. But others like to see Druidry as a religion, with its own clergy and theology. These two very different views are reflected in the interviews that follow.

In a similar way, you will find here contributors who feel Druidry must, by definition, be Pagan, while others espouse a universalist approach which allows the individual to find their own relationship with the spirit of Druidism, whether that be by following it as a Pagan religion or by combining its practice with another way, such as Wicca, Christianity or Buddhism, or by approaching it as one aspect of the Perennial Wisdom Tradition.

Rather than regretting these divergences of opinion, which exist today as strongly as they did twenty years ago, I think we should delight in them. Historians say that the old Celtic tribes showed more differences than similarities between each other, which is one of the reasons why they now question the label. But using the label for a moment, we could say that modern Druidry is truly Celtic in its inability to cohere, in the way it can embrace a wide range of approaches, in its love of braggadocio, in its tendency to enjoy cattle raiding (in its eclecticism and attempts at the *bricolage* beloved of all magical groups and even religions), and in its love of music, story, and celebration. Seen in this way, this book is indeed a celebration – a gathering in the feasting hall of the Druids!

And Druidry's legacy? It has become a vibrant alternative to the more mainstream religions and spiritualities – one which ironically may have been seen as an anachronism, but which has in reality proved itself to be more attuned to the current needs of humanity and the Earth than them all. As I write this, Pope Francis has just made a statement on the threat of climate change, and the Dalai Lama has also just spoken of it at the Glastonbury Festival. The Druids were warning us about this more than twenty-five years ago.

Philip Carr-Gomm
July 2015

Druidry of the Spirit

It is time for the old Earth spirituality of the Europeans to start coming back. We're in real trouble if it doesn't. People really need to start turning to their own ancestors for help. This is what needs to happen. Some people will be afraid of this. Why else did they burn everyone over there? If you're following the lead of the Old Ones and people are afraid or critical of you, then you know you are doing something right.

Anishinaabe, Elder of the Ojibwa

The word 'Druid' has for thousands of years evoked an image of majesty and mystery. Succeeding generations have seized on it and interpreted it according to the yearnings and needs of their time. The Druids of old were philosophers, poets, law givers, healers and peace makers. They were Priests and Priestesses and providers of religious inspiration and generational continuity for the guilds, the clans and the tribes.

This chapter explores the many faces of Druid spirituality as it is currently being expressed in England, Ireland, Scotland, Japan, and the United States. Celtic Reconstructionists, Geomancers, Theosophists, Pagans, ritualists and scholars have added their interpretations to the blend, offering a rich and varied approach to the sacred through the religious and philosophical path of Druidry.

As with all Neo-Pagan traditions today there is an underlying unity to the approaches – a deep reverence for the Earth and the kingdoms of nature, a fierce dedication to self-determination in the areas of personal growth and spiritual development, and a passionate devotion to the Gods and Goddesses of the Celtic pantheons and of other Earth-based spiritual traditions.

Philip Carr-Gomm

Interviewed April 20, 1996
Craftwise Conference, Waterbury, CT

Philip is the Chosen Chief of the Order of Bards, Ovates and Druids (OBOD), an international Druid Order with two thousand members. Philip has a degree in psychology and has studied psychosynthesis, adult psychotherapy, and play therapy for children.

Living in Sussex, England, he is the author of *The Elements of the Druid Tradition* and *The Druid Way*. He is also editor of *The Book of Druidry* and *The Druid Renaissance* and co-author of *The Druid Animal Oracle*.

OBOD traces its ancestry to the ancient Druids, which it considers to have been one of the major inspirations for the Western Spiritual Tradition. It sees itself as drawing on ancient inspiration – from the Megalithic people who built the great stone circles and henges, to the Celts who added their wisdom and artistry, and to the Bardic schools of Ireland, Scotland, Wales, England and Brittany.

The 18th century Druid revival brought the present form of Druidry into being – flexible and relevant to the needs of the day and yet rooted in the heritage of the past. About ten years ago OBOD developed an experientially-based correspondence course, enabling individuals and Groves to study and participate in ceremonies of a like nature, all over the world.

Can you start by describing how you became a Druid and what it means to you to be a Druid now?

When I was a child my father knew the old Chief Druid, Ross Nichols, also known as Nuinn. I first met him when I was eleven and then again when I was fifteen. I was just drawn to it. I suppose it was just automatic, but that sounds like such a technical word. I was fascinated by it. I ended up asking to be initiated so when I was about sixteen or seventeen I was.

I suppose being a Druid means a number of different things to me. There are times when the Druid inside me feels like an instinctive, sort of Shamanistic Druid. When I am out in the forest or someplace like that I can feel him living in me and wanting to work in me.

Then there's the Druid who is the thinker, the philosopher. That's when I am at home in my study with my books thinking about particular issues. That's another kind of Druid who pops up.

That's the 'wet' path and the 'dry' path. Those are old alchemical terms.

Oh really? I thought you meant in terms of the guy who doesn't mind getting wet, being outdoors! In England that would be true!

The wet path is the relationship with nature and the dry path is meditation, study, and those kinds of pursuits; both with the aim of enlightenment.

Great, the wet Druid and the dry Druid! Yeah, it fits. A friend was doing a spell check on her article and for Druid it came up with 'drip dry'. So we put a little cartoon in the magazine of these little Druids hanging on a wash line. So that's perfect. Thank you!

So how were you trained?

I was still going to school when I started to train. What I used to do was I would get off the train on the way back from school a couple of times a week and go round to my teacher's house. He had a house in Baron's Court. That's where Ouspensky lived, I suppose it was the 1930s or something, I don't think they knew each other. He would make me a cup of tea. It was strangely formal in a way. He would sometimes make a sandwich and then he would go to this big cupboard where he had all the teachings. He would take something out and he would read it to me and then he would explain things, on a paper napkin or a scrap of paper. He would draw a diagram of Stonehenge or do something to illustrate what he was saying.

Then he would ask me if I had any questions. Then we would talk about the ceremony that was coming up and that would be it. I'd go home.

Did your parents know this was going on?

Oh yes. Nuinn used to run a place called a Crammer's, which was a kind of private tutorial school for kids who failed. Winston Churchill went to a Crammer's. It's a place where there is no sport, just solid cramming, and five kids in a class. And my father worked as a history teacher there.

So my family knew about this, it was fine. I grew up in a family where both of my parents weren't Christian. They questioned things, they were Agnostic. I went to church in school contexts. I went to Westminster so I was singing in Westminster Abbey every morning you know, which was beautiful.

So that was the training. It sort of drove me crazy in a way because it was apparently haphazard. In other words I would turn up one day and he would talk to me about Stonehenge. I'd turn up three days later and he'd talk to me about the element of Fire, or something like that. It was only years later that I saw the way it all fitted together, when I worked at putting the OBOD course together.

Is there anyone who you are training right now in that way?

No. I don't know if you have read the foreword to *The Book of Druidry*, but in there I talk about how he died in 1975 and he appeared to me in 1984, I was taking a degree in psychology then. I was meditating one morning and suddenly I was intensely aware of him about ten feet in front of me.

He told me that the Druid material was really relevant to the needs of the day and that it needed to be put into the form of a distance course so that lots of people could read it. OBOD was tiny in his day, less than a dozen people, so it was very limiting because you had to go and see him.

Now, at any one time we have about 650 people actively doing the course. There are about 4,000 people who have started it. As far as members it depends how you categorize a member. I would say that there are 2,000 members.

Can you give an overview for Americans of the British Druid scene?

Well, there is the Ancient Order of Druids, which is a bit like the Rotarians or the Freemasons. They do have some ceremony, but they would not call themselves Pagan. They wear blazers and they raise a lot of money for charity. It is said that they have about 3,000 members. That is one type of Druidry which a Pagan American Druid would feel quite uncomfortable with, I imagine. They do have some branches in America. It's mostly male-only lodges with one or two female-only lodges.

Then there is the Ancient Druid Order, which is what OBOD grew out of. That is the group that you see photographed at Stonehenge. They are quite heavily influenced by the Golden Dawn. It's what you might call esoteric. I don't know too much about them, but they never joined the Council of British Druid Orders (COBDO) and they have kept themselves very much apart as a matter of policy.

Then there are a whole lot of much more recent Orders which are really quite small, who come together in the Council of British Druid Orders. One of those is the Glastonbury Order of Druids, the other is the Secular Order of Druids, who each have a dozen or so members.

Their main concern is having Stonehenge as a place for free worship. There is an ongoing debate about that that has been going on in COBDO for about six years and which has never been resolved. There are very persuasive arguments on both sides of the fence.

Put very simply, the argument for free access is that this is a sacred place and you would never bar people from going, say, to a cathedral on Christmas day for example. So to bar people from going to Stonehenge to celebrate the Summer Solstice is criminal.

One of them has taken the British government to the European Court of Human Rights. That's happening at the moment. It's being done by a fellow who calls himself King Arthur.

The argument on the other side is that Stonehenge has become a sort of political focus. It's become a focus of anti-establishment activity and even in the days of my teacher when they did the Summer Solstice there, people would come and throw beer bottles and it was an excuse for what are called in Britain the 'lager louts' to come and jeer. Unfortunately, it has become a sort of magnet for that kind of energy.

So the counter-argument is that now that there are so many people interested in Stonehenge, English Heritage have become the guardians of this site. And that it is appropriate for it to be guarded and to be used. They do allow private ceremonies, you can 'book it' for that.

I have done ceremony there and I was very surprised about how I felt. I went there prepared to feel uncomfortable and feel that we were making a mistake. When we did the ceremony it took me by surprise, I was very pleasantly surprised. I immediately thought, I want to do this again. This is good.

I think we have to accept now that we live in a world that is so full of people... I've been to Glastonbury Tor and it's been full of people camping out, drinking beer, cans all over and all the rest of it. If Stonehenge was completely open all the time there would be people camping there. You would be doing a ceremony and treading on beer bottles. That's the sad reality of it.

If you go to Chalice Well, part of the reason there is that beautiful influence, is that you have to pay a pound to come in and it adds to the protection. We know in magic about the power of the circle and the protection of the circle. Maybe places need it too.

What about the suggestion to have robed Pagan guardians at these sites?

Yes, but how long would it take the establishment to agree to that? The way we are looking at it now is that instead of confrontation in using the site, we are working it so that the feedback we are getting is; 'The Druids came last week and there was no problem with them. There was a very nice feeling from them.'

They have these security guards and we were all thanking them. You start to build up a relationship. Then maybe a year or two down the line you say to them; 'You see how we have been respecting the site. Could we now have a ceremony with 200 people?'

The Druids aren't the problem. The problem is the Travelers.[1]

Right. And this is where I think the other Orders who are lobbying for free access are seeing it from a different point of view. They want everybody to be able to go.

So unfortunately what has happened over the last few years is that these three Orders have pushed their agenda so strongly that it has taken up a lot of time and energy in COBDO. The council has become a self-referring system, spending ages talking about its own structure and mechanisms.

Now the British Druid Order and OBOD have started something called The Druid Forum. We are trying to keep to the ideals of the original council, which is to create a forum for people who are interested in Druidry to come and talk about Druidry. Not to get into voting rights and subscriptions, or presenting 'united fronts', which don't exist anyway because there is such a wide range of opinions. So the Ancient Order of Druids has left the council and the British Druid Order has left, and OBOD has left.

Another thing that's happening is that there is a phenomenon called The Gorsedd of the Bards of Caer Abiri[2] I am a member of that. I was initiated into it; I am the 'real thing'. I think I'm the only American, there's a fellow from Vermont, but he is British.

Oh good! That is growing every year. OBOD had a meeting at

Avebury in the conference center there. And there was a guy at the Stones Restaurant who asked if we would tell him all our festival dates because every time there was a festival they would sell out of food. And the people in the pub said they would lay on extra bar staff at the festival times. This last Spring Equinox was the biggest one – there were over 200 people.

Another thing that is starting to happen is camps. We have run a summer camp for two years around Lughnasad. Philip Shallcrass and Emma Restall Orr, of the British Druid Order, are doing camps now at Calme, near Avebury. Our camps are ten-day camps. The ones they are doing are two or three days. And cyber-Druids have come to England. We are setting up a web page which will be ready in the middle of May. The web page is great. The problem I find with lists, like the Order of the WhiteOak, is that if you are in 'overwhelm', as we tend to be, you get all these messages coming in. I just can't handle the mail. With a web page you can control it more.

Our web page has information about the course and the Order. We also have an art gallery with changing exhibits, a poetry archive – there is a Bard in charge of that, and we are going to try and develop a Poetry Cafe with links to other sites like the Poetry Society in the UK.

If people want to visit our site they will get there and see a Grove of nine trees and they click on the tree and that will take them to the poetry gallery or the art gallery. Then we have an archive – you have been asked to contribute, haven't you?

Yes, and I have.

One development is the growing number of links between Wicca and Druidry. A lot of Wiccans are becoming Druids now. Around the same time that this has happened, people like Ronald Hutton have started to look at the history of Wicca and Druidry around the 1950s. The fact that Gerald Gardner and Ross Nichols were friends and the Wiccans were celebrating the Fire Festivals but not the Solar festivals and the Druids vice versa.

After Gardner and Ross got together in the 50s, Wiccans started celebrating all eight festivals and so did the Druids. And so there are a lot of links. I talked about these links in my introduction to *The Druid Renaissance*, which is coming out in July from HarperCollins.

What I suggest is that there is some danger that we will dilute our traditions if we mix them in a haphazard way. But if we recognize them as discreet, in the sense of unique, to themselves and complete in themselves it will be alright. Some of us will want to work with both and we can combine both. Other people may prefer to only work in one tradition.

This brings me to something that I keep bringing up on the internet and other places. I am an American. I live in America. I walk the land here. I listen to the trees, I look into the water and into the fire and I feel very close to the Native American ancestors. I feel them around me, I hear them, and I get messages from them. I give offerings to them.

In American Druid circles this is often taboo. You are not supposed to talk about Native American anything. They will give you all kinds of elaborate reasons about why, about not mixing traditions and how there is no way you could possibly understand who these spirits were so don't even try.

And yet when I was in England and also through the OBOD magazine I have noticed that people are very interested in Native American spirituality. They want to learn about it and there is no problem there.

Sure. Last year I went to California to do some workshops, and the first night I spent in California I woke up at about three in the morning with this dream that became a waking dream, of a Native American man. He was suggesting what to do in the workshop. He was giving me Druidic things to do. I did it the next morning in the workshop and it was fabulous and it worked.

So I think that in the spirit world they are not so interested in these kinds of divisions as we are down here. There are so many similarities with us and the Native American traditions. The circles, the birds' feathers, the importance of the directions.

Another strange experience I had was when I first came to America. The day before I flew over to New York I had a dream in which a Native American teacher, a man, came to me and said; 'It's good that you are teaching Druidry in America because White people have to learn to connect with their own roots first. And once they have connected with their own roots, then they can come to us if they wish.'

So then I flew out and went up to the Omega Center in Rhinebeck, and I went into the staff room to have breakfast. There was a Native American woman sitting opposite me. She asked what I had come to do and I told her I was doing a workshop on Druidry. She then spoke the words of the dream to me. The only difference was she was female instead of male. It was exactly what had been said twenty-four hours earlier in England when I was asleep.

So I think somehow there is a paradoxical dynamic which we experience as contradictory, but it's not. And that is on the one hand we feel as if we want to root ourselves in one tradition and yet we also want to reach out to all these others. We see stuff in Tibetan Buddhism which is inspiring and which draws us, we see something in Native American religion, in Shamanism, etc. etc.

Or if you are just relating to the land. It's there.

Yes. And you feel it all around you. Sometimes you can get into a quandary when you feel a tension between these two dynamics. But for me it's not a contradiction. It's a bit like a tree that needs to be rooted in the Earth, but can also reach out and touch the sky and other trees and people with its branches. Just as we can have within us dependent needs and needs for independence.

To begin with it's kind of confusing when you connect with your dependent needs and you realize you just want to be parented and you feel very dependent. But you also feel that you want to be independent and go out in the world and do things.

You think how can these two drives exist within me? Then of course you come to realize you can have both, it's okay.

I think we can have a real interest in Druidry and we can practice Druidry and we can love Druidry and we can think of ourselves as Druids. But we can also be interested in and connect with Native American traditions and not be too concerned about the divisions.

You know how OBOD has created a ritual form and Keltria has created a ritual form and ADF has created a ritual form. I think what really raises people's hackles is when you are doing a Druid ritual form and you then start to bring in Native American things.

Yes. I understand that. But I don't have much experience of people doing that so I don't know what it would be like for me.

The best student that I ever had was half Lakota Sioux. She was so connected. When she was talking about Fire she wasn't just talking about it, she was really there with it. We would offer tobacco and we would offer sage and we would offer mead.

For me, because of these experiences with the dreams and coming here, I think there is a kind of bridge-building work to be done. I talked a little bit with a chap called Ed McGaa who has written a book called *Rainbow Tribe*. He is very interested in the connections between Native American religion and Druid tradition.

That brings me to another point. I think that the way I see Druidry in Britain is different to the way many people see it in America. Here I see a lot of Reconstructionism where people are trying to somehow reconstruct Druidry. In OBOD we have a different view to it which is this – that it's very easy to see Druidry as something that existed in the past. We have a few strands that have come down to us in the present day, and we are trying to reconstruct it and revive it.

The problem with that is there is so little material, and also that it is kind of depressing because with every day that passes, the source of your tradition is getting further and further away from you.

But I see Druidry as existing in the spiritual world. And that over thousands of years people have responded to this source in different ways. So you have the pre-Celtic proto-Druids who built Stonehenge and the megalithic monuments. You have the classical Druids of the Celtic period. And then you have the Bardic schools that existed up until the 18th century. And then you have the revival in the 18th century.

Each time had different emphases. Some were influenced by Freemasonry or the Golden Dawn or whatever. But they all were somehow connecting to this spirit of Druidry. So when we look at Druidry in that sense, it becomes something that is in the future rather than the past. Something that we are working towards, that exists in the spiritual world.

That is a much more empowering idea. It means that our task is to connect with the spiritual source and to reflect it as faithfully as we can, using historical material, but also our present day circumstances as well. Not somehow considering the present as inferior to the past. I think some of us have a subtle inferiority complex because we are living today as opposed to yesterday. In the end that isn't productive.

If I could only write about one thing, I think that would be my message. Don't see the source of Druidry as being in the past. See it as being in the spiritual world. Live with this idea for a few months and see.

I think we in America are doing that too or else we wouldn't feel so inspired.

I think one of the nice things about Druidry is this huge diversity of opinion. You can get some guy who is a Christian and who wears a blazer and who is a Druid, and you can get a guy with rings in his nose and long hair who is a Pagan and a Druid and who does completely different things. He walks barefoot from Avebury to Stonehenge. And yet they are somehow inspired by the same source, which is fabulous.

Mael Brigde
Interviewed September 3, 1996
Vancouver, Canada
Via internet

Mael Brigde is the founder of the Daughters of the Flame, a flame-tending group centered on the Goddess and Saint Brigit who under various names was honored throughout much of the Celtic world. She has contributed to a number of Pagan magazines, books, and anthologies, most recently Courtney Weber's *Brigid: History, Mystery, and Magick of the Celtic Goddess* (2015). For two decades she published a newsletter for the Daughters of the Flame, and she maintains the blog Brigit's Sparkling Flame, featuring Brigit-related news, links, reviews, and so on.

The Irish triple Goddess Brigit is patron of smithcraft, healing, and poetry, and the Daughters of the Flame emphasize these aspects to varying degrees in their individual practice.

According to the 11th century writer, Gerald of Wales, a perpetual fire was kept by Saint Brigit and her nuns, sheltered by hedges, with access forbidden to men. Saint Brigit was also associated with healing wells and sacred springs. The women who tended the flames had to use a bellows or a fan, never their mouths, to spark the fire. It was said that after Saint Brigit died, on February 1, 525 CE, nineteen nuns alternated caring for the fire and that on the twentieth day the saint herself kept the flames alive.

Brigit's Fire was ordered extinguished in 1220 by the Archbishop of London. It was rekindled and kept going until the reign of Henry VIII (1509-1541). On Imbolc, 1993, in Vancouver, Canada, the Daughters of the Flame lit a new perpetual fire for Brigit, which continues to burn. Unknown to them, on the same day in Kildare, Ireland, the Catholic Brigidine Sisters lit her flame anew, as well.

In the nearly twenty years since this interview was conducted, women in many countries have taken shifts with the Daughters of the Flame, and many other flame-tending groups have arisen. Mael Brigde remains committed to Brigit and has deepened her studies of the Goddess and Saint and the culture from which she sprang. She is working on a book of devotion to Brigit.

When did you first hear about Celtic spirituality and what drew you to it?

I can't remember first hearing about Celtic spirituality. It just kind of seeped in from the medieval romances and myths and the Scottish and Irish songs that were part of childhood for me. I read a fair bit about not only Celtic but Sumerian religion and when I was twenty or so wished sorely that such religions still existed. Then I met my friend Louise, who informed me that they indeed do, and in short order I was a practicing Pagan. This took a little courage, though, and a little work to overcome early training. I was raised Catholic and besides having the fear of Paganism instilled in me at an early age, I had a much larger problem with the idea of letting any deity overwhelm my life the way the Catholic God had been set up to do for so long. This God had been given by the people around me the authority to condemn much that seemed natural and life-giving, particularly my right to think for myself and to value my intelligence, to believe in my own assessment of a situation over the assessment of someone else.

He'd had stuffed into his mouth prejudices and unfairness of all sorts, and had been given the authority to treat all with disrespect and violence whenever He wanted, as had His representatives – the clergy, and adults generally. In His name I was taught to dislike my body, to belittle other religions, to perceive humans as separate from – cleaved from – nature, to expect cruelty and power from men and shame and foolishness from women. I figured out early that these ideas were not only wrong, but damaging, and I set about replacing them with ideas that celebrated and valued me, my femaleness, my connection to nature and to other human beings on an equal footing, and so on. But early brands burn deep. I had a hell of a time shaking Him off.

My father was a Protestant; my mother was a Roman Catholic. We are a blend of French, Belgian, Irish and Scottish. My father's side of the family was less religious than my mother's, but the prejudice of Irish Protestants for Catholics was present – his family tried to stop the marriage. My mother's French Canadian mother was and is devotedly Catholic, and so even though my parents themselves were not heavily into Christianity my siblings and I were treated to the full package of catechism, church, and, from time to time, parochial school.

Canada itself was largely Catholic in those years, the late 1950s and early 60s. The ideology was everywhere, although the public schools, perhaps because they were administered by the middle class, whereas the Catholic population was overwhelmingly working class, were oriented toward Protestantism.

I didn't dislike everything about being Catholic, or even about the religious life. I make the distinction because there is a sense of community and identity to being Catholic that is much more than religion, and I did indeed identify as Catholic. I hated the queen. I loved Bernadette Devlin, a spokeswoman for the IRA, for her assertive pro-Irish stance.

I found the nuns by and large to be the most sympathetic and lively adults I was in contact with, and whether I ran away from home or skinned a knee, they treated me kindly. So in the early days I fantasized with the rest of my sisters about what sort of nun I'd be, and what habit I'd wear (this was pre-1964 with its great reforms in the Catholic Church) and whether I'd be cloistered or a teaching sister, or what. But I didn't take it too seriously.

What I did take seriously was the sense of community where

I otherwise lacked one, and to this day if someone attacks Catholics I feel personally attacked, and long for understanding to evolve on both sides of this too tall fence. It was with a huge sense of personal betrayal, then, that I encountered the anti-abortion, anti-choice, woman-blaming attitudes that eventually drove me away from the Church and from Christianity altogether.

Another thing I valued about Catholicism, without putting a name to it in the early days, was the ritual. This was part of what drew me into Paganism. I mourned the loss of symbol and celebration that marked important times of year, and when I saw new and, to my eyes, healthier traditions to celebrate, I seized on them.

Currently I am in a period of little ritual and very little pomp or formal acknowledgement of the passages of life. But I now have a strong and nourishing repertoire available to me, and when the need is there, it is extremely rewarding. But let me be frank, although I studied the Celts in some detail at one stage, I am not an expert in Celtic religion.

What actually pushed me into following a Celtic path and specifically becoming a celebrant of Brigit was a trip I made to a Catholic monastery outside of Perth, Australia, in 1985.

On the way to the monastery I passed a high school called Saint Brigit's. I had been into a couple of churches with shrines to St. Brigit, in Melbourne and elsewhere, and I found myself praying to Her as Goddess more pointedly than I had in the past. When I passed the school I said to my companion that I wondered what the students would think if they knew their school was named after a Pagan Goddess?

The idea lit a fire under me, if you'll pardon the expression, and a few months later, I came home to Canada and wrote a little fanzine about Her – one half was about Brigit the Saint, the other was about Brigit the Goddess. I put it in 'AWA' – 'A Woman's APA' (apa=amateur press association) in which I was briefly a member

– and as a result was invited into 'Pagan APA', where I joined a discourse that helped to clarify and form my ideas.

It's now 1996. About four years ago I got the idea that it would be a very good thing if the perpetual flame that had burned in Kildare for hundreds of years might again be lit. Now, I live in Canada, not Ireland, and I don't have a bevy of Priestesses to tend a flame night and day, but I do have a database and a friend who knows computers inside out (Howard Cherniack, who was a founding member of the Reformed Druids back in his university days), and a number of Pagan friends, so eventually this we got organized and birthed the Daughters of the Flame.

This is a group of women scattered across Canada, the U.S., and Australia who take turns tending a flame for twenty four hours, leaving every twentieth shift to Brigit Herself, as was the tradition at Kildare. Whatever other affiliations each woman has, in this network she is a solitary worshipper acting within a widespread community. We don't meet, we communicate in the form of a newsletter once a year, to which any participant is invited to contribute, and we have this link to one another that each of us marks in her own way.

What do you think it was that inspired you to follow this path?

What caused me to follow this path was a need to link with a larger, benevolent, life-affirming community, and to draw closer to myself a sense of deep reciprocity, caring, and hope. A strong affirmation of my rootedness to the physical, natural, wondrous world.

The Goddess I adhere to is one whose people have worshipped Her in a multitude of ways, many of which would raise my hair. She is life, as I see her. Not life the way it is (to my mind) misperceived by so many, as simplistically good or evil, overly inaccessible to understanding or overly explainable in strictly human terms. She is pain and freedom and awakening joy, the opportunity to belong to something far greater than anything offered in terms of rigid rules or disillusioned pointlessness.

The grandest moment of the year is on Imbolc,[3] when I open up my door to the night and thank her for all that she has given, then pour milk across my threshold to the living world outside, inviting Her in, whoever She is, whatever deep and joyous mystery, whatever unplanned liberation she brings, even if it comes in the guise of loss and fear and death.

I believe in the abundance of life, through the most frightening and toilsome passages. I believe in the essential expansiveness of our souls, and these are encapsulated in Brigit, the patron of poetry, of healing, of smithcraft, the one who guides sailors through dark and turbulent seas, who sets the teats flowing and brings birth to the calves and lambs.

The world we inhabit is hidden in a tangle of veils – fear, rage, misunderstanding of who we are and how we are connected and how we can survive and flourish, human and nonhuman, wild and tame.

Facing our own tangles and emerging filled with that ability to give, to receive, to hope and love: that is how I see Her worship as functioning best. She is the beauty and She is the veils, and She is the freedom and unity I keep my eyes on when I struggle through.

Opening the door to Her on Imbolc, giving Her and Her world the nourishing gift of milk and inviting them more deeply into my heart – these are the most joyous religious acts I can ever commit.

Did you ever receive any instruction from a Celtic group? How were you trained?

I wasn't. I picked stuff up from reading, mostly scholarly literature about the Celts and Goddess worship, but a certain amount of popular Pagan literature as well. I mixed with people of varying Neo-Pagan identities, but never found a group I wanted to join, except of course the individuals in my life who were also following a Pagan path.

Can you describe any rituals that you do?

Ooh. This is difficult to answer. For about a decade I had certain daily rituals such as 'opening' my altar in the morning, giving offerings of smoke and clean water, thinking about what I would be doing that day, and then in the evening 'closing' it, which was similar, but also involved giving thanks for everything that had come to me during the day.

This demanded reviewing and seeing things through wider, less grumpy eyes, and was (and is) an extremely useful exercise. In addition I celebrated the major holidays with research and with writing and performing rituals which were often, but not always, shared with others.

The rituals sprang from what I already knew and what I gleaned from my reading about the days and symbols and deities in question, and generally involved poetry, acts that would deepen the connection with the holiday, and an opportunity to relate the symbolism of the day to my own life and those of other participants. They were contemplative, affectionate rituals, whether I was alone or with others, however somber the theme, my affection for the universe generally managed to come through.

I also performed rituals for particular occasions – pleasure rituals, for instance, or rituals of healing, strengthening, firming of purpose, invoking assistance and dispatching fear when individual challenges arose. The pleasure rituals were completely nonsexual, although one was certainly welcome to feel sexual if that's what arose; we just didn't act on it. Instead we were attempting to re-establish our connection with physical and emotional pleasure as separate from sex and performance, and there was not only a worshipful, thankful attitude, we were also encouraged to release any feelings that might come up as a result of connecting with each other and ourselves in this way.

The pleasures involved ranged from tactile: massage, rolling pebbles and pine cones or running silk or hair or feathers across the skin; to olfactory: oils, incenses, foods passed near the nose; to intellectual: poetry read, ideas discussed; to emotional: telling the recipient how loved she is and why, hugging, laughing, crying aloud... I truly enjoyed developing and hosting those rituals and strongly recommend them as an antidote to the anti-physical, anti-pleasure attitude so prevalent in our culture, and to the physical and emotional isolation that results, particularly but not exclusively, for people without sexual partners or children. We need to touch, and to let ourselves feel and enjoy that touch, and to not have all our pleasurable touch be about sex.

As I mentioned before, I have a commitment to burn Brigit's flame once every twenty days for twenty four hours, and I coordinate the efforts of other women who are involved. I perform my commitment in various ways. I light a kerosene lamp and hang it on the porch or change candles every few hours or burn a twenty-four hour candle. I spend the day in contemplation or practically forget I've got the candle burning, the latter is not my most proud ritual, but let's face it, it happens. I also write about the process in my newsletter and in letters to participants, which always feels like a sort of ritual to me. It certainly reconnects me with my intent, and my commitment.

But there are other kinds of rituals. For years I have taken everything I have known about life and re-examined it through what I learn about mysticism, ritual, symbol, worship, deity. I have taken everything I've learned about these and integrated them into my relationship with and perception of life. When I counsel a human being, I am not thinking 'Goddess', but I am seeing Goddess. When I aspire, I aspire in terms of what I know is possible, wider even than I have ever seen, and that is a connection of cosmic proportions, even when it feels prosaic and mundane.

About two years ago, I dismantled my altar and stopped my daily practice and most other rituals except for the flame and those called for by specific situations. I didn't entirely understand why; it was just the appropriate thing to do. I have very recently constructed a small altar again, and begun making occasional small offerings. I am following my guts on this.

So much of my life is imbued with and builds on and adds to my connection to Brigit, to existence, to 'the benign reality' that I don't feel at all that I have stopped the process of connection, only changed the form. Much evolution happens in the shadows, and I've learned to trust the changes even when they are in their hidden form.

I woke up early today to the sound of rain, so strong and constant that after all these months of summer it took me awhile to understand what it was. Then a sound I almost never hear since leaving the prairie provinces nearly thirty years ago: thunder.

Long, low, languorous rumbles of thunder and shimmers of unexpected brightness through the trees. A few minutes later my lover awoke, and we listened together to the building might of the electrical storm. The climax was so intense I was confused – was that just the thunder, or was some huge thing crashing into the side of the building a floor or two above? I lit several candles when I was alone. The rain was still pouring, the room was winter grey. I began cutting pieces of string to make wicks for the Daughters of the Flame.

A few months ago my friend Erynn sent me a candle lit from a candle lit from...the flame of Brigit that's burning at Kildare. I'm sending the flame along to everyone who's burning for Her in our little circle, to share that increased closeness with other worshippers, with the Goddess we love, with life itself. It feels really good to do this on this day. I write an email to Louise; 'Let's celebrate together,' I say. 'Equinox, Solstice, Full Moon, Empty Moon, life...'

I put away my rituals, put away my props because I needed to wade out into life unrestricted by form, to see what fits and what no longer makes sense, and where I want to put more juice.

Life is blossoming for me in a slow, subterranean, powerful way and shoots are pushing up through the earth. It's spring in this weathered soul. Time to give thanks, to dance Beltaine way out of season, to pour out liters of creamy milk, to watch the candles burn in liveliness and glad of heart.

Who knows how my rituals will appear a year from now? But I look forward with wetted lips.

Since this is a book about Druids and the Celtic spiritual path, how do you define those? And do you feel yourself to be a part of those paths?

I don't define Druidism, or even the Celtic spiritual path. My anchors are mostly Celtic, but even the Celts, at any time in their long history, were never separate from the beliefs and influences of the people before them, and all around them. This was no Nazi-like purity, and neither is mine. Whereas I have certain principles and spiritual goals that are unwavering, I believe in fluidity of experience, response, and expression, so that we are at every moment responding appropriately to all the influences around us, rather than reacting in a pre-directed way. Woo, does this sound fuzzy! It also sounds easy, chaotic. Not so, not so... I am trying to live like the plant on the hill, that responds this way when there is light, this way when acidity is too high, that reacts to its total situation at every moment. For a human it is far more complicated.

I don't think in terms of one path or another. I think in terms of doing what feels right (not necessarily nice, but what connects to the deep place that says, 'yep, this'), and for me Celtic Paganism has always been one of the strongest 'yep' spots.

Are there any current 'hot issues' for you that involve Celtic Paganism? Anything you feel particularly strongly about?

I guess the hottest issue for me is the failure to connect the real meaning of one's spirituality to one's life. This can range from using it as an avoidance of life instead of a marriage with it, to talking the talk, but walking willy-nilly all over the place. Of course I don't expect perfection from anyone, and shame only delays improvements in behavior, and mars our relationship to all life. But when people can speak of a connection to the Earth that is worshipful and serene, even write rituals to that effect, and then use disposable dishes at a large celebration because it's too much work to organize dish-washing, or where we have an animal as our totem and do nothing to ensure that it and its kin continue as any more than a symbol or a character in a zoo, where we speak of the dignity of all humans and then refuse to develop a truly honest and courageous and loving connection to ourselves and all other people, well, it annoys me.

It has felt rejuvenating to ponder your questions and I thank you very much for them. I sincerely hope this is of use to you in your work. I guess it's not surprising I work as a solitary in a large group of women. I always fancied the cloistered life, myself. Yet on another level I am extremely gregarious and put much time and energy into relations with others. I look forward to the day when my spiritual self feels safe enough to come into the town and frolic with the folk. I see it coming soon.

All blessings on you, Willow.

Dr. Patrick MacManaway
Interviewed November 15, 1995
Ware, Massachusetts

Following in his family's tradition, Patrick is a medical doctor and healer focusing on Earth acupuncture and geopathic stress issues. He is a Geomancer, a dowser and a member of the Order of Bards, Ovates and Druids.

Living in Scotland, Dr. MacManaway is internationally known for his work and travels frequently to the United States to teach and to facilitate the construction and investigation of sacred spaces.

Patrick's parents, Bruce and Patricia MacManaway, founded Westbank healing and teaching center, out of which Patrick operates.

It is situated in the village of Strathmiglo in Fife, Scotland. Westbank has an international reputation for healing work of many kinds, for complementary medicine, and for its work in developing innate intuitive skills such as dowsing and working with Earth energies.

I know that you have studied Druidism over the years. I'd like to know how you first came across Druidism? What drew you to it?

Growing up in the British Isles one is inevitably aware of Druidism as one of the traditions of those lands. The symbolism and the cultural legacy of the Celtic peoples is universally present to behold. My own personal introduction to organized Neo-Pagan Druidry was through a friend on the island of Iona who hosts the Order of Bards, Ovates and Druids on their annual retreat and who is also a member of that Order.

She had suggested, given my personal interest in Geomancy,

that the Order would be of interest to me.

Do you consider yourself to be a Druid?

I choose not to align myself with any organized religious grouping of any kind for lots of different reasons. I consider that the path that I walk is very close to what we would conceive of as a Druidical path. And I am very well aware that every person who considers themselves to be walking a Druid path would conceive it in a slightly different manner.

Can you describe the path that you are currently walking?

I am a Geomancer. Geomancy is divination of the Earth. My primary energetic alignment is a healing one and my background is in healing and in healthcare. I came to working with the Earth through an understanding of the relationship of people's health with certain subtle forces and energies that move in and through and over the Earth.

Can you describe how Geomancy might apply to an ancient Celtic sacred site such as one might find in Britain, a stone circle or some other site?

I would have to say first of all that stone circles and Neolithic temples in Britain are not legitimately claimed by the Celtic people. It's a very indistinct period of pre-history, but the suggestion is that the neoliths are distinct from the Celts and that the Celts inherited the Neolithic sites rather than creating them, with the possible exception of the third stage of Stonehenge, which is the stage that still stands and is currently observable today. That was right on the cusp between the Neolithic and the Celtic periods.

Now, the extent to which the Celts and the neoliths are inter-merged and interwoven is absolutely unknowable, but the Neolithic period ended when we think the Celtic people began to arrive in Britain.

Could you describe how you would approach a sacred site as a Geomancer?

The study of sacred space of all cultures rests on three

primary legs; the presence of Earth energies, the presence and integration of sacred geometry, and the presence of astronomical alignments, which of themselves give energetic alignments to particular times of the year and phases in the cycle of the solar wheel.

The greatest learning, I would say, is to be derived from the creation of new sacred sites. I have been responsible for several and co-participant in several more.

It is really by working hands-on with the spirit of the place and with the energies present that one begins to unlock both the esoteric and the exoteric mysteries.

One site that immediately springs to mind is one that I was not primarily responsible for, but had quite a substantial input into.

It's a stone Vesica created by a dear friend and magical sister. A Vesica is the shape formed when two circles overlap each other and is the shared area within the radius of both circles. A specific and special example is the Vesica Pisces where the circles share a common radius.

In the creation of this space we were able to witness how exquisitely responsive the energetic patterns of the landscape were to our work and to have a changed and shifted focus on the space.

Astronomy was particularly difficult to do at this site because of the surrounding tree lines. Our calculations did not yield any clearly visible alignments to the eight-point wheel of the year.

However, the center had been shown to us in a very clear way so we went forward with the creation of the space in trust that the alignments were as they needed to be.

What we discovered when the site was completed was that on the birthday of the lady whose space it is the sun sets over the chimney of her home as viewed from the center of the space so there is a direct solar alignment to her Earth space, her domestic space, from the heart space of her sacred space, which I think is absolutely the most beautiful alignment that could possibly be for that. Absolutely lovely. And we had no idea that would be the case until it happened.

You do cleansing and clearing work on people's houses. You are almost a 'Shamanic practitioner' in that sense. Can you talk about how that works?

There is a very close mirroring of our internal energetic patterning and our external energetic patterning. Acupuncturists who are also aware of Earth currents find that the imbalances of Chi (life force) that exist in the clients that they work on are the same imbalances that they find if they go to their clients' homes.

As with every interwoven cycle you can seek change by working both internally or externally. In different cases one or other or both is appropriate. The Chinese seem to make no distinction between the Chi they perceive as running through the landscape and the Chi that runs through a human being.

My experience also as healer is that the sense of the quality and texture and vibration of human energy is identical to that of landscape energy.

For domestic work, or secular Geomancy, one is looking to restore or enhance the quality of life and nourishment that can be derived from the space that people live and work in. In doing that one needs to pay close attention to Earth energies present and also to a multitude of associated factors, which include the psycho-spiritual atmosphere, both that which is current and that which has been laid down in the distant past. One also has to pay attention to the presence and health of any discarnate spirit entities that are there.

Many times one finds that where the Earth currents are stagnant or dissonant then the psycho-spiritual atmosphere that invokes is also stuck and traumatized. That then attracts spirit entities who themselves are in a space of trauma and dissonance and who are Earthbound to that specific space or to a person who is living there. So in working to free and release and re-harmonize the energy in a place one needs to work with many different and related facets.

In sacred space, where the energies are deliberately focused and concentrated, these issues are even more important. Cleansing and pre-ceremonial acts of preparation are immensely important to what can occur in ritual or in path working.

How would you go about preparing an area for ceremony?

Assuming that the space is already physically manifest, in preparation it is important to enter into dialogue with the guardian spirits of the place and to assess the presence and quality of Earth energies and of psycho-spiritual residue that are there.

If one's intent is pure and is in alignment with the desired use of the space by the spirit keeper then one is likely to be guided in appropriate ways. Classical tools that one might use would be prayer and visualization, smudging with sage and with other medicinally active herbs or plant materials, blessing with holy water, purification with fire, purification with earth or other materials.

One looks to tune the space like a musical instrument. If you are working with a guitar you need the strings to be in tune with each other and you also need the guitar as an instrument to be in tune with the other instruments that it is going to play with as well as the human voices that are going to sing with it.

If people wanted to start on the path to Geomancy, how would you recommend that they get into it?

It's actually very tricky. Every indigenous culture around the world has had a Geomantic tradition incorporated into their cosmology. I think it is fair to say that none of those are in a complete form accessible to the English speaker of this time.

There is a lot of interest in certain aspects of traditional Chinese Geomancy called Feng Shui. It's important to recognize in studying Feng Shui, however, that what is generally presented as Feng Shui is only one aspect of it; it is incomplete. It has been taken out of its cultural context and we tend not to get all the layers of the onion.

Westerners are most interested in the commercial exploitation of Capitalism and have selectively taken aspects of Feng Shui to match our present perception of what is important. Traditional Western Geomancy, which is interwoven into the Western Mystery Tradition of Hermetic and European thought, is in many cases written in very hard ways to access. Since Sig Lonegren stopped teaching there is not a school that I know of for traditional Western Geomancy, anywhere in the world.

You can take weekend classes or workshops, but in terms of an authentic training I am not aware of one that is available.

Where can people contact you?

I can be reached through the Westbank Centre, Strathmiglo, County Fife, KY14 7QP, Scotland. And I make frequent visits to the United States where I am available for workshops and trainings.

One more question, since you have been associated with Druids in Britain and you have now met a number of American Druids, can you comment on the differences and similarities that you have noticed?

I think in general in Britain Druidism is regarded with a certain degree of suspicion by the general public. Most British Druid Orders have a fairly low public profile.

My perception in America is that it is less necessary for that to be the case and that there is more opportunity for open public debate concerning Pagan spirituality and magical path working. I can only speak for the Order of Bards, Ovates and Druids as one of several British Druid Orders.

OBOD is quite a large organization, which in my perception is effectively and responsibly promoting the philosophy of Druidism in a manner that is both acceptable and non-challenging to people from all religious backgrounds and walks of life, whereas my understanding of The Henge of Keltria is that it is an organization dedicated to magical path working in the

Celtic tradition. That is quite a stark contrast between two organizations and I can't say to what extent that reflects an American-British difference or if it simply reflects those two organizations.

Is there anything you would like to say to American Druids?

I would encourage everyone on a spiritual path to be sure that their Earth-walk is centered in the time that they find themselves alive in. Whilst we can draw immense riches from looking backwards at old traditions and the deep taproots that they provide, we need to be sure that we are bringing that as a reality into a modern context and that we allow it to move through our everyday lives.

First of all not to keep one's spirituality separate and distinct from one's mundane workaday domestic life and secondly to be prepared to honor one's self equally with one's ancestors.

Lady Olivia Robertson (April 13, 1917 – November 14, 2013)
Interviewed June 16, 1996,
Under the oaks at the Stone of Free Speech
Parliament Hill, London

Lady Olivia was the co-founder (with Lawrence and Pamela Durdin-Robertson) of the Fellowship of Isis (FOI) and of the Druid Clan of Dana. FOI was founded to promote a closer union between the Goddess and each member, singly and as part of larger groups. One of the largest Pagan organizations internationally, FOI has thousands of members all over the world.

All members of FOI have equal status and privilege within the organization. There are no vows, all Fellowship activities are optional, membership is free although there is a price for their quarterly magazine, and members may resign at any time.

FOI welcomes members from every religion, race and tradition. It promotes the ideals of Beauty, Love and Abundance (asceticism is not encouraged). In the words of their manifesto: 'Every human, animal, bird, tree, is an eternal offspring of the Mother Goddess's Divine Family of Life.'

I am Olivia Robertson and I co-founded the Fellowship of Isis with my dear brother Lawrence who is now in the world of spirit and still helping from there. I founded the Fellowship of Isis with my brother and his wife in 1976 and we expected about a dozen members. To our amazement it was the right idea at the right time.

The idea was to unite the good in all religions by emphasizing the neglected Goddess. And we believe in the Goddess, we don't just say She is a thought form or a femininity. We believe the Goddess lives.

We believe in the deities in other words. That there is a world, a whole pantheon beyond ours. We were very psychic and we have had communion, we have had spiritual visions and experiences that the Goddess wanted us to do this work.

We did this at Clonegal Castle. It's a 1625 castle, one of the last that was built. It's on a magical site, built around an ancient pre-Druid well which has healing properties and develops psychic vision. It's between two rivers.

Now, any matriarchal center used to be centered on the main stream of the mother and the tributary. The daughter was the tributary. Our daughter is Derry, the river Derry, which means 'oak'. The Druids sprang from the oak. The main river is the river Slaney and that's the river of healing.

Matriarchal centers were all, for some reason, on the daughter, the tributary. We are in the fork of the two rivers, on the banks of the daughter. We are a power center in Clonegal. From there, because it was the right idea sent by the Goddess, we reach 87 countries, the last being Slovenia, Macedonia and all those.

We have thousands of members in Nigeria. We are multi-racial, I'd like to emphasize, because there can be racism in various cults. We look for the good in every religion, every race and every culture.

You are a founder of the Druid Clan of Dana; can you discuss that?

The Druid Clan of Dana sprang from the Fellowship of Isis. We always ask members to join the multi-racial FOI first because you can get a kind of Druidic racism that says you've got to be English or Welsh or Scots or Irish or you are no good.

So my brother and I had direct initiation through an ancient hermit called Mr. Fox who lived on the banks of the Slaney. He was guardian of a very ancient site. He had total vision and he initiated me by taking me to this well.

I was told to drink from it after which he showed me the old altar. He could 'see' the ancient peoples, how they used to wait for the Sun to rise across water in the East, over some cliffs. So I was shown what the ancient people did by this man who had total clairvoyance. He was an absolutely wild man, but he had been to Egypt.

I also knew the great sage and mystic A.E., George Russell. I am pretty old, I knew W.B. Yeats who was interested in Faery. But A.E. really 'saw' the Gods and Goddesses. And Mr. Fox saw the people.

A.E. actually saw these luminous beings who are beyond time and space, or you can say they include time and space. And I have had that privilege also. There are beings beyond us.

So in the Druid Clan of Dana we are not so much interested in archaeology and in 'who initiated who'. We wish to bring people in direct communion with the deities and we help people to make their own contact.

You said you knew Yeats when you were a girl. Can you talk a bit about that and the influences that led you to Druidry?

Well, the main thing was Mr. Fox and how we used to visit him in a donkey cart. We would spend evenings there and he used to tell me about how he saw the people through his clairvoyance. I also met Golden Dawn people, which were obviously an influence.

My father was a Mason, my family goes way back. In fact I have an ancestress who was a famous lady, she was the only woman Mason. She saw their secret rites so they either had to kill her or get her to join. Her name was Elizabeth St. Leger.

My mother was saying that A.E., this great mystic, could do it naturally, he really got through to the deities. Yeats said he had to have ritual, Golden Dawn or séances, spiritualism to do it.

We went to tea at his house once and I remember we had chocolate cake. He was a friend of the family. I was fascinated because there was a Mrs. Lenox Robinson there, with big black eyes. They were going to have a séance and she was the medium.

I would have loved to have stayed on but we were taken away. My mother said that spiritualism was most 'unwholesome'. They were very pleased because I said that Mrs. Lenox Robinson had eyes like boiled boot buttons. They thought I was effectively discouraged. Little did they know.

Do you know your famous Jacqueline Onassis? I was in correspondence with her about the book *Isis and Osiris* by Jonathan Cott. What interested her was my reference to Yeats because she adored his poetry. And there are masses of unpublished stuff.

He had come through from the world of spirit complaining. You would think some publisher, Doubleday or somebody, would get through due to an ex-president's wife. But his son refused to do anything about it at all. He didn't give a button about Mrs. Onassis. He was an Irish senator.

It annoyed me awfully because a BBC man came down and he came as a friend of Yeats's son. And he said; 'Of course the one thing you realize is that Michael Yeats is President of the Irish Senate and of course he has to think about his father's reputation, hasn't he?'

I said; 'Bloody hell; there is a book of astrology they haven't published. There is all this stuff up in the attic. There's Yeats rampant in the next world wanting it done and because of Michael's reputation as President of the Irish Senate it can't be done?' It's this pomposity that drives me up the wall. They wouldn't give in to Mrs. Onassis so what can I do? Nothing.

I got hold of his daughter, Ann. She said; 'I can't do anything. Father left me his magical equipment and all his books to his son.

'But I knew Michael didn't like them, like many sons he wasn't even interested. He was left a whole lot of stuff that would only discredit him, they all thought.'

They got one book out of it called *A Vision*. They let a man called George Harrap, a publisher, roam around. But the bulk of the stuff is still there. You see, Yeats came through this Swedish medium, Eo Goran, years ago in the 1960s. He described Yeats, his voice, everything. He had never heard of him actually. He called him 'Yeets'.

He said Yeats was walking around, cross because he couldn't get some stuff published. I thought it was maybe a few old papers. And I got hold of Ann who said there were stacks of the stuff.

You also knew Ross Nichols in the 1960s?

Well, I never belonged to an Order because I would never take secret vows or anything. But I always went to Ross Nichol's ceremonies. He was friend who used to stay with us and give us lectures and seminars at the castle.

I used to come up to this very place, Parliament Hill, by Hampstead Heath, with my friend and it was very interesting. They all wore white and it was very synchronized. It was very Druidic. You didn't get anyone wearing animal's heads or horns. I think that would have given people fits.

They were more like well-educated archaeologists. Scholars and gentlemen. I remember it used to irritate me frightfully; Ross was the only one who was decent enough to give women a role. The other Druids hadn't any Goddess at all.

He introduced the Celtic Fire Festivals. He had Imbolc for the Goddess Brighid. He used to read the wonderful Isis declaration from Apuleius. But Brighid was always given the silliest poem, read by a woman. It rather went like this [*Olivia speaks with a thick Irish brogue*]; 'Ah, sure now, we invoke the golden-haired blue eyed Brighid, the sweet Brighid who gives us the good cow's milk.' This ghastly image. She is the Great Goddess, the Triple Goddess, not Saint Brighid. She read it with an Irish accent rather like somebody behind a bar, an Irish girl.

We've come a long way haven't we?

By God we have. At least he did read the greatest invocation to Isis in literature, at least he appreciated that. You Americans know far more than us because you research your stuff. We think we know it all you see, at least the English do. Not, of course, the

Irish who *do* know it all [*laughter*].

When is Michael due to retire from the Senate?

It won't do any good till he is dead. We mustn't wish for that. He has his reputation to the grave. And then what's on his tombstone. When people have a reputation they stick to it. 'Respectability' it's called.

Can you talk about Druid training from your perspective, what you think it is or should be or could be?

I never want to influence other people. People have their own training courses, we haven't. We expect people to develop direct clairvoyance and communion themselves, not only with higher beings but with the spirits of nature so we do magical journeys. I don't use the words 'path working', I don't like the word 'path' or the word 'working', it suggests hard work. We like the word 'magic'. We believe in magic. We do direct, natural magic. People get their inspiration directly from Source that way.

When you look at the Druidism that you see around you now, the various Orders that you are aware of, are there any problems that you see? As an elder, what are the things that the younger ones need to work on?

Well, what I would say is they have to realize that this entire world is a mirage. It's like a video, it's not real. The real world is beyond our five physical senses. The true Tír na nÓg we call it in Ireland, the Land of Youth.

If you have the most horrible Druids that you are busy in-fighting with or horrible family or horrible lover, or anything, you are only playing with their shadow self, their unreal self. If you can get to your inner source of being you will see the divine in all and you won't fight with people because you will know why they are so horrible and you will suddenly to your amazement find that they think you are horrible and you will laugh. And you don't fight. Right? That's what I would say to the young. Tune in to the divine in everybody – especially the people you hate. You will have a good laugh and you will get on fine.

Where would you like to see the Druid movement go in the future? What is your vision for that?

My vision is that I believe a new generation who are in touch with Light Beings from outer space, spirit people, deities, will do it directly. They don't have to swallow alive all these books and books. They will read nature's lessons directly. I feel in that way you will have your millennium because whatever disasters come upon the Earth, your spirit is there all the time.

You have to learn to contact your own true self, your spirit. Then you can contact the spirits of earth, trees, plants and water. I believe it's the only way for humanity to survive now with all this pollution and destruction.

The Fellowship of Isis is dedicated to honoring the feminine aspect of deity. Can you talk about where we have been and where we are now in terms of the Goddess movement?

Well, I think the mistake in the Feminist movement was that they paid the worst compliment to themselves and the best to men because they copied men. I believe the Goddess is divine as Goddess and She is perfectly manifested through female beings. That suggests polarity and long live men. Vive la difference!

I believe that to love the Goddess is to love the God because only a woman can convey both sexes together. At the point of conception there is this little embryo, it may be a little boy, and it's inside her. Therefore the Goddess contains all and therefore women have a natural tenderness and love and caring nature. So we want to exercise that.

But that can be a bit boring. I am not a mother. I like the psychic and spiritual side. And I do believe that men are terrified of women as Witches. They are terrified of the supernatural, of the next world, of clairvoyance, of astrology, the lot, because women are good at it. And they hate everything connected with us like that lovely Star Trek episode where what they most feared was a Witch, a cat, a bat and the moon.

I believe that women suggest all that to men, my brother

believed that too. And why we have been kept down, why the Church stopped us from being Priests, was because we have natural power, which they stunted.

The world is heading towards natural disasters. I believe that the spiritual beings from the stars and everywhere else are helping women to bring through a new race, a new humanity of every color and sort who will have their true center in their spirit and will thereby control their bodies in perfect health and happiness. But who also don't mind if they do what some call death and I call transition.

I believe there is a new race coming. It's rapidly developing among children who have natural E.S.P., natural power of psychically projecting and healing. All these gifts come naturally now which usen't to because people aren't punishing their children for being psychic. 'Psyche' means soul.

When I look at every single Druid Order of any size that I am aware of, you are the only woman who is the actual, official figurehead for a Druid Order. Emma Restall Orr is now co-Chief of the British Druid Order, which happened last year. She is co-Chief with a man, Philip Shallcrass. I am Vice President of The Henge of Keltria. ADF has Vickie Meith who is Vice Arch Druid, which happened about two weeks ago. Speaking strictly in the little Druid universe, why do you think it is that the Druid Orders will always talk about how the women do so much work and have so much authority yet the Arch Druids are always male?

I can tell you exactly why. The Druids are very Patriarchal. You see the moon was controlled by the women and the older Witchcraft. The Druids were rather respectable; one of them was a secretary to Julius Caesar. They became Christians and they followed the Sun, the ways of the Sun and the day.

Even today I am terribly amused by seeing some Druid Chiefs who when they talk to me have these handmaidens around them, bringing them their beer and actually waiting on them. I mean, they are Patriarchal. I was co-founder with my dear brother, but now he is gone and I am not going to look around for a bloke. There's too many of them.

I think we women have to assert ourselves in Druidry because of its natural intellectualism, archaeological attitude, and because it always was very male. But in the New Age we have got to develop the ancient Druidry of natural affinity with nature, with stones and grass and trees. You can't do that without the Goddess. And I am happy to represent the Goddess Dana, Queen of the whole Earth.

Is there anything you would like to tell American Druids in particular?

Yes. I remember an ancient Druid, and I quote him, who said; 'There can't be any Groves in America because there were no Druids in America.' Bang that's it. And still there is a lot of racism. You are supposed to be a sort of Celtic Aryan really. I have known people who were furious at seeing some Japanese climbing up Glastonbury Tor. They said; 'How dare they.'

Well, I am the opposite. What I want to tell Americans is that they are the Rainbow People. They are of every race. And they can be Druids as much as anybody else if they follow the ways of nature and of the Goddess.

Before the Patriarchal Druids were around there were the Matriarchal Druids who were the old Wise Women. And we have Groves in America. And you are welcome to join and bring the Goddess into Druidry for the new era.

You were at the Parliament of the World's Religions in Chicago. Now that some time has gone by, what have you distilled out of that experience?

Well, what kills me laughing is that I had a death threat. I was representing the Fellowship of Isis and I was the only woman of a non-Christian, a non-respectable religion on the platform. There were six or seven thousand people, only eighteen people spoke. Only two were women, one a very severe looking Baha'i lady and myself.

Now the Pagans had objected to this. They didn't want to have any more women or Pagans on the platform so they shoved a list of Pagan organizations under the name of Olivia Robertson. I didn't mind, but the people said; 'Why are you representing us?' and I said; 'I don't know I guess there is nobody else to do it, so I'll do it.'

So I got up on the rostrum and I invoked the Goddess Isis. The Chicago Tribune and the various television things said that the people on the platform sat with stony faces, they refused to applaud me. There was a Cardinal, a Papal Legate, Buddhists, that lot. And even I'm afraid the Baha'i lady, I saw it later from the video, never clapped. I got an ovation from the floor.

But anyway, when I came out I was wanting to talk to the people. They were all saying thank you for speaking up for the Goddess when a very tall handsome gentleman of African descent, beautifully dressed, came up, seized me and said; 'Move, move, move!' I didn't know what he was talking about. I thought they thought I was Irish, I.R.A. or something.

So he brought me right up the moving stairs to my friend, a Benedictine monk. He was surrounded by husky looking chaps who looked as if they did baseball, seminarians. And they stood around me in a ring. Then the security man left me. I thought what a funny place this is.

The next year I went and stayed at Saint Procopius Abbey with the good Benedictines and I said; 'Look, why did the security man behave in this way?' And he said; 'But you had a death threat.' And I said 'What?' He said; 'Oh yes, you were going to be shot.' And I said; 'Oh Muslims, thinking they didn't like ancient Egypt.' And he said; 'No, Christians!' It was terribly funny I thought. I was rather pleased, I was delighted. Nobody has ever tried to shoot me before!

I was just on a panel at Rites of Spring, a Pagan gathering in Massachusetts with Oberon Zell, Jackie Zaleski, Andras Corban Arthen, and myself. Oberon and Jackie and Andras have all received death threats. We were supposed to be talking about the future of the Craft and what they were saying was that sooner or later someone is going to be killed.

Yes, I agree. Because we are the new religion. You see we are like the Christians were in the year one. The Pagans felt they were threatened so they went and fried up Christians in the amphitheaters. Now the Christians know intuitively that we are the coming religion and this is what they are afraid of. And the nastier they get the more we can be sure we will prevail. But we accept the good in them.

In the FOI we have two Catholic Priests. One is a monk and the other a brother, a Jesuit and a Benedictine. So we have nothing in FOI against the good in Christianity, love and all the teachings of Jesus. But I think these people are terrified because they are afraid of the supernatural. They are very schizophrenic. They think everything is the Devil.

There is one thing I would say to Pagans, don't get schizoid or paranoid against the Devil. See the good in others and you will get on OK. I think this paranoid fear of the dark, of death, and fear of other people, leads to persecution. It's a sort of mania and it's not easy to overcome.

I think it's bad to hate people and to be afraid. One could get like that, being attacked and threatened. I don't mind a fig. I rather agree with what Jesus said; 'They know not what they do.' They are just scared of us. We'll turn them into frogs maybe [*laughter*].

Can you talk some more about the Goddess Danu?

Yes. She appeared to me in a vision. I believe the Goddess was in the center of the Earth. The Earth has a sun inside it, as we all know now. Usually I see without any trance, but this was the other way. I fell down as it were, a pit, a tunnel. It was beyond sleep, deeper. And there was this divine being.

She was a very tall lady with long golden hair and every thread was separate and luminous. She had a long face, rather

Gothic looking, pale, with a slight rose tint in Her cheeks. She had these wonderful blue eyes and a very aristocratic face with a small mouth, pinkish.

She was wearing a cloak of the most marvelous blue. It wasn't royal blue and it wasn't turquoise. It was between the two, luminous blue with a bit of sun in it. And it was elaborately embroidered with gold all the way down. And I noticed that Her hair and the elaborate gold sort of blended and came right down.

I got a state of happiness which I never in my life have had before. But I have noticed that whenever we do a Druid rite of Dana this happiness comes, which only seems to come with Dana. She didn't give a name so I thought it was Demeter or somebody. But then years later She came through a medium, a friend of mine, Rosemary Ryan, at the Bridge House in Clonegal. This Lady appeared and gave the name of Dana, but still I didn't accept it.

But then I went to a famous healer, a seventh son of a seventh son, John Doran, and he described this vision of this Lady. He knew nothing about my experience. Then She appeared in full Celtic regalia with Her hair elaborately plaited with pearls, wearing a gold cloak lined with silver.

What amused me was, he is not clairaudient, he is just clair-voyant. She produced a sort of scroll that spelled out D-A-N-A and I thought, well, I have to call Her Dana. That's it. Oh yes, She gave a message, she said; 'I am the mother of all beings, go on, do well, preach my name.'

I had already founded the FOI so I didn't know what I could do for Dana. But then we founded the Druid Clan of Dana. It was Hers you see. So that was how I got it directly from The Goddess. That respect of The Goddess.

Can you talk a bit about the Druid scene in Ireland?

It's popping up now in various places. It's all little groups. They came later than the British. The British were firmly entrenched and only recently have there been Irish Druids. We were the first and then some others popped up. But when I say we were the first I am sure some groups were there, practicing away in secret.

Are there any people in Ireland that you know of, who are keepers of tradition and who have been passing this down through their families?

I think you get wonderful phonies. People initiated by their grannies or their fathers. But believe me, Mr. Fox existed. Some people say he didn't, that he was like Dorothy Clutterbuck and Gerald Gardner, but he did. I really couldn't tell you about others. I wish them well but I don't know about them.

Susan Henssler

Interviewed June 15, 1996
At Primrose Hill, London

Susan is a farmer, painter and the co-ordinator of the Bardic tutoring program for the Order of Bards, Ovates and Druids (OBOD). She also is web mistress of the OBOD website.

What religion were you raised in? Can you describe the religious training you had growing up?

I was very fortunate to be raised without any particular religion, in an atmosphere of enquiry and freedom of choice. Neither of my parents was religious and I received no particular religious indoctrination at all. As a result of that I am very fortunate to be in a position of regarding all religions as a sort of an anthropologist in that they are all equally strange and equally valid from my point of view.

You mentioned to me earlier that you had some Hermetic training. Can you talk about your early years with the Western Mystery Tradition?

I haven't had any formal training. I would say that for me discovering *Kabbalah* was a very exciting thing. It was around that that I began my own formal exploration of spiritual work. But I have had a natural spirituality or metaphysics all my life. I found *Kabbalah* interesting and appealing because it was not religious, it was metaphysical and spiritual rather than religious.

I studied Magic, mainly on my own for about twenty years, before I came to Druidry. I would define Magic as the art and science of creation.

Was it a particular system of Magic, like The Golden Dawn or some other?

Most systems of Magic these days are derived from The Golden Dawn so yes, I certainly did study The Golden Dawn system, again without believing in anything or taking anything anybody said as a precept or dogma. I've had a very interesting time exploring a lot of different approaches.

So how did you find Druidism? Or how did it find you?

That's sort of a funny story. When I came to England I knew nothing at all about the whole Celtic side of the Western Tradition. I am from the United States. I was born and raised in New Jersey and I lived in New York. I came to England seven years ago. I came here not knowing anybody involved in spiritual work.

The one person I was told to get in touch with was a fellow named John Michell who I had never heard of. He was a friend of a friend and I just called him up and it turned out he lived not far from me. I used to go and have tea with him. We would talk about *Kabbalah* and things like that and I gradually became introduced to the whole Earth Mysteries side of things.

I also began hearing about Druidry so I said to John one day; 'You must know some Druids, what is this Druidry all about? Who should I go talk to?' and he said to go talk to Philip Carr-Gomm because he was the best Druid he knew.

So that was that. I telephoned Philip and in the meantime found a couple of his books, which I was very impressed with. I went down to Lewes to meet him and was again really impressed with him and his approach and I decided forthwith to join OBOD. It was the first organization of any sort that I have ever joined and I joined it exactly because it doesn't have a dogma or a religious attitude. It doesn't preach and it doesn't teach.

Since you co-ordinate the study program, can you describe it?

Yes. The OBOD course is a distance learning course in three parts. It teaches the general approach to the Druid way in three segments; the Bardic, the Ovate and the Druid. If you want to find out more about the course visit our website (http://www.obod.co.uk). Any search on the word Druid will lead you inexorably to it. Or you can write to us.

The study program is an experientially based course. The essential thing is that it's more about the art of not teaching and about helping the student to find their own inner teacher, their own inner connection. It helps them define their own inner path and their own inner journey.

Many people have said that starting to work on the course felt like coming home. That's a very interesting thing. It seems to connect people with their inner selves in a way that no other program I have ever encountered does.

One of the things that American Druids sometimes find hard to understand about OBOD is the way that one can be a Christian and be a Druid at the same time. Can you talk about that?

Well one of the things that some of us in OBOD have said is that OBOD Druidry is not a religion so much as it is a way of life. It is a spiritual path and a way of working with the world, its metaphysics and also a guide to action and right action and conduct in the world.

It isn't a religion in that it doesn't tell you what to believe. You don't have to believe in Deity of any sort although in the course of the work you are introduced to and given a lot of exercises to do with the Celtic Deities. But it is not required that you believe in any of these things.

It's a way of life rather than a religion. We have many members of the Order who are Christians and Druids, who are Jewish and Druids. And who are Buddhist and Druids and Atheists and Druids. It's a way of balancing and integrating one's inner life, on the inner planes, and one's outer life, how one lives one's life. One of the things that is taught is creative expression so that as we awaken to who we are inside we also develop channels to express who we are on the outside. We open up channels to inner guidance and inner teaching as we become more centered and balanced within ourselves.

As one becomes centered and balanced in one's self one learns about relating to the world – to the planet, to the brothers and sisters that we have among the humans and the animals, the plant kingdom and the mineral kingdom. All parts of the single being that the planet is.

What kinds of transformations have you seen people go through as a result of taking the course?

I've seen quite a lot. For example some people might begin with a very incredulous attitude, a skeptical attitude towards the spiritual life. Perhaps the only contact they have had is what other people have told them, religious dogma and so forth. These people find their own inner spirituality.

Other people think of themselves as very spiritual people and have been working in spiritual paths for many years and for them the course may offer a greater grounding in the real world of relationship and of physical work with the material world.

Everybody becomes more integrated within themselves. Clearer about who they are, what their particular path is. I find that as people get free from dogma and free from thinking that somebody else is going to tell them what to believe they find within themselves the really crucial thing, the really valuable thing, which is the way of knowing for themselves at any moment what is right for them to do. And what path is right for them to take.

There are some American Druid groups that put a great emphasis on scholarship. It seems that the OBOD course puts more emphasis on the inner life and on the intuition. Can you address that a little bit?

That has to do with what one considers Druidry to be. If you look at it as a historical entity, as the scholars do, then you have to go on the documentation and you concern yourself with what people in the past believed and how people in the past thought about themselves and their world and their relationship to it.

For me and for us in OBOD, Druidry is a living thing. It is an essential part of the human spirit by whatever name. So what the ancient Celts happened to think or do is certainly of interest and is very valuable to uncover, but that's not what Druidry is now.

In OBOD, and in spiritual life in general, one of the first things you have to learn is not to concern yourself with what other people believe. And that includes your ancestors or anybody else's ancestors. You have to find out what is real for you, what works for you, what concepts embody truth for you.

That inner search is what Druidry, in its true sense, really is. That is quite separate from the historical item of Druidry as it existed in Celtic cultures in the past. Druidry is a living stream that has continued. It is not something that existed in the past and then stopped and that we are now trying to revive.

Druidry has continued to exist as long as humans exist. Druidry is that inner knowing, that inner quest that every human being has as part of their innermost self and that motivates all humans in their search. Whether they phrase that search in terms provided by a religion such as Buddhism or Christianity or whether they find their own terminology to phrase and quantify their own inner search.

Anyone who is serious about the study of philosophy would put it in those same terms. They are looking for that inner truth. So how is what you are calling Druidry any different from philosophical inquiry, which has been going on since the Greeks at least?

I think because it has the outer side of it as well. It's not purely an inner search. Part of the Druid tradition is a tuning to the wisdom that is made available to us from the natural world, and connecting to that; the sun and the moon and the trees, the sky and the earth.

An important part of the experience of Druidry for me has been visiting sacred sites in Britain. That has been incredibly important, especially as an American. There is very little of a tradition of sacred sites that the European culture in America is involved with. There is very little sense of place.

So the connection with the earth that I've had through places like Iona where I go every year on retreat with the Order, Stonehenge, Glastonbury, and Avebury where I go half a dozen times a year, has become very significant for me. It's the first time that I have really felt the living energy of the planet. I've always had a very close relationship with nature and the natural world. I grew up in the country, living a very natural country life. But I never really had the sense of place that I have connected with through Druidry and through being here in Britain.

In the States I have been finding that by working with the Native Americans. They have been there for at least 40,000 years and they definitely have a sense of place. A lot of Druids in America find that extremely controversial for some reason. They have a very hard time with that.

Here in England we look at the association of Druidry and the Native American tradition as a very natural and positive thing. We certainly applaud whatever route people take to find something that works for them, that is meaningful. I quite understand how Americans feel, as transplanted Europeans. How they feel detached. They haven't really connected to the land of America because it takes hundreds of generations to do that and they have disassociated themselves from the land of their ancestry. I think working with the Native American tradition is a great way of resolving that.

You see, if people think that Druidry is something from the ancient Celts they lock themselves into that. If that is where their interest lies, if that is what is rich and satisfying for them there is not a thing wrong with it. But I personally wouldn't say that Druidry is limited to that.

Are there any problems with Druidry in Britain? Anything that needs working on?

We certainly do have our scholars who say that: 'You people aren't *real* Druids because you are making things up as you go along.' There certainly is a very strong tradition of scholarship within the Celtic field. But that isn't a problem because they are doing what they enjoy doing and everybody else is too.

What is your vision for the future of Druidry? Where would you like to see it go?

I do see Druidry becoming a more international, multi-faith kind of thing. I think that what we are calling Druidry is something that is actually emerging all around the world. I see that through my connections with the internet. It seems to be a more genuine kind of spirituality that comes out of a more inner directed rather than outer directed search.

What I see happening in the future is Druidry strengthening because it can be the means whereby we bring our spirituality into the world of action and the world of matter. It is also conversely the way we understand the truly sacred quality that is inherent in matter itself. It's a way of reconciling the inner and the outer world of the spirit and of the material world and of the world of nature and of the divine. And it sees the human being as the resolver. The human being as the Druid is the one who can resolve this terrible split in the Western world between the material and the spiritual, the inner and the outer life.

As each person learns to be their own Druid they can heal this rift in themselves and join in healing the world.

Mara Freeman
Interviewed August 9, 1996
Via internet

Mara has had essays on Celtic spirituality published in Parabola, A Magazine of Myth and Tradition: Sacred Water, Holy Wells, spring, 1995; in Word of Skill, fall, 1995, and will be published in an upcoming edition of The Sunwise Blessing. She has also had articles in Gnosis Magazine, the Journal of The Henge of Keltria, Talking Leaves, and The Trumpeter, a Journal of Ecosophy, in Canada. In Britain her essays have been published in Dalriada and Touchstone magazines. She is a contributor to *The Druid Renaissance* edited by Philip Carr-Gomm (HarperCollins, 1996).

Mara has given seminars on Celtic spirituality since 1986 at places such as the University of California, Santa Cruz, California Institute for Integral Studies, Esalen Institute, Chinook Learning Center, Elderhostel at Shenoa Retreat Center, and at conferences including Spirit of Place and the annual Conference for the Association of Transpersonal Psychology at which she is a regular presenter.

In 1986 she produced a multi-image mystery drama using slides and sound entitled Between Earth and Sky – An Initiation, which has been staged throughout the West and South-West. In 1993 she created a series of path working tapes and has just released an audiocassette series of Celtic storytelling; Celtic Tales of Birds and Beasts and Tales of Love and Transformation, stories told to the accompaniment of harps, pipes, whistles and more. She has three books in progress: one on magical trees of the British Isles, one on eco-psychology and the Celtic tradition, and the third is a collection of folk-tales.

Mara has performed story and dance productions for schools and libraries, is a licensed marriage, family and child counselor with an M.A. in psychology, an astrologer, a hypnotherapist and a shamanic healer, and is a member of OBOD in the Bardic grade.

Since the year 2000, Mara has had two books published: *Kindling the Celtic Spirit – Ancient Traditions to Illumine your Life through the Seasons*, HarperSanFrancisco, 2001; and *Grail Alchemy: Initiation in the Celtic Mystery Tradition*, Inner Traditions, 2014. In 2001, she created Celtic Spirit Journeys, which provides tours and retreats in the British Isles and Ireland.

She can be found at www.chalicecentre.net and www.celtic-spiritjourneys.com.

Can you please talk about your early religious upbringing?

My father was Jewish and married a non-Jewish woman whose family had come from Ireland, my mother. Although I never heard the details, I gathered there was some opposition to the match from the more Orthodox members of my father's family. The result of this was my parents' very 'modern' lack of interest in religion. They were more identified with being Socialists. So I was never subjected to any religious ideology or training, although in England during the 1950s and 60s, public schools taught Christian hymns, prayers, and doctrine across the board, so I got a hefty whack of Christianity, most of which was harmless enough.

One thing stands out though – as a small child, I remember asking my father where God was. He threw out his hands in an expansive gesture – we were in the garden at the time – and replied, 'God is everywhere!' I liked that a lot, and I liked singing All Things Bright and Beautiful and Christmas carols and Easter hymns, too, and drawing pictures illustrating Bible stories. But most of all, I liked walking in the countryside.

I was an only child and given a lot of freedom in a safer era than today: from the age of ten I would take buses or trains out into the countryside alone and wander along the country lanes singing to myself, very happy to be out of the city. I've always loved maps, and used them to seek out ancient sites, such as burial mounds and castle ruins.

How did you first connect with Celtic spirituality?

I was raised in Southern England, in the seaside town of Southsea, but I started to connect with Celtic culture at the early age of nine. This was precipitated by an event at the junior school I attended. We saw some crackly old film on the class projector for geography, I believe it was. It was called, The Four Corners of the British Isles and one of the corners was Stornaway on the Hebridean Isle of Lewis. The less than-romantic image was of women gutting herrings or suchlike, but the soundtrack played a few bars of a Hebridean air, and I was shocked into life by its mysterious beauty. From that moment on, I wore as many plaid clothes as I could persuade my mother to provide; gathered vocabulary through story-books to give me enough semblance of a Scots dialect; and announced I was changing my name to Heather! This lasted until my teen years.

As a young adolescent, I spent hours in the local library, poring over books of Celtic legends and sheet music, and at school would sit looking at a map of Scotland under the desk while other lessons were going on. I took *Teach Yourself Gaelic* out of the library, too, which was quite a challenge. Since I had rather hands-off parents, no-one had any influence on this unusual obsession. As an adult who, both through psychotherapy and clairvoyance, works with past-life phenomena, I cannot help wondering about past-life influences here, although I have never explored it. I was very unhappy at high school and Celtic mythology was a way out into more happy realms.

I lived for books that took me into other worlds. One series, the now-famous Narnia chronicles by C.S. Lewis, is full of Celtic influences that I didn't realize then. And later, when I was fifteen, I discovered *The Lord of the Rings* and not long after,

Graves' *The White Goddess*. Medieval romance grabbed me, too, where I first started sensing the Grail mystery that I now teach in workshops. I always loved Christmas carols, and I chose a book called *Medieval English Lyrics* for a school book prize, and as I read it, I became aware of an older, deeper mystery that lay behind the Christian sentiments: the archetypal marriage of holly and ivy or the wounded knight in Down in Yon Forest There Stands a Hall.

At Bristol University, where I was much happier, I began expressing these mysteries in ritual and drama – a May Day dance ritual at one time and a short poetic play called The Three Faces of the Moon Goddess. A lot was happening in the West Country in 1969-72. I attended the first wild and wonderful Glastonbury Fayre. John Michell published *The View over Atlantis* and the whole Earth Mysteries thing began. I went to the first Ley-hunter's moot ever, and my boyfriend and I would pore over ordnance survey maps with pencil and ruler, then set forth into the Somersetshire countryside to dowse energy lines, bent coat-hangers at the ready.

I journeyed to Wales where we hiked over boggy moorland to the heart of the Preseli mountains where the blue-stones of Stonehenge were taken from. Many times I hitch-hiked to Glastonbury before it became the New Age mecca it is today, and communed with the windy spirits in silence on the Tor.

After graduating, I began writing a book on the folklore of trees, but I soon began to feel isolated, and inspiration drained away. My friends had all left Bristol, and I was afraid the world was leaving me behind. I moved to London and became a high-school teacher of English, but I always cherished a dream of living a country life – in a cottage in Wales. At age 28, I did move into the deep country – but not Wales. A holiday led me to the coast mountains in central California where I lived for twelve years, very close to nature.

My twelve years in the mountains deepened my love of the

Earth, so for me, being in nature feels the most natural way to worship, in the very presence of a Divine force that teaches me so much. I recently came across some words of Jung, in which he said; 'I never doubted that the physical world is spirit seen from without and the spirit is the world viewed from within.' That phrase sums up my world-view more than most I've come across in recent times.

I never felt very comfortable with, for example, Starhawk's description of spirit as 'immanent' in Earth. 'Immanent' literally meaning 'staying in' implies that 'Spirit' is something separate from 'Earth'; it's dwelling within, but is not the same as Nature. The way Jung puts it suggests the seamlessness of the inner and outer worlds.

When I am spiritually connected, there is no inner and outer. And as I write that, I am reminded of the extraordinary Zen liturgy that goes: 'That which is form is emptiness, that which is emptiness form.'

I see so many connections between all religions – so many facets of the same diamond – that I am glad I had no one-way religious upbringing at home, just my Dad throwing his arm out and saying; 'God is everywhere!'

By 1985 I had married, and feeling a deep longing to connect with my British roots again, I travelled round Britain and Ireland for several months with my then-husband, a photographer, where we gathered material for the multi-image show I made on our return, called Between the Earth and Sky – An Initiation. He shot images of sacred sites and seasonal rural festivals, while I wrote poems and songs for the script. When we returned, we moved to Santa Cruz, California, where I made the show, and we travelled around the country showing it wherever we could.

Since then I have been deeply immersed in the British Mystery Tradition, giving workshops and writing, and my love for this path grows stronger each day. I still hope to return – when the time is right – and live in that cottage in Wales.[4]

How were you trained? And are you a member of a particular Druid group?

As the above indicates I wasn't really trained. I learned path working from a friend at Bristol when I was nineteen. I learned to deepen psychically in California. Only this month did I join a group – OBOD – after meeting Philip Carr-Gomm in England last year when we met to discuss my contribution to *The Druid Renaissance*. I liked Philip a lot, and the energy surrounding his Order felt very much like 'coming home'. I wanted to feel part of a group of like minds, so I'm starting off in the Bardic grade, and have joined the NOBOD email discussion list.

What are your rituals? How do you worship?

I don't really do any rituals, maybe because I'm not affiliated with a local group, but more probably because I'm not really a 'hands-on' sort of person, preferring the imaginal world of the soul. I've noticed that people who like altars, and circles and magical tools, etc. usually have more Earth in their astrological make-up than me (I'm triple Water). On my somewhat solitary path, I do path working, journeying inward usually in the presence of a particular guide who is associated with the Grail mysteries, but whom I sense doesn't want to be talked about in cyberspace!

I may travel extensively in a shamanistic manner through sacred landscapes of the Celtic tradition, but I tend to let the journey take me where it will, rather than following any pre-set formula. That's how I connect with the inner planes. When I am in Nature I feel gathered up in a force so much greater and more wonderful than the human world that I am in a constant state of worship at the beauty that floods all my senses. All my manic activity in human society fades into the background, laughingly knocked into proportion, and I am restored to a state of peace, equilibrium, and, very often, pure joy. That for me is the purest form of worship.

How do you define Druidism? Or the Celtic spiritual path?

I'm assuming you mean 'define it for myself' as there are plenty of fine discussions of Druidry to be studied in books, the best most recently, being Peter Berresford Ellis's *The Druids*, and to enter into that discussion would take more time and space than I have here. I am well aware that the original Druids were multi-faceted people of wisdom and power, holding many exoteric positions in society as well as performing sacerdotal functions. Like most modern Druids today, I tend to pull out from the original matrix of beliefs and practices the importance of their regard for Nature, as priests of the polytheistic religion of the Celts.

To me, Druidry and Celtic spirituality is a clear mirror wherein the outer and inner worlds reflect each other. I can be filled with awe at the beautiful juxtaposition of holy well and tree in, say, the Cornish countryside; and I can also experience the numinosity of the inner archetypes of well and tree that arise from the collective unconscious.

The local and particular are revealed not only as full of meaning in themselves, but also as holograms of the Original Tree and Well, and ultimately, the primal forces that these images represent. I believe the consciousness of the Celts was expanded far beyond what we can experience today. I am fascinated by the matter-of-factness with which ordinary people described their encounters with faeries, tree-spirits, and the like, and the way experiences of second-sight were so common.

To me, reconnecting with Celtic spirituality means reawakening our almost-atrophied organs of perception, so that more of the hidden worlds can come into view. Having said that, I don't think these experiences should be sought as sensational phenomena; but the awareness our ancestors had with the now unseen worlds bespeaks of a connectedness with the great web of being that transcends time and space, and being part of a greater whole, casting off the Cartesian legacy of separateness, is what is most important to me.

I have just finished writing an article (for Parabola) on the Scottish country-people's culture in the last century, mostly using Carmichael's *Carmina Gadelica*. The way every task of their working day was regarded as sacred, from building the hearth-fire to shearing sheep, to greeting the morning and celebrating the rhythms of the year, has so much to teach us about how we can bring back a sense of meaning and connectedness with the Divine in our fragmented lives today. I am continually overawed by the spiritual wisdom of the Celts, and how they were able to align their lives with the Divine.

How do you think this is unique from or similar to Wicca or the Pagan revival in general?

Well, I may be speaking from my ignorance of other paths here, but from the little I know of Wicca, it is very different from the Celtic tradition because Gods and Goddesses from religions all over the world are invoked. In me this creates a form of spiritual indigestion! A well-meaning group of local young people where I live have just started a group called, Clan Cymraes SilverMoon: the very name with its garbled concoction of Welsh, Scottish and English, says it all. It all seems 'made up', a post-modernist nightmare of the desperate modern attempt to shore 'fragments against our ruin', that T.S Eliot spoke of in his poem, The Wasteland.

I've also come across other Neo-Pagan paths that emphasize body at the expense of spirit. Sex, desire, hedonism, seem to be the most important things on the agenda. Seems out of balance to me. I recently received a letter from British author Nigel Jackson who spoke of his disillusionment with some Neo-Pagan movements he described as purveying 'woefully simplistic and half-baked spirituality'. Sort of how I feel. There's a kind of feeling of 'anything goes', a 60s-era flower children's abhorrence of anything smacking of structure, tradition, scholarship and – God forbid! – discipline. You can just make it all up, dance beneath the full moon, and – voila! – instant religion. (Here ends rant!)

What is your vision for the future of the path? Where would you like to see it develop?

I have a deep dislike for large movements and it seems to me that growth equals dilution when something as subtle, nebulous and elusive as Druidry/Celtic Spirituality becomes popular. I don't want to see it 'develop' if that means more and more people read Llewellyn books and become overnight 'Druids'. Having said that, however, I do see the value in the spread of Druidry if it proves an attractive vehicle for those rediscovering that the Earth is sacred, and wanting to gather in Groves to deepen their spirituality and actively work towards restoring and creating Earth-honoring practices. I would rather see it deepen and lead more people to the mystical path than spread, become faddish, and then, inevitably, go out of fashion.

Rev. John R. Adelmann (Fox)

Interviewed November and December, 1996
Via internet

Reverend John R. Adelmann, known as 'Fox', has been active in the Neo-Pagan movement for thirteen years. With degrees in Engineering and Anthropology, his background includes Deep Ecology, Native American spirituality and Germanic magic, Shamanism, Wicca and Druidism. He is the founder and Senior Druid of Shining Lakes Grove, ADF, one of the largest and most active Druid Groves in the US. He is also the newly elected Arch Druid of *Ár nDraíocht Féin,*: A Druid Fellowship (ADF), which practices and promotes Druidry worldwide. He is actively working to empower Druidism as a living faith and Neo-Paganism as a viable and accepted religious alternative in today's mainstream culture.

Fox has written many articles for Ripples, the quarterly publication from Shining Lakes Grove, for News from the Mother Grove, an ADF newsletter, and has frequently written letters to legislators and other powerbrokers.

Can you please describe your childhood and your religious education?

I was raised in the foothills of the Appalachian Mountains of rural Southeastern Ohio in the sort of small town where a stranger couldn't pass unnoticed and people never locked their doors. Summer days would often find me wandering the countryside of dense forest and rolling pasture, ever close to the natural world.

The spiritual life of my youth was rather ordinary. I attended the Protestant Church of my parents, mostly because they insisted that I do so, for I was far more interested in the adventures of a boy's life in the country. The memories of those young years are filled with seemingly endless hours of fidgeting on hard pews, washing dishes at Church dinners, embarrassing performances in Christmas pageants and misbehaving in Bible school classes.

In my early teen years I began to take more of an interest in the social side of Church life. I sang in the choir, joined the youth group, and went caroling at Christmas time. As a young adult I finally accepted the faith and became baptized into the Church. This, however, was to be all too short-lived.

One of my favorite subjects in high school was biology. I dreamed of becoming a wildlife biologist, hiking and camping in the wilderness, stalking some elusive creature to learn its secrets. In my sophomore year a new biology teacher came to town and began teaching us evolutionary theory. A year later this radical was dismissed from his position, to be replaced by a fundamentalist teacher who returned us to the safer study of anatomy, classification and phyla.

But it was too late for me. That year had opened a new world to me and I gazed at my surroundings with a new-found sense of wonderment at the intricacy of life. I found myself confused over the conflict between the teachings of my faith and those of the scientific world. Given the choice between a world view based upon faith, in which any conclusion was possible but not necessarily true, and one based upon empirical reasoning, carefully stacking one theory upon another, I came to the conclusion that science was the better ally in my quest for truth. I abandoned the Christian world view to those whom, to my way of thinking, needed the delusional crutch of faith.

I spent the bulk of my college years as a rational materialist. I believed that the world was only made up of that which could be scientifically measured and made a hobby of debating, and occasionally destroying, the Christian beliefs of my classmates. I was perfectly confident that I understood the workings of the world. That was, until I signed up for a class in cultural anthropology.

Anthropology instantly became my new passion. I signed up for every class that was offered and though I had completed an engineering degree, I spent an extra two years in school devoted to the 'study of man'. It taught me the history of the world and cultures far removed from my common beginning. I began to recognize the significance of faith in bringing beauty and wonder into human life and the tremendous power of spirituality. An intense yearning for a return to a more tribal society began to grow within me.

I learned of the western world's arrogance toward traditional cultures and of the incredible environmental damage that we had unleashed upon the globe. I learned that the thinkers of every age had been convinced, as I had been, that they knew all, only to be proven wrong a few decades later. I began to understand that the history of human knowledge has been a steady progression of 'occult' ideas into the accepted body of human understanding. Faced with this new uncertainty I concluded that I had been the one who had been closed-minded, all the while convinced of my own enlightenment. I had refused to listen to descriptions of very real experiences of the unknown, choosing instead to rationalize them away as coincidence or hallucination. I resolved to open my mind to the world, to suspend disbelief and to enlist experience as my guide.

Over the next few years I became very involved in Deep Ecology, the environmental movement and Native American spirituality. I taught myself to live off of the land, became an environmental activist, made my own clothes and shoes, and generally tried to lead a life in balance with the natural world. Ultimately, this interest led me to spend a year with the Shawnee Indians.

Life with the Shawnee was a dream come true. For the first time I knew what it meant to have an all-encompassing faith, where every action and thought had relevance to the spirit. I developed a great fondness for the feeling of belonging, for tribal life among a supportive community and knew a profound kinship with all beings of the world. During this time, as the result of a vision, the Natives dubbed me 'Chakwiweshe' or 'Fox'.

But, alas, the idyllic life didn't last... Little by little it became apparent that I, a man of purely European descent, had intruded where I was not completely welcome. The native people have suffered so much at the hands of my culture and still bear the scars. Although they made every attempt to welcome me among them I began to feel like a guest whose visit had gone on for a bit too long.

It all finally precipitated into a confrontation with a man that I had taken as my adopted brother. He told me that I should leave Native American culture to his people and to seek my own native heritage. I protested that my people had not lived in harmony with nature or in tribal communities for so long that surely there was no trace to be recovered! Luckily I was quite wrong.

I began my search for my own native roots as a solitary practitioner of Germanic Magic. I learned and worked from books that were available on the subject. That went on for about three years until loneliness for the sense of belonging that I had known and concern over the undercurrent of racism in some Germanic sources caused me to become disenchanted with my solitary work.

How did you first hear about Druids?

One day I discovered a very small advertisement in the back of Mother Earth News magazine inviting 'intelligent nature worshipers' to join a group called *Ár nDraíocht Féin*, A Druid Fellowship (ADF). I was intrigued and sent away for my membership.

At about the same time a friend invited me to accompany him

to a series of classes on Wicca. The class ultimately led to my being welcomed into my first Coven. We were wonderful together, sharing our hearts and creating powerful magic in a way that I had never experienced before. I stayed active in Wicca until three years later when life events forced me to move away from my dear companions.

During those Wiccan years I had continued to read the writings of the Druids, finding an increasing appeal in their thoughtful approach. I resolved to begin working exclusively in the Druidic tradition and to found a Grove of my own. My dream was and remains to foster the creation of a modern tribal society of loving folk, living in spiritual harmony with the world.

It was slow going for a while. My wife Jaguar and I spent the first few months holding meetings in the back of a bookstore, meetings to which nobody came. Finally a few people met with us and decided to join, giving us a tentative foothold in the community.

Two and one-half years have passed since then. Our little Grove is now ADF's largest with seventy-five members and a congregation of about one hundred and fifty. We have grown and diversified as more and more people have stepped forward to help with our work. We are highly active, gathering between four and five nights per week and have become the dominant Neo-Pagan group in our region. We now have our sights on the purchase of property and a building to give us a permanent home.

Can you talk about your Grove and its activities?

The spiritual life of our Grove centers on a localized Celtic pantheon and is deeply rooted in reverence for the land in which we live. Our tradition is based upon the study of ancient Indo-European, and particularly Celtic, practices, but has been tailored by ecstatic experience and spiritual guidance to yield a faith uniquely suited to our land and people. We undertook this work not out of an escapist desire to live in another age, but rather out of a sincere wish to understand the world and live according to our cultural heritage as the modern descendants of the ancient Celtic people.

It is our belief and experience that the Gods and Goddesses of our people have traveled to this land, either with our ancestors a few generations ago or in response to the calls of American Neo-Pagans over the last few decades. These deities traveled with our ancestors from place to place across the face of Europe before the dawn of history and our restless migrations continue to this day.

In time the people of the Shining Lakes found their way here, to the watershed of the beautiful Huron River in southern Michigan. We have made our new home in this landscape of forest, field and marshland, dotted with hundreds of lakes.

The ancient Goddess of this land is embodied in the river that flows through it. She has made herself known to us by the name of Ana. She is the bringer of life and abundance to the land, welling up from the depths with powers of regeneration and fertility. She is the mother of all who dwell here and she is the central figure of our pantheon and spiritual life.

Ana is honored in many ways by our people. She is visited at her source by those seeking the blessing of a child or the aid of her restorative powers against an illness or sorrow. She visits us in dreams and visions and speaks to us on the tongues of our bards. Each year, on Beltaine morn, we gather at her source to honor her and her parents, Danu and Bel. We cast into her depths offerings of silver, crystals, flowers, and carvings. Before sunrise we sing songs of honor and praise, and speak from our hearts of our gratitude for our beautiful home.

We gather her water as it wells forth from the depths, untouched by the light of day, and walk to a nearby rise of land crowned with oaks. Together we welcome the first sunrise of summer with song and catch the golden rays in her sparkling water, re-enacting the original union which we believe led to the birth of the universe. Newly fertilized by the light of the sun, this water is kept by us for use in rites of blessing and healing.

When we began the work of establishing spiritual connections with the land we quickly realized that we needed to gain an understanding of the spiritual character of our people. The work and discussions that followed culminated in a night of trance and divinatory work reaching out for a God to come forward to stand as our divine ancestor, a father to stand with us in a sacred marriage to the land.

The God who answered our call is Lugh. He is a close cognate to the mythological *Lugh Lamhfhadha* or Lleu of the Old World. Since we believe that the Deities grow and change over time we never identify our deities as identical to those frozen in textbooks. Lugh is our protector, guide and inspiration. We seek his help and advice often through the year and especially honor him at our annual Lughnasadh gathering.

Tradition has taught us that the ability to live in peaceful harmony with the spirits of the land hinges on a very special bond between our folk and the mother Goddess. At the Summer Solstice of 1995 we conducted a rite of sacred marriage between Ana and our father God, Lugh. Her acceptance of him signified that we are welcome to remain in this place and have been accepted as her children.

Each Summer Solstice this bond is reaffirmed in a ceremony conducted in the forest. At that time newcomers to our folk are invited to join in the sacred pact. This relationship comes with a heavy obligation as we strive to live responsibly as her respectful children. We consider ourselves to be the protectors of the watershed and the many species with whom we share this home.

The spirits of our ancestors are also very significant in our world view. We consult and honor them continually as we go about our busy lives. At Samhain we go out into the forest at sunset and invite them to join us in a joyful trance dance where the spirits of all generations entwine. We consult them when making decisions and seek their guidance in all matters of import.

The God who helps us to make contact with the dead is *Manannan mac Lir*. He guides our loved ones across the boundary between the worlds and cares for them until their return. He is a beneficent and gracious host in the Otherworld where they enjoy great banquets and are free from disease. The Grey Walker is key to all of our rites involving the dead and we call to him by ringing bells and blowing on a conch shell. Those who aspire to the arts of magic and particularly that of shape changing have been known to seek him along the quiet banks of our many lakes, where his birds, the crane and the heron frequent.

At the social center of our tribe is the Goddess Brid. She seems to be very similar to the textbook Brighid with the exception of the latter's river Goddess aspects. She tends our spiritual hearth and rules over the laws of hospitality. She is key to our success, watching over the social glue that holds our group together.

Our God of youth, beauty and romantic love, Aren, is a cognate of *Angus mac Oc*. He appears to us at Beltaine and rules over our springtime rites. According to our mythos he joins in our springtime revelry and catches the eye of Ana. As star-crossed lovers they pursue their desire in a short-lived, but passionate affair that ends each Samhain as he flees in the form of a swan.

There is one additional God who is a part of our world for whom we have no name. Despite nearly a full year of searching for him our contacts continue to be fleeting but awe-inspiring. He is the Lord of the Wild who holds dominion over the wild lands and the animal kin beyond our cities and towns. He usually appears in stag form, but too little is known of him to be sure of his full character.

Each spring and fall we send out a hunting party in an effort to know and honor this important God. We take no weapons on these journeys, but travel and camp as if we were a party in pursuit of the wisest of game. We travel through the wild country of our homeland in silent reverence for the natural world. We find our way through the use of augury, watching the flight of birds, the behavior of deer, listening to the sounds around us and the voices in our souls.

Also important to our people is a group of entities that we collectively call 'the Allies'. They include the spirits of the Native American dead who once called this land home, their living descendants and their Gods. We offer them respect as honored guests though we do not worship them. A number of their descendants are among the members of our new tribe, and are invited to share in our celebrations around our sacred hearth.

The rite on each high day starts in the forest at sunset and lasts until after the following sunset. Once per year, at *Beltaine*, the flame that is tended in our Grove shrine is extinguished. The new flame is lit using a bow drill and is consecrated with nine sacred woods. Prior to all our rites, regardless of the weather, we gather to kindle the ritual fire from that sacred flame and keep a vigil over it throughout the night.

Our year begins with the celebration of *Samhain*. The main rite is on the day following the fire vigil and centers around honoring the dead and the Otherworldly God, *Manannan*. We hold a public feast in their honor and speak fondly of their memory.

At Yule we celebrate the return of the sun. At this time we also celebrate the children in our community. Some years we perform a sacred drama of helping the sun return, decorate a community tree and gather food and clothing for the homeless.

Imbolg is the holiday of the Goddess Brid. We celebrate the first signs of spring and our impending rescue from the cold grip of winter. Huddled around the winter hearth, we also work to strengthen the social ties of our community.

Spring Equinox is our time of seed blessing and preparing for the work of summer. We gather to celebrate the fertile power of the Earth and talk about our plans for the coming busy season.

Beltaine is a rite of the fertility of the Earth and the joys of youthful love presided over by the God Aren. We hold a lively Maypole dance and revel in the delights of the springtime. We choose a King or Queen for the day, by drawing pieces of bannock cake from a basket. This individual voluntarily sacrifices him or herself for the fertility of the land and the health of the people by thrice jumping the ceremonial fire.

At the Summer Solstice we re-enact the sacred marriage between our people and the land, embodied in the marriage of Ana and Lugh. The two aren't actually reunited until *Samhain,* but we choose this time to encourage the return to the proper social order. The sovereignty afforded by this rite is particularly important to us through the remainder of the summer and harvest season.

Lughnasadh is the time of our annual gathering. We host a Pagan festival in our watershed and people from near and far join us in our revelry. We conduct the traditional rites of the first grain harvest and of praise to Lugh. We hold athletic competitions to select our Grove Champion and we feast and laugh, forming new bonds of friendship in the community.

The final rite of the year is the Fall Equinox, our harvest celebration. We gather to feast and give thanks to the spirits of nature and the deities for the abundance that our hard work through the summer has yielded.

You were recently elected Arch Druid for ADF and seem to be taking the group in some new directions. Can you discuss that a bit?

I am new in my leadership position within ADF, having been elected only six months ago. I am the first elected Arch Druid for our organization and face the formidable task of stepping into the shoes of my talented predecessor, Isaac Bonewits, our founder and Arch Druid for the past twelve years.

When I joined ADF I was drawn by Isaac's vision of an open and accessible religious community founded on scholasticism and an emphasis on excellence. Over the years I have remained a strong supporter of that vision and have worked to do my part in implementing it. Since much of Isaac's vision has been incorporated into my own goals, the ultimate direction of the organization should be largely unaffected by my taking over the reins.

Where substantial change will be seen is in the steps taken to reach those long-terms goals. I have set myself to the task of spending the first year or so of my nine-year term on issues of organizational structure, communications and management. While these are the least exciting portions of the job, I believe that they will be crucial to facilitating the years of growth that are ahead of us.

One of the areas of innovation thus far has been our communications structure. One of the major challenges to ADF has always been our concept of distributed leadership. Our board of directors or 'Mother Grove' is composed of officers who are scattered across the country. Our leaders rise through the ranks from positions of local leadership and many of them, like me, still wear both hats. This makes our time resources precious and presents some serious logistical problems.

The challenge of finding a cost-effective way for us to get our work done has been answered through extensive use of the internet. While this medium presents its own set of problems it has greatly increased our ability to share a large workload, even when some of the officers have never even met. This effort has also allowed us to lay the foundations for our next organizational expansion, when we will likely have international officers who have arisen from Groves overseas.

A second area of the organization that has received substantial attention in these first months is our study program. For a variety of reasons the participation of our membership in the ADF study program, which centers on clergy training, has always been low. With the election of a new Preceptor we have set ourselves to the task of reorganizing and refreshing the entire system. We have totally reorganized the administration to facilitate quicker response to our students, are strengthening our existing clergy training, and are in the process of designing additional programs for non-clergy training in fields such as Bard, Diviner and Healer.

Another area that has seen major change is our publications. ADF's newsletters and magazine have been a source of angst since our early days for members and leaders alike. To correct these problems we have consolidated our publications into a single quarterly magazine and have updated our publishing effort to take advantage of more sophisticated technologies. Our new Chronicler has assembled a competent staff of individuals and the early returns of these efforts are quite promising.

In the near future we will be examining other aspects of ADF such as our Guilds, special interest groups and Groves, looking for opportunities for improvement. With the implementation of the new study program the Guilds will see a burst of activity. Shortly thereafter I plan to devote some of our creative energy toward strengthening our existing Groves and expanding their number through Grove organizing efforts, education, and communications improvements.

I have long had the desire to see ADF offering more specific spiritual and theological resources to our membership. I believe that the only way for us to make a substantial contribution toward mainstream acceptance of our ways and the long-term survival of our ecosystem is for our membership to experience Druidism as a transforming faith and spiritual way of life. Though still in its infancy, we have begun to concentrate on efforts to generate training materials and access to spiritual resources like never before. The first step, which is nearing completion, is the creation of an introductory course in Druidic magic, spirituality, and scholarship for our new members that will be called The Dedicants Program.

A much more substantial effort is just in the concept stages. Over the years we have developed a tremendous base of knowledge and experience in our scholars, diviners, ritual leaders, liturgists and magicians. We are beginning to organize them in an effort to pool their wisdom into the creation of a unique magical system and religious Order to train those who seek our ways. I predict that this effort will ultimately do much to empower and transform ADF into the fellowship of which we have dreamed.

If I were to look at the organization at the other end of my term I would confess that I have great hope for the future. By the time that I retire ADF will have established itself to an even greater extent as a Neo-Pagan institution of competence and faith. We will have greatly expanded our positive impact upon the Neo-Pagan community worldwide with permanent facilities doing great works of charity, magic and public education. With the will of the Gods we will have obtained land for the construction of our College of Druidism and will have established a reputation for producing some of the world's finest Clergy, Bards, Healers and artisans.

Joining hands and efforts with our neighbors in other Neo-Pagan organizations we will together bring great change and hope for the future of our world.

Now

Reverend John Adelmann aka 'Fox' continues to live in the Huron River watershed on his farm in southern Michigan. He remains active in the leadership of *Ár nDríaocht Féin* holding the rank of Senior Priest and title of Archdruid *Emeritus*. Today his most formal duty as Preceptor of the ADF Clergy Council is overseeing the education and training of all new Priests and Initiates.

The ADF, now more than 30 years old, continues to grow and expand with membership around the world and nearly 80 local Groves in North America, Europe and Australia. Leadership of the organization has passed to the third elected Archdruid, Rev. Kirk Thomas. The local Grove that Fox founded, Shining Lakes

Grove, ADF, continues to celebrate the seasons of the year and the relationship between the folk and the land much as he described 20 years ago, but now under the leadership of his successor, Rev. Robert Henderson.

Ceisiwr Serith
Interviewed August 13, 1996
Via internet

Ceisiwr is the author of *The Pagan Family* (Llewellyn Publishers, St Paul, MN 1994), a handbook for raising Pagan children. He has also written numerous articles, most recently a number on Proto-Indo-European religion, and several on the Gaulish God Cernunnos. Since this interview, he has published *A Book of Pagan Prayer, A Pagan Ritual Prayer Book, Deep Ancestors: Practicing the Religion of the Proto-Indo-Europeans,* and *Back to the Beginnings,* an attempt to recreate Wicca from scratch using the best scholarship available today.

Can you please describe your religious upbringing as a child? What was it like for you at home?

I was raised Roman Catholic, with a year and a half of Catholic school, and a year or so as an altar boy. I recently saw someone write that you can't really count as an ex-Catholic unless you were a pre-Vatican II Catholic. Well, I qualify.

How did you first find out about Druids and what drew you to that path? Or Celtic spirituality if you don't call yourself a Druid.

Druidism in general I encountered along with my studies of ancient Paganism. I became involved in ADF when I heard Isaac Bonewits speak at a Pagan gathering when he was first organizing the group. His concern for scholarship impressed me; I had subscribed to Pentalpha Journal/Druid Chronicler for a short time, and found the scholarship level of this work to be refreshing. When he described what he wanted to do with ADF I knew it was the group for me.

Celtic spirituality attracted me first when I read the *Mabinogion*. I had been a Wiccan for a few years, and had read in many places that Wicca was Celtic. So I read this Celtic text, and discovered just how un-Celtic I had been. The stories, especially the Four Branches, were strongly appealing. They are still my favorite Celtic texts.

I started out in high school, forming a Coven with a friend. We were actually not intending it to be serious; we were going to be the school's Witches. It never went very far; we only initiated one other person. But in doing the research I got hooked.

In college I studied Eastern religions. I found both the experiential side and the scholarly side to be great fun. This gave me a scholarly bent, which I have continued and, I hope, refined since then. Most of my time as a Pagan has been as a practitioner of family Paganism. My family is my group, and we practice the important aspects of the domestic cult. For a year and a half I was a member of an ADF Grove, a fun experience which did wonders for my ritual writing skills.

How were you trained as Druid?

I am essentially self-trained. I have attended workshops and gatherings in which I received some training in such things as Neo-Shamanism, drumming, and ritual writing, but most of my work I have done by myself. My time in the Grove gave me the opportunity to bounce ideas off other people, and to see rituals I wrote performed. That was a great training time, and I am grateful for it.

How do you personally define Druidism or Celtic spirituality?

Worshipping the Gods as they wish to be worshipped, my motto is: 'As Paleo as possible, under the circumstances.' We know quite a lot about how the ancient Gods were worshipped.

Since ADF is a pan-Indo-European group which uses 'Druid' loosely to include the priests of the other Indo-European cultures – the Flamens, Brahmans, and Godhi, I include the principles of Indo-European religion in general in my Druidism.

You have written a lot about Pagan families, can you describe how you worship with your family? Things other Druids and Pagans can do with their kids?

The short answer is; 'read the book.' What I describe in there is essentially what I do with my family. The important thing about family worship is that family worship is important. In fact, it is the most important aspect of Paganism. In ancient times, most Pagans did not serve as priests or priestesses. There were professionals to do that. What the everyday Pagan did was to honor his ancestors, the deities he was personally attached to, and the local land spirits. You can be a good Pagan and do just that. In fact, you can't be a very good Pagan without doing that. Don't let your Coven, or your Grove, or whatever, become a substitute for your home worship.

The real worship side of family Paganism should take place daily, with prayers and occasional offerings. Make the seasonal festivals more celebratory than worshipping, with the exception of Samhain, which should have a solemn aspect. Set up a family shrine with images associated with your ancestors and patron deities, and pray there daily. Have bedtime prayers. The repetition wears the Pagan nature deep.

You have written quite a bit about Pagan prayer, can you discuss that?

The ancient Pagans were big pray-ers. That is something that many Neo-Pagans have lost, I think because they wrongly associate it with Christianity. A good place to find examples of Pagan prayers is in the Greek tragedies. The characters there pray at the drop of a corpse. We have records as well of Roman and Vedic prayers, and even a few Pagan Celtic ones.

The prayers we have show us that there is a standard format to Pagan prayer, at least to Indo-European prayer. First the God is identified. With so many Gods to pray to, it important to make this clear right off the bat. You can be straightforward: 'I pray to Mithras,' or more subtle, 'God of Contracts, I pray to you.' This is followed by titles and descriptions of the God. What you are doing here is explaining why the deity should pay attention to you.

You are leading up to your own request. Did the God do

something like this in the past? Then he is more likely to do it for you, so remind him of it. Plus the reminders of the God's deed amount to praise. Gods like praise. Once you have finished with the deeds and titles of the God, then you can go on to your own request. When that is over, you mention what you will do in return – you can promise an offering, for instance.

This last bit is so important that it cannot be overemphasized. It is the essence of Pagan worship. The Proto-Indo-Europeans had a great word, *ghosti-, which meant 'someone with whom you have a reciprocal obligation of hospitality'. Our words 'guest' and 'host' both come from it. Now here is the great mystery of Paganism: We are *ghostiēs to the Gods. We have a reciprocal obligation of hospitality with them. Sometimes we are the hosts, and we give them gifts, with open hands. Sometimes they are the hosts, and they give us gifts. Their gifts are greater, because it is fitting for a powerful host to give great gifts to a less powerful guest, and it would be presumptuous for the less powerful to attempt to reciprocate equally.

This guest-host relationship is a cycle, as important to us as the cycle of the year or of the moon. In fact, it is more important, because it is the cycle in which we, as humans, are most intimately related to the deities. It is how we relate to them.

This is all prayer. To give an offering is a prayer. It is an act of communication with the Gods. It shows them that we know what our duty is.

You seem to lean heavily towards the Indo-European interpretation of Druidism, can you discuss the rational for that?

ADF is a pan-Indo-European organization. As a member of it I naturally take an Indo-European view. From a personal point of view, I do not really view Druidism as an Indo-European thing. I see it as the Celtic manifestation of an Indo-European thing. It is unfortunate that we have so little preserved that is from the Pagan Celtic period. That means that we have to interpret what we have from later periods; myths preserved by monks, folk customs and tales, etc. – as well as what we do have from the Pagans; archaeological remains, a few prayers, travelers' reports. The best way to interpret them is to compare them to what we know about related religions. This will help fill in some of the holes. For instance, the Irish Nechtan guards a well of power. Boand approaches it improperly, and is wounded as a result. Similar stories are told of the Roman Neptune, and the Indo-Iranian Apam Napat. The names are even cognates. This adds to the depth of our knowledge about Nechtan, and assures us that this story, preserved by Christians, has been preserved accurately.

I myself follow not only the Celtic religion, but also the Proto-Indo-European religion. I find the deities (Dyēus Ptēr, Perkwūnos, Xausōs), the rituals (circumambulation, the honoring of the fire, facing east to pray), and most importantly the concepts, especially reciprocity between the Gods and us, appeal to me on a very deep level. It is only natural, then, that when I approach Celtic religion I would see it through an Indo-European filter.

Are there any problems in the Druid community that you are aware of?

I am not well enough acquainted with Druidism as a whole to answer to that, except to say that Druidism is in a way beset by romanticism. This has its roots in the origins of modern Druidism as a 19th century Meso-Pagan group, as well as the popular view of the Celts as 'misty and mystical'. The Meso-Pagan influence also shows up in some groups, with aspects of such frauds as Iolo Morganwg still being taken seriously.

ADF is currently undergoing a transition from a religion led by its founder to one led by its members. The result will certainly be a period of definition. I have my own ideas as to what that definition should be (concern for scholarship, pan-Indo-European emphasis), and I hope to be of some influence in the debate.

Are there any issues within Druidism of particular concern to you?
There is a serious lack of scholarship within Neo-Paganism in general. This can best be seen by checking the bibliographies of books on the subject. We are all reading the same books. Worse, we are all reading each others' books. The result is an intellectual in-breeding that can lead to disaster. An error is made in one book, and repeated from book to book with no one bothering to check the original sources. The most absurd things end up being popularized this way. It is OK for someone to believe whatever they want. It is not OK for them to project that belief into the past.

There was no peaceful matriarchy. 'Samhain' does not derive from an Aryan God of death. The Druids were not noble philosophers. These things can be determined.

The ancients believed certain things. Let us find out what they were. Then, if we do not want to believe them too, we can found our own religions from knowledge.

I do not believe this tendency stems for dishonesty. I think it has many causes. Some people are of the opinion that Paganism has always been about finding one's own path, and worshipping the Gods as one pleased. Until the 1960s it was not. But that is what is being published nowadays, so of course people will think it. Others would like to be scholarly, and may even think they are, but have not been taught how to do it.

OK, so this is my pet peeve. But it has a huge effect on how non-Pagans see us. Until we overcome it, we will never gain their respect. Until we do, we will not have earned it.

TopazOwl
Interviewed September 14, 1996
Via internet

TopazOwl is a member of The Henge of Keltria. She has degrees in education and equine science and is currently pursuing her Masters in counseling psychology. She once taught in the public schools and now owns Black Horse Consulting, a transformational life coaching and shamanic counseling practice. She lives on a 12-acre horse farm with her partner Shawne, four horses, two rescued does, and three rescued cats.

Can you please describe your religious upbringing at home as a child?

I was raised a Roman Catholic, of course; most Irish-American households are Catholic. Although my maternal great-gran was a Blackfoot Indian who converted, my father was Irish, and my mother is Scottish/Irish/Native American. We went to church every Sunday, did the whole route – I even went to parochial school until the 6th grade. But there were always the little folk Magics done by my grandmothers. Of course, growing up with such, at the time this seemed totally normal, an every-day part of my life.

It wasn't until I grew up that I realized this wasn't 'normal' American Catholic stuff, that these things were remnants of a much older culture and belief system. And my Irish gran (my father's mother) loved to tell the stories of our family, our history. I listened intently when she told these tales; it gave me a sense of who I was. Everybody needs to be able to know where they came from, in order to know where they're going.

I was allowed to explore other paths from an early age; this was considered part of education in my family, and no source of knowledge was ever withheld from me. I discovered the Roman and Greek mythologies, which always seemed more 'true' to me in the aspect of several Deities rather than one, and some were even female! Catholicism never did quite 'speak' to me, and when I was still very young I adopted the Greek Goddess Artemis as my idea of Deity, or rather, She adopted me, was it the fourth grade? Hard to say now, and I continued to learn. I was a Goddess-worshipper and a polytheist from a very young age.

I also delved into some Native American spirituality for some time after I discovered that I had the blood, which was quite by accident, in a conversation with my half-Indian grandmother. Seems the family was a bit embarrassed by our Indian blood, and it didn't come up in conversation very often. I never even realized this was part of my heritage until this conversation one day. My grandmother that day spoke of her mother and her heritage with pride, though, and something deep inside me latched on and went with it. I studied all I could find on the Plains Indians and also became interested in the local Native American culture, the Iroquois.

My family helped develop my love for the natural world, my respect for all things that share this Earth with us. We used to care for birds that were hurt and always had some sort of rehabilitating wild animal in our house, it seems. My paternal grandparents were farmers and taught me much about land use and plants, and names of trees and plants, and the activities of animals, and both of my grandmothers were especially knowledgeable about uses for wild plants.

I have to say that my father was probably my best teacher. He was very open-minded when it came to spiritual things, and he always realized that I had certain 'gifts'. One day he took me to meet a friend of his, they worked together, that I would term 'Shaman' or 'wise man' now, but at the time I only knew this man to be knowledgeable about things I wanted to know. I'm sure that, even subconsciously, my father wanted my random Magical abilities to have some direction, and I remember him telling me that this man knew much more about things I should particularly know than he himself did.

I spent some time developing my 'talents' under the tutelage of this man, who was, incidentally, half-Cherokee, without realizing what I was really developing. I think I was only twelve at the time, and had no real base of comparison. He taught me how to meditate, trance, and direct power. He taught me how to actively listen to my Spirit Guide, who has been with me since I was born. Of course I used to call my Spirit Guide my 'guardian angel' when I was quite small, my sisters tell me. My Catholic upbringing gave me no other term for him. They say I used to talk to him all the time, when I was too young to realize that this was unacceptable. I did not realize at the time that with this teacher my father introduced me to, I was laying the groundwork for my later beliefs and magical workings.

I am reminded in relating this of a particular incident; he one day asked me to tell him what image he held in his mind. All I could 'see' in his mind was a long, straight wooden structure that reminded me very much of a telephone pole. Well, I felt rather silly saying so, and thought I was probably wrong, but he was waiting. So I said, 'I'm not sure; it looks like a telephone pole, but I know you can't be thinking of a telephone pole!' He burst out laughing, and I was so embarrassed because I just knew that laugh had to mean I was wrong. Finally, after he caught his breath, he said, 'It was my fault. I was thinking of that long, straight ash tree outside, but I was concentrating too hard on the trunk!' Well, that ash tree was the exact size and shape of a telephone pole until you got to the leafy branches at the top. That incident became an unintended lesson on proper visualization (for both of us!) but it also taught me to believe in myself and what I was 'seeing'.

But a young teen with the Power and just enough knowledge

to use it is a dangerous thing sometimes, because youth can be too self-centered. I used my powers to get what I wanted, without regard for the consequences. I got involved with other young Witchy types that had very little conscience, who were in it for kicks.

After a while, I decided to abandon it, because I knew I didn't have the self-control I needed to use it wisely. I continued to read, to learn, and kept running across wise people who would teach me more and help me gain the control I needed. When I was sixteen I met a man who taught me a great deal about Magic, but he used me more, and as a result I became embittered and reluctant to pursue this path or my Magic actively for quite some time. In adulthood, when I felt more ready to accept it, more responsible, I resumed a more active spirituality when I discovered that I could practice a solitary Wiccan path, which I did for some years.

So, I guess you could say that, though my religious upbringing was technically Catholic until I was a teen, I had quite a mishmash of influences. And, you know, sometimes dealing with the negative side of the Craft is good training for the positive.

How did you first find out about Druids or about Celtic spirituality?

I have always been an avid reader, and my first introduction to Druids was through literature. I remember asking what Druids were when I was quite young – and got all sorts of answers, none of which were quite correct. The closest answer I got was that they were the priests of an ancient people, but mostly a fantasy, and no one seemed to be able to tell me more, or were reluctant to tell more. And, at the time, Druids were not viewed in a very good light by most people. But it didn't matter; I was obsessed, for every time I read or heard 'Druid' the very word thrilled me and I couldn't explain why. But it was difficult at best to learn anything of them back then, and most of my reading was fiction and yet certain things can be gleaned from fictional tales that ring true, especially if the author has done his or her homework.

I spent lots of time in my local library, searching for books on Witchcraft and Magic and all things occult. I read the Arthurian tales in various forms, never realizing for the longest time that my favorite character, Merlin, was a Druid. It is surprising in retrospect that there was so much 'occult' material in this small-town library for me to learn from, but there was a large Masonic Order in town, maybe that's why.

I finally learned the truth of Druidism and Celtic spirituality when I took English and Irish history courses and anthropology in college, and everything in my life, all I had learned, began to come together in a wonderful synthesis. Here was something I had been searching for my entire life, finally something that made sense, and I realized that all I had learned and all I had done had led me to this point, this epiphany; and I had finally discovered a spiritual view that accepted all nature beliefs, that accepted and incorporated my own spirituality. A view that spoke of balance and being one with the natural world, the spirituality of my ancestors, that would even theoretically accept and incorporate the spiritual view of my Native ancestry also, by its very nature, and it spoke to me, resonated in my being like nothing had before.

I find that Druidism and Native American spirituality have much in common. Many people say, 'Well, yes of course they do; they are both the resulting religion of pastoral/hunter-gatherer societies,' but there is more to it than that. It's hard to explain; I guess you have to work with both to understand. There is a feel to both that is quite similar. Recently one of my sisters has found that the Native Spiritual Path is the one that 'speaks' to her heart, and we have had several discussions on the similarities and differences of our respective paths.

Anyway, I spent the rest of my time reading everything I

could find on the Celts and the Druids; some scholarly, some not so, but all with something to urge me on, to keep me going, learning. I was practicing at the time what I termed 'Celtic Wicca', but it really was a blend of things from my lifetime studies that could only go under the heading of 'eclectic Paganism'. And the more I learned of Druidism and Celtic spirituality, the more my own spiritual practice leaned that way.

I found and joined The Henge of Keltria about five years ago. I signed up for the correspondence course and continued to study on my own as well. And while I find that in many things I am beyond the material presented in the course and hence have been sporadic in my correspondence (meaning I should have finished it a few years ago), still it is helpful in some ways, especially for little tidbits, and occasionally a different outlook.

As a Druid I have been trained by my life, by the right people being in the right place at the right time for me; my family, friends, and others. No, I haven't been 'officially' trained by some guru priest/ess; no Coven or Grove or organization claims me. I have been trained by the world around me, and my own quest for Truth has brought me to where I am now. I expect that will not change; I'm not much of a 'joiner'. The things I do, the way I practice comes from someplace deep inside me, like a sudden inspiration, 'imbas', if you will – and then later, I find out that what I have done is 'correct', is the way other, more 'trained' people would have done the same. Tapping into the collective consciousness, perhaps, or some past-life memory? I don't really know; I only know it works.

Are you in a group? A Grove? If so please describe it.

I do on occasion work with a couple of people who are close to me, but we are not 'officially recognized' by any organization. There is nothing structured about us. I have dubbed us '*Tuath de Capall Dubh*', which is really more the name of the land we live on and care for, and everything and everyone that abides here. I think of us as more of a clan than a Grove, for various reasons.

How do you define Druidism? The Celtic spiritual path?

Definitions are hard. My definitions keep changing, adapting, and to have a definition written is to have it there staring you in the face forever, even if your perceptions change down the road. But I'll give this my best shot, having added that qualifier.

Druidism is a way of life. For some it is a religion. But either way, it is a belief system that honors the natural world in its many manifestations, a system that can work with other religious beliefs or stand just as well on its own as a religion. It is a personal belief system that is different things to different people, yet all working loosely within the structure of the ancient Celtic world-view, but that is the beauty of it. No one's perception of it is quite the same. It has become my world-view, a world-view that honors the Nature Spirits and the Ancestors and the Gods – and to me this means all of the ancestors, my ancestors, which are not just Celtic, and the Gods of all of my people, and the spirits of every place.

It is (or can be) a living system, an adapting spiritual system within ancient Celtic cosmology, the spirit of the old Celtic ways. It is a scholarly and difficult path, but has many personal rewards. It is not static; does not stand still – but it requires one to find the balance in life, the balance between all things. It is a path for those who wish to pursue Truth as a way of life, a path for people who are naturally curious and want to grow, both in knowledge and spirit.

Peter Berresford Ellis has put forth in his book *The Druids* that the ancient Druids were a caste within Celtic society, the learned class, and I tend to agree. And it seems to me that the modern Druids continue this tradition. Those of us who follow this path are certainly well-educated in our own areas of expertise; many of us are scholars, teachers, philosophers, scientists, etc. – we are still the learned class. Some would say I am being elitist to say so, but it's true.

Where do you think this path is presently headed?

Of this I cannot be certain, because there are so many variables, but I see many people going back to the land, living in harmony with our natural world, the way it was meant to be. But that isn't just Druidism; it's Paganism in general. I think that Druidism as a legitimate belief system in the eyes of the mainstream has a long way to go because when I see people using Paganism as an excuse to do whatever they want, and many do, they hurt our respectability, because we are included in this Pagan label. But I think our numbers will grow; I think there is a need for us, and for this world-view, in this day and age. I think there is a need for living harmoniously with the land, and rediscovering our rich heritage.

So many of Celtic descent in America feel displaced, because we have lost so much of our ethnic identity by being absorbed into the culture that was already established here. This never happened to, say, the Italian immigrants, because they fought hard to keep their culture intact, remained clannish, and so preserved much of what we lost. I think it had a lot to do with keeping their native language alive...but I digress.

I see us eventually following the path of the ancients in an improved manner, something more in line with where we are now, because our belief system can't be static; it has to evolve with our culture or it will die. To know the history is all well and good, but to be such a purist that you can't do anything 'new' is counterproductive – and highly un-Druid-like. We must accept and work with people of all positive-path nature religions, and we must work with the land we live on and the spirits that live here as well as our ancient Gods. We must adapt our belief system to suit our current life.

And we can't forget that the Celts are not a defunct people, that there are still Celtic people in the world that we can learn much from. The Irish and the Welsh and the Scots are remaining Celtic people, and within many of the folkways of these current cultures are the thinly-disguised practices of the ancients, handed down through the generations and Christianized. We can't allow these practices to die out, and we can't allow these people to be absorbed.

Where would you like to see Druidism go in future?

I would like us to stop being so stuck in the time and location loops, thinking we can't honor the spirits native to this land, that they 'belong' to someone else, that they are the exclusive right of the Native culture. The spirits of this land are just as legitimate if not more so to us as the ancient Celtic Gods, and deserve our respect.

I was born here, in this land, my feet walk this part of the Earth, and all things are connected. After all, I doubt very much that if the ancient Druids had come to America, they would have ignored the spirits of this place. I think rather that they would have incorporated them into their already-long list of deities. We need to see that – for how can we live on this land without really knowing it intimately and still call ourselves Druids?

There needs to be a synthesis, because in America we aren't just Irish or Spanish or English or Native – most of us are blends, and it is my belief that our spirituality should reflect that, reflect who we are. Druidism can be that vehicle, that spirituality.

I would like to eventually see the Druids of today regain the respect given to the Druids of yesterday, and that can only happen when we show the world that we are worthy of that respect, that we aren't just a bunch of crackpots in white robes. We've come far, but there's still a long way to go. We are currently viewed by the mainstream as just another cult. We have to show the world that we are not without the strictest morality when we don the Druid robes, that our ethics are beyond reproach, and that we are extremely knowledgeable in many areas. Of course, first we have to actually be so. I would like us to become 'the Truth against the world' once again. It's a tall order, but it's something to work toward.

Are there any problems that you are aware of in the Druid

community?

Well, we can get hung up in the history and the purely Celtic aspects to an extreme. And while it is important to know where we have been and understand the framework in which we work, we do not need to remain there. For wouldn't that be moving backwards? After all, the ancients continued to learn and incorporate other things into their framework.

There are so many 'purists' who say you have to do this *this* way and you can't do that. Why? Because it isn't classic 'Celtic'? Who really knows what 'classic Celtic' was? We are the new Druids and maybe we were the old ones, and haven't we learned from our mistakes? And we can make this what we want it to be; we can learn from and evolve through, or we can stagnate in, the history.

And I think there is a lack of unity. I understand that Pagans are gun-shy when it comes to organization (I am myself), but how can we be a significant force in the world without a unified front? There are so many factions, so many separate groups; ADF, OBOD, Keltria, and the list goes on. And this is a good thing most times, for in this way we challenge each other and everyone needs to be challenged to grow, but there is no organization between groups.

When you consider that the ancient Druids were a force in Celtic society because of their unity, their organization under one Arch Druid, much like the organization of the Catholic Church, and, as another example, the Iroquois Nation is a united people under one council, with all the checks and balances built in, and yet they are still independent nations, it just seems to me that, with our divisions, we are sometimes just spinning our wheels.

There should be at least a council of elders, a representative from each organization that meets maybe once a year and discusses policy. If there isn't, if we aren't unified, then we can only be viewed as just a bunch of separate cults, and we have no clout. Why couldn't we set up a system like the Iroquois

Confederacy, and like the ancient Druids had? It would not hurt our autonomy, and would perhaps help us to unite. As it is, we have several heads of several organizations; we are scattered and divided, and if they have come up with a universal council, I have yet to hear of it.

And you know, there really is no consistent training for clergy, and while I realize that some of the organizations are working toward something like this, the fact remains that any Joe off the street can start a Grove, a church, write a book, and this only serves to diminish our respectability. There really should be a recognized course of training that is universal and accredited.

Are there any issues of special interest to you? Bones to pick?

The misinformation that abounds within the Druid and general Pagan community about Celts in general and Druids in specific is really annoying.

And it seems like there is always this jockeying for position when Druids get together; everyone always playing the one-upmanship game; who knows what and how much and they seem to feel the need to prove that they are so knowledgeable and wise every time they open their mouths. And while I understand that deep knowledgeable discussion is often the reason for Druids to get together, still, it is arrogant in the extreme to have this attitude even in discussion. Silliness. A truly learned man or woman need not prove him or herself to anyone.

And some of us need to realize that the ability to poke fun at oneself on occasion is a sign of security and maturity, and the inability is a sure sign of the opposite. And the folks who tell me I cannot be a real Druid, for various ridiculous reasons. Like, I am not from a long line of Druids, we have re-created this and so we are only playing at it, or I'm a woman, etc. That last bit is preposterous, as we know, and yet it's surprising how many folks still believe that. The patriarchy annoys me, and the people who expound patriarchal attitudes without even realizing it. I guess it all comes down to ignorance, which is the most annoying thing.

Or if I am not worshipping the Celtic Deities exclusively then I am not practicing Druidism – but again, would Druids moving to America have ignored the local spirits of place or the Gods already installed here? Or the people who also question my right to be worshipping the Celtic Deities when I don't live in Celtic lands. I've heard this mostly from Europeans, but that is also my heritage, and I refuse to ignore it or feel 'unworthy' just because someone questions my right to it. I can't figure out why certain people think their Deities are exclusive to them. Some Native Americans are like that, too, saying the Whites can't honor the Native Spirits. Preposterous. We can honor any spirits we wish to, and who has the right to question which Gods choose to speak to us?

Another thing I find annoying is the contingent that expounds the twenty years of training thing – you know: I have not been training for twenty years and can't be considered a Druid, well, I am of the opinion that much of that ancient twenty year training included the general things we now learn in high school and college, and also includes things we have explored on our own, and our life-lessons. Therefore, I have been training longer than twenty years, if you want to get technical.

Christian-bashing within the Pagan community really bothers me, too. When people do that, they show the same intolerance that they abhor from people in the Christian sect. There are good people and there are assholes in every religious path, and this kind of attitude of lumping all members of a group together and generalizing only demonstrates that the basher is really just another one of those assholes, in my humble opinion. Tolerance is important, for all paths lead to center. To lump all Christians into the asshole group is totally unfair.

Being a Druid is a mindset, a way of life. I know several folks who could fit the description, but are reluctant to be labeled. I don't need to shout it from the rooftops. If we live our lives as an example, we are more likely to be accepted for who we are and not what we believe in. I am one; it is simply what I am, and while I continue learning and growing in my Celtic and Magical studies, I am still what I am, what I always have been, had I only realized what to call it. My talents were bestowed upon me by the Gods, and I have a responsibility to use them wisely. I feel that following the Druid path is the best way to utilize them.

Is there anything else you would like to add?

One night in winter, years ago, I decided that I needed to find my animal totem, so as to find guidance from the animal spirit that I needed the most at this stage of my life. The Horse has always been with me, but I knew that there was someone else now, and I needed to find out. It was a very cold, clear night in January or February and the full moon was just coming out of eclipse at midnight, her renewed half-light shining off the crystallized surface of the icy snow. Thinking; 'What could be a more magical time?' and taking the eclipse of the moon as a sign, I scratched a protective circle in the snow around myself and asked the Gods to show me my animal totem this night. Then I sat down, shifted easily into a meditative state, and waited.

I was fully prepared to wait all night if need be, but that wasn't the case. Not long after I had sat down, I suddenly felt the slightest whisper of a touch on my ear, which startled me out of my light trance in time to see a huge Great Horned Owl silently drift past me like a ghost in the half-light. I was thrilled to realize that the touch I had felt was the tip of her wing brushing my ear. Sometimes the Gods are not at all subtle in their response, eh? That is the way my name came to me, and I have studied and worked with Owl Magic ever since.

And yet everything must have a balance, and it must be that I had gone too far in Owl Magic to the exclusion of others, for I was recently approached by the Hawk, the Owl's diurnal opposite, the balance. Two Midsummers ago, as it was nearing dusk, I felt a strong desire to climb into an old willow on one of our farms while my friend was chatting with someone near one of the barns. I sat and talked with her a long time, comfortable and safe within her branches, and soon there was no difference between the willow and I; I had her long flowing hair of branches and leaves, I was encased in her bark, I swayed with her in the wind. Then she told me that I must leave her now and walk to the far field; that something awaited me there. I removed myself from her and walked, and everything looked different somehow around me; that entirely altered, hazy-golden quality to the air that I have come to associate with excursions into the Otherworld.

I finally approached an old dead oak tree, and noticed a big nest sitting in a fork near the top, and in the nest, quietly watching me approach, was a young Red-tail Hawk. I walked up to just beneath the nest and looked at him, knowing this was the reason I was sent here. He studied me for what seemed a long time, and I studied him in wonder, for Hawks do not usually hang around in human presence and I was delighted. There was a sudden understanding that passed between us, something that can't be put into words, and he immediately plucked a feather from his breast and sent it spiraling down to me. As I caught it, another, older Hawk burst out of a nearby oak tree and soared off toward the woods. I smiled and thanked the young Hawk, and turned and made my way back across the open field to where my friend had been talking, the spell broken. He asked me where I'd been, and told me he had been looking for me, but hadn't been able to find me anywhere – very odd; I was in plain sight, or would have been normally.

Since then, the Red-tail Hawk has followed me everywhere, and the Owl still makes an occasional appearance also, so that I know I'm on the right path, and have found the balance.

Tony Taylor

Interviewed December, 1996
Via mail (with thanks to Mary-Alice, Tony's wife)

Tony Taylor is cofounder, with Pat (Sable) Taylor, of The Henge of Keltria, Inc., a non-profit religious corporation, which is the largest Celtic Neo-Pagan Druid Order in the United States. Founded in 1987, Keltria functions as a positive-path tradition dedicated to preserving Mother Earth, honoring the ancestors, revering the spirits of nature, and celebrating the Gods and Goddesses of the Celtic tribes.

Keltria emphasizes evolution of body, mind and spirit, which it fosters through a quarterly journal, a correspondence course, information booklets and classes, and its network of Groves and regional gatherings in the United States. It has members in Canada, Europe, Australia, Africa, South America, and Asia. Keltrian Druids cultivate a spiritual relationship with the members of their individual Groves, which provides them a family and tribal context.

Keltria is different to other Druid groups in that it is specifically Celtic. Keltria is an initiatory tradition and during initiation certain mysteries are revealed. Additional mysteries are revealed at various elevations.

Tony is editor-in-chief of Keltria: Journal of Druidism and Celtic Magick, the first Pagan journal to pay for articles. Submissions are solicited in the areas of Celtic religion, philosophy, herb-craft, folklore, poetry, storytelling, ethics, history, and culture. Graphic artists are encouraged to submit work with a Celtic focus and are also paid.

Among Keltria's list of publications is *The Book of Ritual*, which is available through The Henge and provides a walk-through of Keltrian rituals for the eight High Holy days of the year. Included is an overview of the tenets of Keltrian Druidism, as well as practical instructions on how to set up an altar and the use of ritual tools. Tony is co-author of *The Book of Keltria: Druidism for the 21st Century.*

How were you raised as a child?

I had an unusual childhood. My mother worked to support the family while my grandmother raised me for my first twelve years. I was not indoctrinated into any distinct religion – neither my mother nor grandmother were particularly religious people in terms of attending organized services. They were both extremely tolerant of others. This non-judgmental behavior, which is unusual for the human race, was exhibited almost daily in a quiet and consistent manner which seeped into my psyche. It is the most important lesson I learned from them along with patience, humility, and a sense of dignity, which serves me well in relating to others as a community leader.

While I was a child, the household moved almost every year, which had two results. First, with little time to establish friendships with other children, I spent a great deal of time alone and learned to entertain myself. Secondly, with little boy raucous energy usually non grata in the house, I spent many hours exploring nature on my own. I became at peace with myself and gained a deep respect and love of nature.

At about twelve or so, I began to seek a spiritual path, first being introduced to the Missouri Synod Lutheran Church, both because it was in the neighborhood and is a prominent religion in Minnesota, where I was raised. I was baptized Lutheran when I was twelve and confirmed in the American Lutheran Church at fourteen.

At about sixteen I realized that the Lutheran Church wasn't my path and I walked away from religion until I graduated from high school and entered the Navy. While in the Navy I began to really question what my religious views were. I seriously considered many paths including the Reorganized Church of Jesus Christ of Latter Day Saints, which is a Church similar to the Mormons. Further investigation included the Baha'i faith and Taoism as well. Reading about Confucianism was particularly interesting and had a strong impact on my philosophies. My childhood exposure to non-judgment allowed my mind to be open to cosmopolitan concepts. It slowly dawned on me that I was trying to find something that I fit into rather than figuring out what I believed.

Then, I changed the focus of my search. I defined my beliefs in relation to Deity and what the Gods were like in my estimation. My first contact with Neo-Paganism occurred in 1972. At that time Wicca was gaining popularity and those practices were close to my convictions. Then I found Druidism, first as a philosophy rather than as a religion. Later I began to explore the religious aspects of Druidism more deeply.

How do you personally define Druidism?

I define it differently than most people because I see it as an important difference in philosophical perception. That difference being that the Druidic view of the world regards things in terms of triads. Rather than defining things as right or wrong, good or evil, which is the dualistic approach, I see Druidry as approaching situations from three different perspectives, which is like a three legged stool – sturdy. If you attempt to balance a playing card on two fingers, it can be done. However, the slightest shake or breeze will topple it. Introduce a third finger and it's much more stable. Mentally there are formulas which can be accessed quickly. For example, comparing the disciplines of mind, body, and spirit or Ancestors, Nature Spirits and Gods, as well as past, present, and future. Fundamentally it's to look at the world from three very different perspectives, to me that is the foundation of Druidism. The Druids of old valued scholarship and diplomacy; those are aspects of Druidry that are emphasized in our practice and daily lives.

Can you describe how you were trained as a Druid?

In the early 1970s training was a difficult process compounded by being stationed in Hawaii. I self-identified as a Druid, however, as far as I knew, I was the only one on the island. The only other Pagans, *per se*, were in the native population and they wouldn't talk. If they did speak, it was only to say they didn't want to talk to a *haole*, so most of the time I educated myself. I read and studied everything I could find on related subjects and corresponded with anyone who had the time. My reading was slow and methodical; I'd read a page in a book and then ponder its relation to everything I experienced in the world around me. In the early years, little was available regarding anything Druidic. It was a challenge.

In the early 1980s, after reading *Real Magic*, my previous wife Pat contacted the author Isaac Bonewits. Isaac indicated he had an interest in starting a new Druid organization and was looking for support for a national movement. Certainly that correspondence was influential in our joining *Ar nDraiocht Fein* (ADF) in its first year.

During the ensuing years, I also maintained acquaintances with folks who practiced various types of Wicca, which provided the opportunity to experience those paths. Some were very traditional in their focus and others were quite eclectic, yet I found all of them to be akin to what I was doing in Druidism. It was like a pair of gloves that are the same yet different. Almost opposites in terms of energy, yet alike and comfortable.

What led you to found The Henge of Keltria?

At the Pagan Spirit Gathering in 1986, four or five of us, after careful consideration created a list of concerns regarding *Ar nDraiocht Fein*.[5] That list was taped on Isaac Bonewits' van door. It was meant to be humorous in a way, mimicking Martin Luther and the Ninety-Five Theses that he nailed to the Wittenberg church door. At the same time there was serious side. It outlined thirteen concerns, numbered 1-12...95, which we felt were important enough to be addressed by Isaac and the ADF leadership. In our estimation a number of these issues warranted immediate attention. During the course of the following year, none of the identified concerns were adequately addressed, so Pat and I decided to leave ADF and found our own organization.

Our studies had convinced us that Druidism was a Celtic phenomenon while ADF embraced Druidism encompassing the entire Indo-European world. Though other Indo-Europeans performed similar practices, they didn't have an organized priest class referred to as Druids, therefore, Keltria would be specifically Celtic in its focus.

To be a Grove associated with *Ar nDraiocht Fein* required conducting public rituals. Rituals held in city parks and other public spaces were compulsory. We believed that spiritual attainment and religious activity should be a private affair. Casual gawkers and people not participating are distracting and inappropriate therefore Keltrian rituals would be invitational and take place in someone's home or a private space outdoors.

Ar nDraiocht Fein had no magic rites at that time; there were no mysteries. The scholarship of ADF was stimulating and a wonderful thing to be a part of, but mysticism, which is an important part of religion, was nonexistent in their practice. A magical rite reserved for trained initiates needed to be created addressing the mystical needs of the participants. Through a combination of research and inspiration, certain Celtic myths were selected and adapted for ritual performance. That was the birth of Keltria's initiation, elevations and Vervain Rite.

How do you worship?

The foundation of Keltrian ritual is formulaic. Precise words are not important, allowing for the creativity and personality of the individual. It is the intent behind the words rather than the words themselves that are significant.

We meet on the eight major festivals, which are celebrated with a ritual and a pot-luck feast. These rituals are open to non-initiates and are held either outdoors or in a home. The cycle of the year is celebrated to honor a God and Goddess of the *Tuatha dé Danann*, whose specific attributes are appropriate to that particular festival. Other Keltrian Groves are free to choose any Celtic pantheon they wish to honor. We also honor our Ancestors and revere the Nature Spirits in our rites.

At the major festivals each participant receives a remembrance, some little simple thing to remind people of the God and Goddess of that rite. It is essential that the mythology and attributes of each Deity of the pantheon is known and understood, hence our focus on scholarship. It could be something as simple as hazelnuts for *Boann*, candy hearts for *Angus Og*, or a crow's feather for The *Morrigan*. The concept is that each person will think of that particular God or Goddess whenever they see that object in their ordinary lives. Humor is also encouraged. For example, one *Samhain*, we handed out miniature baseball bats to represent *The Dagda*.[6]

We also celebrate the sixth night of the moon with a ritual called the 'Mistletoe Rite', which is also open to non-initiates. It provides a communion of food, drink and fellowship. The Nature Spirits are invited to consecrate the food and the Ancestors are asked to consecrate the drinks for the ritual. Two chalices, one of water and one of mead, are blessed by the Gods and Goddesses of the Grove. The participants partake of these foods and libate everything that is brought. We discuss topics of religious significance, questions and answers are addressed, and perhaps some storytelling or other related activity. The Mistletoe Rite is also an opportunity for the Grove to do healing work.

Another ritual is the Vervain Rite. Vervain was gathered in ancient times when neither sun nor moon were in the sky. This is the magic working ritual for initiates only. We gather after sunset on one evening during the third quarter of the Moon. The principal content of that ritual is one of the mysteries revealed during initiation.

Two other rituals that we celebrate are considered Tribal Rites. They are 'The Feast of Age' and 'The Feast of Remembrance'. For the Feast of Age we borrowed a mythological story and transformed it into a ritual. It is usually celebrated between Lughnasad and the Autumnal Equinox, which are traditional harvest times. The mythological Feast of Age was hosted by *Manannan Mac Lir*, God of the Headlands, and *Goibhniu*, God of Brewing. Manannan provided magical pigs which, when eaten, gave the Gods immortality. *Goibhniu* brewed ale which, when consumed, gave the Gods invincibility. Finally we honor the cloak of *Manannan* which was often loaned to mortals so they could pass unseen. We ritualize the cooking of the pork and partaking of it and the ale. A cloak is passed to each person who wraps up in it and declares the immortality of spirit, the invincibility of our convictions and the ability to pass through the mundane world without arousing attention.

The Feast of Remembrance can be observed on any traditional celebration of the dead. It is usually held near *Samhain* or Memorial Day, which is a modern-day secular American holiday. It celebrates, remembers, and mourns all who sacrificed their lives in the name of their religion, from the Druids at Mona/Anglesey and the Native Americans to the Jewish brethren who died in the Holocaust. We remember anyone, throughout history, put to death because of their religious beliefs.

Will you describe how your Grove operates?

Our Grove operates with leadership remaining constant. Participants, particularly initiates, help plan pageants or other activities appropriate to the season. Before the start of a ritual, all participants are asked to volunteer to perform various ritual parts. The Grove leaders select volunteers based on the anticipated flow of the ritual, the capability of the individual, and the needs of the individual to perform tasks for their own spiritual development. For example, someone working on their Bardic skills may be selected to lead a Tree Meditation or lead the singing.

Occasionally initiates aspiring to Grove leadership positions are invited to lead a particular ritual. However, responsibility for the Grove remains with the designated leaders. Grove leaders are usually man and woman; however, same sex leadership is acceptable.

My particular Grove, *Caer Duir*, works specifically with the *Tuatha dé Danann*. Keltrian Druidism believes that only a single pantheon should be utilized within a specific ritual. In order to provide for a greater understanding and a deeper spiritual relationship with the Gods, our Grove stays with the *Tuatha dé Danann*.

What is your vision for the magazine? What are you trying to do with it now?

In 1984 we began publishing a journal called Wodenwood, a newsletter for the Pagan/Occult/Witchcraft Special Interest Group of Minnesota Mensa. After its first year it metamorphosed into a Neo-Pagan newsletter and then a journal. When we founded Keltria in 1987, the focus of the journal was narrowed to specifically Druidic and Celtic subjects. At that time the name was changed to Keltria: Journal of Druidism and Celtic Magick. We have never missed producing an issue nor been late with either publication during the ensuing years. That may be a record for the Neo-Pagan community, in that we have been in publication for over twelve years.

Today, the purpose behind the journal is to provide an outreach mechanism to promote Keltrian Druidism as well as to educate people concerning Celtic Earth-based religions. We publish articles on various subjects with a Celtic focus and particularly in reference to Druidism. The Journal is divided into three major disciplines; Bard, Seer and Druid, which correspond to the three Celtic Worlds. For example, 'Bard' relates to the concept of Ancestors and the Celtic World of Sea, 'Seer' encompasses Land and Nature Spirits, and finally 'Druid' includes the Celtic World of Sky and the Gods and Goddesses of our tribes. These headings provide a forum for us to present those disciplines and philosophies.

Over the last five years, the journal has developed a focus on Celtic scholarship. We work very hard to keep its quality high. It is now distributed all over the country and we continue to grow. In fact, the last issue sold out due to the number of new subscribers. For many, the journal is their first exposure to the Neo-Pagan Druid movement.

You are something of a 'cyber Druid', would you comment about Druidism in cyberspace?

It's an exciting technology that is changing almost daily. Many people who have not been exposed to Druidism discover us via the internet. Through e-mail, we are able to communicate with people interested in Druidism anywhere in the world both quickly and inexpensively. It is common for us to find international communication when we check our e-mail in the morning.

The World Wide Web is an opportunity for Druids of various paths to link together in concert to help each other promote Druidism. Through the pages at our website we offer information for novices and experienced practitioners as well as links to other Druid organizations throughout the world. We now reach larger audiences that may not have the opportunity to discover the possibilities offered by Druidism any other way.

I do see bulletin boards and on-line discussions as a problem area. It is too easy for people to be anonymous and make offhanded comments that they wouldn't otherwise make if they were in a face-to-face situation and personally accountable for their words.

Not being able to see facial expressions or hear nuances in a voice has the potential for major misunderstanding. One person's joke may not be another's, which perpetuates hard feelings.

Unlike the fine art of letter writing, the time to carefully consider words is not taken. As an editor, I know how many times a piece of writing needs to be rewritten to clearly communicate a concept, sometimes more than half a dozen. Very seldom, if ever, does the idea appear on the screen fully formed and perfect on the first try, like Athena stepping out of Zeus' head. I avoid on-line discussion groups because they are time consuming and I don't like to see the discourtesy that often takes place. People fail to show respect for other people's beliefs or practices mostly from misunderstanding or being too casual.

Is Druidism experiencing any problems today?

Nothing major that I can perceive, many Druid Orders are in existence and for the most part, there is open communication and co-operation among them. In some respects the explosion of Druidic interest may confuse some newcomers with a plethora of organizations and practices.

One of my concerns is that many people assume that Druids belong to the realm of fantasy like unicorns. This could be due to the British Romanticism of the 18th century. For whatever reason, many seekers discover Wicca first and end their search. If Wicca doesn't adequately address their spiritual needs and concerns it may not occur to a person to look further in the Neo-Pagan movement and find that Druidism may better serve them. The Druid movement needs to do more education and outreach to attract those people.

Another concern is that when I meet people who only have cursory knowledge about Druidism, they assume that it's strictly patriarchal and excludes women. Keltrian Druidism isn't that way. Our practice has balance between the energies of the Earth Mother and the Sky Father and in the nature and relationship of the Gods and Goddesses that we celebrate. Female members share equal status and responsibility with men.

What is your vision for the future of Druidism? How would you like to see it develop?

This is a tough question. My perception of Druidry is that it's a growing and evolving philosophy and religion that will change as the needs and concerns of its practitioners do. To speculate how it will develop in the future limits that evolution in some ways. The limitations of the mind should not limit the possibilities of the future.

On the other hand, my hope for Druidism is continued growth, both spiritually and in numbers. I anticipate that continuing archeological and linguistic scholarship regarding the ancient Celts will lead to more revelations which will bring us closer to the Ancestors, Nature Spirits and the Deities we revere. Couple these hopes with the continued education and outreach endeavors of not only Keltria, but the many other fine Druid organizations in the world and Druidism is looking at a bright and positive future indeed.

Druidry and Politics

*In our shortsighted desire for life, we have disrupted the whole
biosphere, the living mantle of the Mother. In our attempt to defeat
death, we have created a true waste. Of all the Mother's creatures,
we alone may be able to accomplish that defeat, and the world would
not live but die. Then indeed would Arawn weep, for there would be
no young children or tender blossoms to play about his knees.*

Joan Carruth, The Epistle to the Myopians, *The Druid
Chronicles (Evolved)*

2:8

*DESTRUCTION IS BETTER: It should never be forgotten that the
forces of breakdown are as important as those of building in
producing the balance of the Multiverse. Without the bodies of dead
plants and animals to feed the soil, the biosphere would soon be
impoverished. Therefore did the Ancients of Blessed Memory
remind us that it is better to destroy that which is in need of
destruction, rather than merely complaining about it.*

2:7

*CREATION IS BETTER: The wise Druid always proposes a
solution to a problem at the same time she or he calls attention to the
problem itself. However, it is not uncouth to merely identify the
problem if one genuinely does not have a solution oneself. But in
such a circumstance, the praise goes mostly to those wiser ones who
eventually solve the problem.*

Dru Earl, The Te-Mara, Commentaries on the Mishmash (Of
Hasidic Druidism), *The Druid Chronicles (Evolved)*

Druids in all historical eras have been the guardians of wisdom
and preservers of tradition for their tribes. Modern Druids as a
group are working to preserve natural habitats and to moderate
the effects of development on the planetary landscape. In Britain

especially the opposition to the encroachment of roads into previously unsullied areas has been an active concern, and the debate over how to protect and honor ancient sacred sites has been at times passionate.

Human politics have customarily been of concern to Druids as well and modern Druids are no exception. From Tim Sebastian's ecumenical outreaches to the efforts of the Council of British Druid Orders and the Druid Forum to create dialogue within the Druid community as a whole, the debate has been lively and controversial. American Druid Orders have yet to create a unified council to address common concerns, but the elders of the various Orders are keeping in close touch and attempting to foster each other's projects.

Liz Murray
Interviewed June 14, 1996
The Bryanston Court Hotel, London

Liz Murray is co-author, with Colin Murray, of *The Celtic Tree Oracle* and has been a Druid for twenty years. She was a member of the Golden Section Order, she is an OBOD Druid, a member of the Universal Druid Order, a Bard of the *Gorsedd of Caer Abiri*, and liaison officer for the Council of British Druid Orders (COBDO). COBDO evolved out of discussions between four Druid Orders which had been at Stonehenge in 1988, the year that a five-mile exclusion zone was set up around the monument to prevent access by worshippers. The original intent of the group was to discuss the problems at Stonehenge and other issues involving the Druid community. The Council meets quarterly and now has about a dozen member groups. A new Chair is elected yearly and there are a number of other semi-permanent officers. COBDO hosts an annual pan-Druidic ceremony at the time of the Summer Solstice on Parliament Hill or on Primrose Hill in London.

What religion were you raised in and can you describe your religious upbringing?

We were Christian. In terms of religion I think what my parents gave me and my brother was a basic sense of right and wrong and of morality. We were taken to church and we had religious education at school as well, but it wasn't rammed down our throats. By the time we were teens and we had decided to go off and explore other things we were quite free to. In fact my mother at that time was exploring some other things as well so it was quite easy.

When did you first encounter Druidism?

Through meeting Colin, I met him through work and he was talking about these weird and wonderful things which I felt were interesting. We started a relationship and in the process I was learning a lot. He gave me odd bits of information, out of context, which made them even more fascinating.

What was the Golden Section Order?

That was a Celtic and Druidic society that he founded. The basic idea had been there since the 1960s and it really got going around the time that he and I met. That was about 1975, the year Ross Nichols died. Maybe that, in a way, led to there being some people around who had been members of OBOD, and others, who encouraged him to do something and that was what he wanted to do. The GSO was founded to study Celtic myth and lore. It published a magazine that brought together people with Celtic interests, Christian, Pagan, whatever. Geographically closer there was an inner Druid group that conducted ritual and attended talks and lectures in London and sometimes in other parts of the country. It was officially laid to rest a year or so after Colin died. The London Druid Group to a certain extent rose from the ashes of the GSO. It actually derives its authority from the Universal Druid Order. Joint meetings were held under both names for a while and then that group of people began calling themselves the London Druid Group because they felt they had an identity and they wished to go on meeting regardless. It subsequently worked as the UDO.

How is the London Druid Group different from other Druid Orders? What is unique about it?

I would say that it is one of those groups that involves a more Masonic element in its membership. As I am not that knowledgeable about that, since I am not a Mason, I really shouldn't say more about it.

How did you get your training as a Druid? Can you describe that?

The GSO didn't really have a structure to its training, it just happened. I learned various things from Colin and other people. It was probably more like the proper Bardic training. It was what one saw and heard rather than what one read, that is a very traditional Bardic training isn't it? Not relying on the written word, but hearing and doing, learning from your elders or from people who know things that you don't.

Something I am interested in in Druidism is that there are people who are very scholarly who can quote chapter and verse which book they got something from. They want to know who wrote what and what page is it on, all that kind of thing. Then there is another school that believes in 'Imbas', which is the fire, the poetic inspiration that comes from within. Since you weren't trained from books did they expect you to rely on your intuition more? Or were you just learning what other people were telling you? The intuition certainly came into it. The GSO to a certain extent was a network; it didn't have a grading or an examining system. It simply brought together people who had certain interests and therefore wanted to join on to the network at whatever level they wished. For me the intuitive side has played quite a role. Colin had it, I had it, we respected it in each other as a couple, very much so.

Can you describe any of the activities that the GSO was involved with?

Yes. The four Fire Festivals[7] used to be held in different parts of the country, the Oaks, Gog and Magog, at Glastonbury, were one of the places. At each of the rituals you would get people who came from that part of the country who would look forward to that particular one each year. In Glastonbury for example, there were a number of local people who came including Jamie George and Rollo Maughfling. There was a varied little group that attended the rituals. We would just go there and visit, and do May Day at the Oaks.

What was the focus of your ritual at the Oaks? Why did you choose that particular location?

I think maybe because it was quieter. The places most people go in Glastonbury are the Chalice Well or up on top of the Tor. I think Colin just realized it was a quiet little spot where you could commune with the oak trees and be surrounded by grass and trees. You weren't surrounded by all the passing tourists and strangers. We'd light a *Beltaine* fire and we also used to have a portable maze, which was a square, a Cretan maze, which we could lay out after pegging it with twigs. It was made of colored ribbons for the different quarters. That was why we made it square – it was easier to measure out the lengths of ribbon with stones or twigs holding the corners. We had the maze at all the festivals actually. It was a kind of meditational tool if you like. People could go into it on their own, as their own spiritual journey, but at some stage of the ritual we'd get everybody going into it at once. The paths were only about a foot wide. Everybody would go into the middle, turn around and come out again, galumphing about in their Wellies. So it was a communal thing, but it was also something you could use personally. We would do the *Beltaine* fire, couples would link hands and jump over it. The fire was particularly important at that one.

Where did you go after the GSO?

Colin died in 1986. Throughout 1987 I was attending meetings of what was the linking of the GSO and what later became the London Druid Group. OBOD (The Order of Bards, Ovates and Druids) officially started in 1988. Philip Carr-Gomm had been working on it for years before that, but I got a letter from him that year inviting me to go along. I've done all three grades, taking it slowly with some gaps in between. I found it very interesting.

You co-authored a book called The Celtic Tree Oracle. It was unique at the time it came out. Can you talk a bit about how you and Colin conceived of it and what you hoped it would do for the world?

It was really more what Colin had conceived of. I'm still puzzled as to how he actually first got into it and developed his own particular theories about it. My motivation was quite simply that he died suddenly, when he was on the verge of signing a publisher's contract, and I just wanted to get it out there for him. I suppose that to have a book out that is sold in various parts of the world is not bad as a memorial.

Did you and he work actively with trees? What sort of things did you do with them?

Notice them. Sit by them. Plant some. He took as his Druidic name 'Coll', which is the Hazel and which also linked to his given name. After he died I felt very much connected with Birch. I think I felt at that stage that it was my Bardic name. They say that in Druidism when you are initiated into a given group you may, to begin with, choose a name, but eventually a name chooses you. At that stage I felt that Birch had chosen me. I think it was because I was experiencing a situation where I had to make a new start and a new beginning. I was alone and the Birch is number one in the Celtic Tree Alphabet. Then I finally realized, and this had never occurred to me or to Colin before, that my name is Elizabeth and the Birch is commonly known in the Gaelic as *'Beth'*. It just suddenly all came together. There are several Birches that I remember from my childhood, three of which are still there, near my mother's house. I always noticed them, played round them, and saw them through the windows.

You are liaison officer for the Council of British Druid Orders (COBDO). Can you talk about the history of that organization, how and why it got started? And what happened after that?

It all started in 1988; I didn't get involved until the beginning of 1991. It appears that there were a whole load of people in three different groups, down at Stonehenge, who all for some reason or another were looking for other people. Whoever they thought they were looking for or why they thought they were there, in the opinions of each of the three representatives of those three groups seems to vary, but they found each other. So the idea came up that they should continue to meet and try to form a group, and shortly after that OBOD was invited to join as well. And that's how it all started. There were four founder-members' groups, which was how it remained until the first meeting I attended in 1991. That was when it was decided that they should start to contact other groups, let people abroad know that they existed, bring other groups in Britain into it, and try to find out where other people were. So I got appointed liaison officer to try and do some of that.

What was the ultimate purpose of bringing all these groups together?

I think that is something we are trying at the moment to go back and work out. At the time it probably just seemed enough that suddenly there they were, talking to other people from other groups. Up until then that hadn't happened so much. Now there is a certain amount of having to think back to what did we think it was about at the time? And should that be the same now or does it need to change?

Some of the member groups have left. Can you talk about how that happened?

There were disagreements over certain issues. How they should be approached, how important they were to the different groups. I think the encouraging thing is that in most of those situations the different groups actually are still communicating, phoning each other, meeting with each other, and talking about other issues. Maybe that is actually what COBDO has achieved which is still there. Whether people are inside it or outside it, we are talking to each other. If it had never existed we probably wouldn't be. And because of COBDO the different groups are putting on events knowing they are for a wider community than just for their own group. It's very hard to think back to where we would all be if we hadn't had this. But because of it a lot of networking has gone on.

If these groups do remain separate, will COBDO be able to continue?

I have no idea. Two of the groups are proposing an alternative with a slightly different slant to it called the Druid Forum. I think we are all waiting to see how that develops and how they set the agenda for that. Other people have other ideas about how we could get together. If we end up with all of those we are all going to be rushing around going to meetings every weekend!

One of the divisive issues, a sensitive area, has been Stonehenge. Can you talk about that a little bit?

I think I have narrowed that down to two things. The situation as it is at the moment is not right and we need to get something more sensible, more accessible. It's got to be sensibly dealt with by everybody who goes there. The other thing I have had since the beginning of this year is a feeling in my bones that the day when that happens is actually close. Quite how that is going to happen or which people's actions will achieve it in the end I don't know. But I think we are very close to it.

Do you have a personal vision of where you would like to see Druidry move in the future?

I hope that we keeping moving, that we keep talking to each other and learning more from each other, that we take a broader view, learning more about the different manifestations of Druidry and the different aspects of belief.

We have talked about this before, do you see British Druidism moving away from the Meso-Pagan, Masonic kind of influence or do you see it continuing in that vein in order to be more attractive to the Christian contingent?

I don't think it will be there in order to be more attractive. I think it will be there because even if we need to eliminate some of that which has come in more in the last two hundred years, it will take some time to weed it out, to straighten it out and to get it into people's minds that maybe things should be a bit different.

So you are thinking that Druidism in Britain will become more Pagan rather than Christian in orientation?

The Druidic period or the Celtic period actually overlaps with the coming of Christianity. I think there will always be some Christian influence. But maybe the particular brand that got in there two hundred years ago needs to be sorted out.

One of the things that American Druids notice about British

Druidism is that it doesn't seem to be particularly Celtic. We work with Celtic Deities in America and we work with the Three Worlds[8] etc. What part do you think the Celtic tradition really plays here in England?

It does play a part in it. It could be there more. I think with the GSO it was there a bit more than with some of the groups that are around at the moment. The trouble is, you see, that all the groups in COBDO, the groups that I have been associated with, are English. This means we do have this slight problem that people in the Celtic regions say to us; 'You are not Celtic because you are English.' I think that maybe explains why the Celtic influence isn't there so much and why it would be difficult for us to go for it too much. It might be seen a little bit as being above ourselves as English people, by the people in those regions, Druids and others. We might be seen as pretenders.

Do you think that Druidism has any problems right now that need to be addressed?

No, I don't think so. We have referred to the fact that COBDO is having some discussions and disagreements, but I think that may be a necessary stage to understanding each other better in the future. My theory is that if the 1700s brought the Druid Revival to this country then I think what is happening now is a worldwide Druid Renaissance. There seems to be more communication and more literature being produced. There are groups popping out of the woodwork. Maybe some of those groups were there in the past and I just didn't hear about them, but there seem to be an awful lot more, in the last eight years or so. So I think it's alive and well and growing.

Is there anything that is a burning issue for you regarding Druidism or the Celtic revival that is going on right now?

Taking it very personally for me I want to go on, meet people and learn things. That's my personal agenda I suppose. Wherever they come from, whichever group they are from, whether we argue or agree. I find it extremely stimulating and I wish to go on being stimulated!

Postscripts 2015

Well, a lot of time has passed since this interview was given. I'm still a Druid, sill involved with COBDO and a number of other groups. I don't know whether I was right or wrong about Stonehenge. 'Very Close?' Public access at Midsummer was actually restored four years later in 2000 and has continued since.

The Celtic Tree Oracle is currently going into a new edition in German. I still very much think of it as Colin's book rather than mine and I wish so much that he had lived to see, and be part of, all the other developments in Druidry that have happened over the decades (even if that meant that I hadn't played such a part).

However, that initial inspiration from him set me on a wonderful spiritual path, with so many amazing experiences and adventures along the way. Thank you.

Arthur Uther Pendragon

Interviewed June 16, 1996
At The Bull and Last, Parliament Hill, London

Arthur Uther Pendragon, known as 'King Arthur', is head of the Loyal Arthurian Warband (LAW), a group that has been actively campaigning to open Stonehenge for free access to all pilgrims.

The LAW has three degrees – Shield, Quest, and Brother Knight. The Shield Knights regard themselves as reincarnated Dark Age Celtic warriors of the Round Table, sworn to reunite the Celtic nation in its hour of need. The Quest Knights are similarly reincarnated, but have yet to revert to their 'true and former name'. The Brother Knights are of the 20th century, fighting also for Truth, Honor and Justice.

The LAW fights for ecological issues, Libertarian concerns and above all for Stonehenge access.

Arthur Pendragon is a member of M.E.N.S.A. and rides a bike. He is the Pendragon of the Glastonbury Order of Druids, the official sword bearer of the Secular Order of Druids, the titular head and Chosen Chief of the Loyal Arthurian Warband, a member of the Council of British Druid Orders, A Bard of the Free Gorsedd of Caer Abiri, Sword Bearer to the Cotswold Order of Druids and Champion of the Free and Open Gorsedd of Caer Badon.

He is a published poet and has been commissioned to write articles for two national newspapers. He is generally regarded as part of the warrior arm of the British Druid movement and as a political activist.

How did you become a Druid? How did that happen?

I've always been a Druid. So 'how did you become a Druid' is to me a rather silly question. I've always been a Druid, not only through this lifetime but through several others. Yeah. I'm a Druid.

And how did you find out that you were Arthur?

I've always known that I was the reincarnation of a battle Chieftain and of a Brythonic Celtic Chieftain. It was only when somebody else put it into words, in 1986, that I reverted to what I believe is my once true and former name of Arthur Uther Pendragon.

You are active both in the environmental movement and in the movement to open up Stonehenge?

Yeah. I'm active in the environmental movement and I am also active in the Civil Rights movement because basically my Order are sworn to fight under the ancient virtues of Truth, Honor and Justice. If I think something is wrong I'll stand up against it. If I think something is right I'll stand up for it.

A lot of the fighting I do for justice involves court cases and I don't see any better place to fight for justice than through the courts. Subsequently I have taken actions in the European Court, in the High Court, in the Crown Court and in Magistrates' Court.

As you have rightly said I am active in the environmental issues and also I am fairly active in the spiritual side of Druidry. I take an active role spiritually as well as that of a battle Chieftain, leading other people's forces other than my own into battle.

Can you describe some of the environmental issues that are being faced by Britain and specifically what you have done about them?

Basically what I have done is I have gone out there and invented perhaps the first Druid conundrum for two thousand years. When I went to Newbury I was faced with a problem. Who was the real Druid? The protester in the tree risking his life or the guy on the ground in the white frock from another Druid Order?

Well the answer I came up with was the guy in the tree in the white frock wearing it and that was me. And that's what I've done.

I've got arrested three times. I've done three Magistrates' Courts and I've done two High Courts because of Newbury. What I am talking about is non-violent protest over the anti-roads campaign.

Basically our 'green and pleasant land' is being destroyed by people who want to make money out of it. It's all about money and political corruption. And some of us are standing up against it. Some of the Druid Orders in Britain are saying, hey, we are there with you. Others, of course, are sitting on the fence. I am one of the Orders that are out there doing it.

So you are opposing the building of roads?

No, I'm not opposing the building of roads. I am opposing the devastation of our countryside to build *more* roads. It's totally different. If anybody wants to repair that road out there that's fine. Anyone wants to build a new one right through the middle of that heath I'll oppose it. It's a totally different issue. I'm not anti-car I'm just pro-countryside.

There are proposals to extend Whatley quarry. The proposals will make it the biggest quarry in Europe. I'm opposed to that so I took part in a demonstration to oppose it. I am opposed to them digging up the Mendips and also because it will affect the water table and probably destroy the Roman springs at Bath.

I am also opposed to a lot of the new roads that are proposed to go through a lot of our sacred sites. So whilst being opposed to them I will not simply sit around and say; 'I am opposed to this.' I will take part in demonstrations and peaceful protests to stop the roads going through.

In the case of the proposed Newbury bypass I spent a month living up a tree, basically saying you will not chop this tree down while I am in it. And subsequently I have done five court appearances because of it.

Was this the tree that got its own post office box?

Most of the trees have post office boxes. All the camps have post office boxes. My camp, Camelot Camp, was set up after the eviction of Pixie Camp. Pixie Camp had a post box. The whole thing about the media saying; 'A tree had a post box,' is absolute rubbish.

How does a tree get a post box?

That's a really silly question. You build it! You build a post box and you tie it to the tree!

That's it? So then the mail gets delivered there?

Yes! Once you build a post box they deliver the mail to it. You can't deliver the mail to it if it hasn't got a post box!

I am sorry. I have never heard of anything like this in America... The other big thing that you have been involved in is the whole Stonehenge issue...

Yeah. I'm taking that to the European Court. It's actually listed that on the 22nd of March papers were sworn out by King Arthur Uther Pendragon.

Basically Stonehenge is a temple as we revere it. It's also a monument as English Heritage looks at it. From their point of view it's something to make money off of. From our point of view it's something beyond that which is spiritual, which is where we wish to worship four times a year.

Long, long ago there were Druids who were prepared to worship while the people were kept out. That's like having the vicary without the congregation. There are no Druid Orders now, to my knowledge, that are prepared to do that.

We are all saying that everybody has a right to worship four times a year – Solstices and Equinoxes. And we will stand by that. Because of that I am taking them to the European Court and I have been arrested about seven times at Stonehenge and I have spent the night in police cells and I have been let go without charges on two occasions. I sued a constable in Wiltshire for wrongful arrest and unlawful imprisonment.

Last year we had a new law to play with – The Criminal Justice Act. Last September I beat that. I was charged with Trespassory Assembly. I beat it. This year I beat Aggravated Trespass. There are new laws that have just been brought out. Basically they are politically oriented, The Public Order Act and the Criminal Justice Act. They were rushed through Parliament.

In the case of the Public Order Act it was to beat the miners' strike. In the case of the Criminal Justice Act it was to target people not only such as myself but anti-hunt saboteurs, ravers, festival goers, Travelers, anti-roads lobbyists, basically anybody who wouldn't vote Tory in the first place. It's a politically orientated law and some of us are willing to stand up against it.

And personally I don't care if they jail me for the rest of my natural life. If something is wrong I am going to stand up and fight against it. And that's where me and my Order are. We fight for Truth, Honor, and Justice.

We are not going to say we are against the by-pass and then not do anything about it. And it's not only the Druids who are getting involved now. Also the Green Party are getting involved, which is a political party on a national level. Also Friends of the Earth and other organizations. They are actually getting involved in direct action.

The revolution has come. It's a democratic revolution. It is people saying enough is enough. As it goes I will be a candidate for the Green Party in the next general election.

What you are describing sounds to me like an Order of Knighthood rather than an Order of Druids?

No! I am the head of two Orders. One is the Loyal Arthurian Warband, which is a Druid Order, and the other is an Order of warriors who fight.

But weren't the Druids the great peacemakers who would walk out in the middle of a battle and all hostilities would cease?

Right. So let's let them do what they want and get away with it. I'm saying it's now time for Druids to stand up and be bloody counted. And a lot of them are. Those that aren't, it's like the wheat from the corn. They will go by the wayside. Those that aren't prepared to stand up and be counted and stand up for what they believe in have no right and no voice and no right as far as I am concerned to say they are Druids. To say that they believe in something when they aren't prepared to do anything about it.

That's not peacemaking. That's a cop-out. That's sitting on a fence. All you do if you sit on a fence is you get castrated and that's not where I'm at. And to be quite frank I have no time for the Druid Orders that say; 'We are opposed to this but we are not actually going to do anything about it because we are too scared to rock the boat.' Well, I'm not too scared to rock the boat and I don't believe the Druids of old were ever too scared to rock the boat.

A Druid speaks the truth. All we have to do is follow our own truth and be honorable to ourselves. My Order is sworn to Truth, Honor and Justice, to speak the truth, to honor your spoken word and to be just and fair in all your dealings. Anyone who can't live up to that has no right in my Order.

Where did that code come from?

From me, that's only one part of my sacred oath. Honor was a very big thing to the ancient Celts. It still is now. It's a very big thing to my people. You dishonor them and they might as well curl up and die. When you talk about the Celts, when you look around at the World Atlas you will see the re-emergence of nations on an almost daily basis such as Bosnia, Croatia, Georgia, Latvia, so why should it be so different and unexpected that the Celtic nation also is re-emerging and saying, hey, we know where our roots are and we are willing to stand up and fight for it.

There is no difference to my mind between our tradition and that of the Native American and the Aboriginal peoples throughout the world, including Australia. We all have the same basic religion and the same basic belief. And it's now time to find your roots and come back. Otherwise you might as well put a board on and say the end of the world is nigh and walk up and down the high street.

You are either going to fight for Mother Earth or you are on the other side. It's time to stand up and be counted and say which side you are on and do something about it. The Earth has suffered too much.

Rollo Maughfling
Interviewed June 18, 1996
On the Tor in Glastonbury, England

Rollo is Arch Druid of the Glastonbury Order of Druids (GODS). The Glastonbury Order traces its roots to 2700 BCE, the tentative date for the giant earthworks south of the Tor, known as the Glastonbury Zodiac. The labyrinth that rings the Tor has been dated to 1500 BCE and the legendary Druid Abaris, thought to be Pythagoras' teacher, was said to have taught there in 500 BCE.

In 500 CE, according to English tradition, Arthur, Merlin, and the Knights of the Round Table played out their sacred drama in the region of Glastonbury as did Morgan Le Fey, Guinevere and the other ladies of legend.

Glastonbury is famous in Christian circles for the Holy Thorn said to have sprung from the staff of tin merchant Joseph of Arimathea who, according to legend, brought the boy Jeshua Ben Joseph to the area on a trading voyage.

The area is also the home of the Chalice Well, an ancient site associated with the Grail legend, and of the White Spring, said to be the entrance to Annwn, the Celtic Underworld. Thus Glastonbury is sacred to Pagan and Christian alike.

What religion were you raised in? Can you describe your religious upbringing and what it was like when you were a child?

I was born and brought up down in Cornwall, in the very southwestern tip of England that's renowned for the places of the early Christian saints who if you actually start to look at any of their lives were really quite extraordinary people. They were spiritual warriors and healers and very interesting people.

They had families, settled, made friends with people and were accepted. This was seven hundred years before the coming of the Roman Church to these islands and all the dominance and persecution that was to follow on that. Where I was brought up in Cornwall we still had the wild places where the Cornish saints had established little churches.

So in those days, the early 1950s, there wasn't a large apparently Pagan movement as such. Being brought up on the moors there in an apparently Christian background, was what one considered the norm. This is the way society worked then.

But behind all this were the stone crags and the beacon fires and the Gorsedds of Cornish Bards and the Cornish Druids. I lived just over the hill from the Grand Bard of Cornwall, a fellow called Morton Nance. He was the compiler of the Cornish dictionary and a very great name in Cornish Druidry. I used to play with his children and grandchildren.

We didn't seem to call that Pagan then, it was just what we did. We went out on May Day to the holy hills of Cornwall, places like Trencrom and such like, and celebrated. Thousands and thousands of people came to these Midsummer bonfires and listened to the blowing of the horns and the reading of the scrolls and the parchments and the poems in the Cornish language. We just took this to be a natural everyday occurrence.

It was years later before we realized that part of this is was what is described as 'Pagan'. I have been fortunate because in that western part of Cornwall Wicca and Druidry and Christianity were so much inter-wound.

There is an old book called Hunt's *Popular Romances of West Penwith*.[9] I am talking about a little strip of land about four miles by two. It's a thick book, about three or four inches thick which contains, for instance, the story of the Witches of Zennor, a little tiny village in the southwest of Cornwall.

This huge thick book has thousands of accounts of Witches and healers and saints and Druids and all sorts of curious folk, just in that tiny little strip of land. That was the background I came from.

At the same time in the school where I was brought up we used to have regular religious lessons. But instead of the way it is with most people, what they were most concerned about was the coming of Saint Joseph of Arimathea to Cornwall and how he was received by the villagers and by the Druids and how he was taken with the Holy Family from village to village and introduced to all the elders and to people all the way up from Cornwall to Glastonbury.

This ties in with one of the particularly important legends for the Glastonbury Druids, which is the coming of Saint Joseph of Arimathea with the boy Jesus and learning at the Druid Colleges here before going back to the Holy Land.

Joseph of Arimathea was a member of the Jewish Sanhedrin. He was also a Roman Decurio, an honorary Senator of another race who acts as an agent of Rome. Our traditions say he was married to Princess Ann, a very ancient and beautiful and powerful Cornish Princess.

She is the one who comes into the Leonardo prints of the Virgin Mary. She was supposed to be the aunt of Mary, the mother of Jesus. Joseph had rights on the lead mines and the silver mines that are up on the edge of the Mendips. It's a place called Priddy, the location of the last Gypsy fair in England. These are very inter-woven legends. At this point there is no hint of any battle between any of these people. There is no hint of dominance and persecution, women overpowering men or men overpowering women, or of one religion trampling on another religion. That's the beauty of these very old Celtic legends. All the three religions seem to be bound and woven in together.

When did you realize that you were a Druid? You were nominally raised as a Christian so how did it happen? And how did you receive your Druidic training?

It really took off for me when I was about sixteen or seventeen. I left Cornwall where I was born and brought up, and went up to London to seek my fortune. Curiously I ended up living across the road from the antiquarian writer and researcher John Michell whose books on Ley lines and stone circles are certainly household names in the Earth Mysteries field around here.

He took the research of Alfred Watkins in the beginning of this century that showed how hills and valleys were in line with stone circles in straight lines across the Earth's surface, aligned with sunrise positions and such like. John worked on this and added further to it and popularized it in this era. I would say he is one of the greatest contributors to modern Druidry.

He also managed to decipher the revelation of St. John the Divine, which when interpreted numerically gives the numbers of the proportions of certain sacred structures such as the Pyramids and Stonehenge and Glastonbury Abbey. And that the numbers used in their building would be from what we would consider to be Druidic origins, long before anyone started to use words such as 'Masonic' for them.

The numbers describe the whole conception of a received vision of the structure of the universe in which the Earth and Moon and Sun relate in terms of their mean diameters and widths of their orbits and the rest of it. It was a cosmic pattern which the ancients had received and built into their architecture. This was later reproduced, presumably in trance, by St. John the Divine.

The key to that whole business was rediscovered by John Michell. This is why he has the title amongst Druids of 'Bard of the Eternal City', which is only given once or twice in a millennia.

I lived across the street from him. It's difficult to appreciate now but in those days Ley lines were something that just a few people at the end of the street in Notting Hill Gate were talking about. It had something to do with U.F.O.s and the psychedelic thing that was happening at the time. Most other people hadn't heard of it. Now I think it's worldwide.

Did you study with him?

Yes, as much as anyone does with somebody who has the vision and has been gifted with the knowledge and has the ability to transmit it. It was subtle. I didn't sit down in a classroom and learn anything with him. He had written various books, which anyone could read. But as far as what we are talking about, which is the Druid way, so many of the teachings are quoted in the books as being oral.

It has to do with means of sharpening perspective and vision to be able to see. Sight has always been a very important thing for the ancient Druids. I think you can only perhaps learn that when you have been in community with Druids for perhaps over twenty years and some of these gifts or secrets are passed on. You can't go there on a Tuesday at four o'clock and learn it. It's only when you are in the situation that you can learn it. This is also why our Order is not particularly into doing correspondence courses or teaching by that method. We believe it happens live in the field or it doesn't happen at all.

Yes, it's hard to relate to the land when you are writing on or reading a piece of paper. So then what happened? Did you join an Order?

Whilst I was busy learning all this stuff I also had the good fortune to run into an extremely witty and generous and very learned in the old ways fellow by the name of Alex Sanders, who for a long time was King of the Witches. Here we have an interesting thing which always seems to come up. Names which appear over and over again.

Yes, Alex's name does tend to pop up.

He had been about three years in London when he had the vision that he should initiate as many people as he could during that time. He was from a very old medieval Witchcraft tradition. He didn't have to teach. He probably taught a lot of people who didn't learn very much except 'Eko Eko Azarak, Eko Eko Zamilak'.

In other words you could read the book and become a Witch and you could repeat these formulas over and over again and hope that something would happen, that your friends would come round and maybe even like your cooking or something, and that, they thought, was it, for being a Witch.

There were other people like Alex who had far sight and all of the rest of it. He could conduct discussions with other beings in a comprehensible way, Fairies and Angels. You could be there and watch him do it, but after that you had to learn to do that for yourself.

But not everybody was taught that because not everybody was capable of seeing it on that level. It was just nice that there were people who were hosts and taught some young people and maybe in the next generation after that some good ones would come up so it was worth it in the end.

I studied with Alex for a bit. He then said; 'You will be welcome in the ways of the Witches and you will always be welcome with me, but your path is the Druid path. And here is your initiation into the Arch Druidship.'

Did you know what a Druid was?

At that time all I remembered was from Cornwall. He was initiating me into an Arch Druidship that was very much connected with Glastonbury and with Stonehenge. It took me twenty years to walk the path; I'd had comparatively little experience of either Glastonbury or Stonehenge at that time.

Then what happened?

Well, I've been living here on and off for about twenty five years. I was perhaps one of the first people from the 60s that came to Glastonbury and opened up this little quiet market town with the crumbling Abbey at the bottom of it and this beautiful green hill up here and the lovely Chalice Hill and the Well and the rest of it. Again, it's now known the world over.

There is a rock festival up the road as well, which is a pretty terrific thing. It's a disguised Eisteddfod. You have great people playing there and you have great theater and there is great magic going on there. And there is the stone circle where we preside every Summer Solstice as well.

This is the way it was with the old Druids. You started with a festival basis. It wasn't just five Druids reading out of a book. It was the Druids surrounded by thousands of people who were camped there to do King making and dispute settling and contests and games and spiritual and musical and artistic skills. Everything was going on for two or three weeks at those festivals.

So how did G.O.D. get formed?

It should actually be G.O.D.S. We ourselves write it G.O.D.S. But people like to misprint it. It was 1988 when we decided it was time to go public. I had, of course, been here since the 60s. Curiously enough we did the ceremony to go public here on May Day 1988, on the Tor, because we always perform the dawn May Day ceremony there. As we discovered afterwards May Eve 1988 was the night that Alex Sanders went on.

So he was your official ancestor?

I suppose from the point of view of a mentor, but John Michell probably influenced me more deeply. As with older people, when you are fortunate enough to meet them they do give you your stuff in this life. The illuminating conversations you can have are very often catalysts five years later, or even seven or ten years later.

So what is unique about G.O.D.S vis-à-vis the other Druid Orders?

On Summer Solstice 1988 we went to Stonehenge because we felt very strongly that the spirit was at Stonehenge. There was a somewhat old fashioned Druid Order that used to work there. Because of the Stonehenge festival and various things that had been going on, unfortunately, this great divide came between us and an old fashioned Druid Order which was only answerable to itself and did not want to discuss any of its business, least of all with people who looked like hippies and travelers, scruffy looking but not necessarily unintelligent at all.

In fact this was the trouble. They couldn't quite understand it. The whole traveler thing that happened in this country was that suddenly a whole lot of people were thrown headlong into the intuitive side of Druidry and Wicca. What you learn when you actually live in the hedgerows, in nature, all day long and all night long under the stars, with the birds and the animals and the rest of it.

Picking it up from the soil.

Exactly. So these people were slowly becoming instinctively and intuitively very knowledgeable. And these Druids would talk to them and treat them as if they were nobody because they hadn't read so and so's book or something.

Class warfare?

Yes. So this was happening at Stonehenge and of course the government and the police were taking total advantage of it. Let's use this as a riot situation. They actually stormed in and broke up the Stonehenge Festival, smashed up wagons and things. Pregnant women and little children were being beaten up. The 'Battle of the Beanfield' and all that.

I had heard that the stones were being desecrated, that people were chipping off pieces.

Lies. Utterly lies. That's just like the Romans saying that Druids burned people in wicker cages. That type of thing. Three years later, 1988, everybody who had come to the festival previously decided they would come on foot, leave the vehicles behind. No festival, just come as a pilgrimage to watch the sunrise on the Summer Solstice and be at the stones.

Fair enough. We get there. There's the old Druids going around in the middle trying to ignore everything. And there's always young people waiting to see what's going to happen for the sunrise. And police, the usual thing, pincer movement, advance on both ends of the road next to Stonehenge and start driving everybody up into the middle with their riot shields.

Everybody is getting pinned between barbed wire fences, between the National Trust land on the one side and the English Heritage land on the other. People are getting hurt. The fences are coming down. And they are using this as an excuse to send police through the English Heritage arena to try and close the fence at the middle and beat them up from there.

Nobody had done anything; it was just a total riot training exercise. The police were put on stand-by, told to go to Stonehenge. We saw it being done and we saw the Druids still carrying on their sermons and trying to ignore it all. It was just disgraceful. Had we had a free hand about what we could have done there we would have gone down to the fence and done a Druid ceremony with the people there and told them to keep calm.

So at that time our Stonehenge work came into being. It has meant, if you like, trying to whack up an umbrella to protect an emerging Pagan and Druid movement in this country against, not the Romans or Saxons or Normans this time, the Tories.

When you do ceremony what do you try to do? What do your ceremonies look like?

Well, whatever the season is we are just trying to do the rite of the season, as such. Now we are in a situation where we are down to half our service, if we are lucky, on the side of a road next to the Heel Stone at Stonehenge.

When we come to Glastonbury Tor on May Day we've got perhaps an hour or so. Morris dancers usually come with us; it's only a small space on the top of the hill. It really depends on the location, but there's always seasonal invocation, world healing, chanting, dancing, music, poetry. Whatever blends into the theme of the season in the particular place that we are at.

Do you feel there any problems within the Druid movement itself in Britain? Or are there any problems that Druidism is experiencing internationally?

No, I wouldn't say so. We've got the British government into court at the European Court Of Human Rights because they used the Criminal Justice Act against pilgrims to Stonehenge. I dare say we will take the Heritage Ministry to court as well. That's the actual ministry that looks after ancient monuments.

I think by that time we may get a change. The difficulty we have had is basically with the Freemasonic Empire. There is a fellow called Russell Kerns, who in early 1988 published a book called *Stonehenge: A Freemasonic Temple*.[10] For years academics had been arguing about whether Druids came to Britain in 1500 BCE, or whether they were descendants of the indigenous proto-Druidic megalith builders who built Stonehenge and other ancient stone monuments circa 2500 BCE. Suddenly out of the blue in 1988 CE this guy writes a book about whether Stonehenge is a Freemasonic temple, when Freemasonry itself had only been in existence since 1717 CE. You could hardly get a more ridiculous idea for a book.

Anyway, after this book you got this wave of Tory officials from the government, brothers, sort of taking this seriously. It also happens that the head of the movement at this time, Lord Montagu, was head of English Heritage. This was at the time of the Gulf War, which he was involved in.

They had this crazy opinion that they ought to be thinking about what they ought to do to Stonehenge since this book had been written. It wasn't that they knew what it was about or what they were supposed to do with it, they were damned if anybody else was going to. And this is why we have to go to Europe to get our temple back.

It's only for four days, Summer and Winter Solstice, and Spring and Autumn Equinox. They are going to make money out of it as a tourist racket the rest of the year anyway. They just put it on the internet apparently, a virtual reality Stonehenge.

What is your vision for the future of Druidism? Where would you like to see it go? Both in Britain and on a planetary scale.

Well, you know, the more Druid movements get going the more you increase the amount of human potential and personnel available and you start to recover more and more ancient knowledge, it turns up physically. Evidence that wasn't there before suddenly becomes available. Or you get insights about how ceremonies were done and how they worked with the power of sunlight and with the power of sound etc.

Suddenly out of hippie; 'Oh yeah man, groovy,' it moves into some sort of real science of a spiritual nature which some people are learning how to work. I think that as this religion, or whatever name you choose to give it, gets more and more global and links up with the ancient indigenous societies all over the world we have a chance of re-kindling all the ancient sacred power points and bringing about a greater consciousness to get rid of pollutants.

The 'dark Satanic mills' as Blake had it. There is one near here, Hinkley Point nuclear reactor. We're supposed to look after that for the next twenty five thousand years. We've hardly been able to look after Stonehenge for five thousand years.

We're dealing with that too. First they made us pay to build the reactors and now they are making us pay to de-commission them. Then they are going to make us pay to store the stuff so that we can have 'cheap, clean renewable energy'. It's a real mess...

Is there anything going on with Druidism that is a hot issue for you at the moment? Anything other than Stonehenge?

Not really. I think that for the next two years this business of getting Stonehenge open again for worship, at least on the Summer and Winter Solstices and the two Equinoxes, is very important. I feel it is an important site in the power network of global ecological, spiritual sites. And the fact that it is being suppressed is definitely a wrong thing.

Once it's open again and Druidry has got its shrine – it's source – back, then we will know what to do next. There has got to be a code of behavior established for how to behave at Stonehenge. You don't mess on the stones because English Heritage gets paranoid about it.

There are some stone monuments where it's okay to sit on the stones, we have one here at Glastonbury that is structured especially for that. But at the moment the prevailing ethos is that you shouldn't sit on the stones, they are eroded enough as it is. I don't think that sitting on a stone hurts it. If you take a pick ax and smash it then you have hurt the stone!

But people have hacked at those stones over the years.

But this has not happened in this present age. Obviously, a major place like Stonehenge needs custodians if there is going to be orderly access. There need to be marshals and stewards and a chain of command in such a way that if large numbers are coming someone will be guarding the stones. People taken in rota, how many can be in at one time, queues, that sort of thing.

What about the ones who sit around getting drunk or stoned, which is something I have observed at the Rollright Stones on the Solstice. Those people are not going to stand in a queue patiently and nicely like sheep.

This is why you have to have people like King Arthur Pendragon who instill respect. You have to. You have to be strong. There are a lot of ways of defusing. It's only when people don't want to talk to each other, this freezing out business where people think they are better than others that the problem occurs.

I've lived through the good years in this country when we had spiritual festivals and people came to them from all over. It was a lovely time. All the litter was cleaned up afterwards. You didn't get these problems. It doesn't have to be like that. I've seen very tough looking individuals on the outside who as soon as you start to explain to them gently what such and such is about they are so grateful. You explain it to them and they say; 'Oh sorry, I should have thought about that shouldn't I?' And you give them a litter bag after that.

But when everybody was deliberately split up by the government and not allowed to associate freely anywhere, and everything that happened only happened because people did it in the dead of night as a dare, that's when all the rubbish came in and it apparently became impossible to clear this up. Then the government tried to lay on our doorstep that we were 'Medieval brigands' when in fact we were ancient Britons and Indigenous Celts.

There does exist among young people in this country a very good grapevine, a good network. I think that is what the Pagan and Druid network should become. Not isolated little cells of people. We need a public, open situation in which our ancient monuments are respected by everybody in England.

Note

Since the above was written, Rollo and his Arch Druidess partner Donna have been successful with others in seeing Stonehenge fully open to the public once more. Since the year 2000 there have been ceremonies and celebrations for all at the Summer Solstice, attended by up to 37,000 people, the largest such events for 1,500 years.

Tim Sebastian (29 April, 1947 – February 1, 2007)
Interviewed June 24 1995
At The Red Lion, Avebury, England

Tim Sebastian was the Arch Druid of Wiltshire, Chosen Chief of the Secular Order of Druids, a conservation officer for the Council of British Druid Orders and a Bard of the Gorsedd of Caer Abiri (Avebury).

The Secular Order of Druids (SOD) is a non-hierarchical Order that aims to revive ancient tradition in a modern context. To this end they have held Druid rituals at 'raves' and have staged a series of inter-faith councils to promote Pagan-Christian dialogue.

What does it mean to be a conservation officer?

It means that I am responsible for environmental matters such as conserving trees and conserving land. It also means that I have an extra task, which is conserving Druidic heritage in Britain.

What first inspired you to become a Druid?

My name is Roman. Sebastian, after Saint Sebastian, Diocletian's plaything who found Christianity and was pierced by arrows. That's me. I was brought up in a Roman Catholic monastery from the age of eight until I escaped at the age of sixteen. Thank God.

My parents sent me there. I never forgave them for it; it was a Roman Catholic boarding school. The Black Monks, the Xaverian Brothers who came from America, may they rot in Hell. I forgive them now, but I didn't then.

When I chose my confirmation name I chose Saint Sebastian because of all those times in the monastery where I really did feel I was being pierced by arrows. When I became a Druid I chose to use my confirmation name rather than my real name.

I have rejected Christianity on all levels other than I think it's a system that has as much a right to exist as we do. I believe in the Goddess, I'd rather live under a matriarchal system than a patriarchal system. And I also think the time is long past where we need to have these stupid arguments about Christianity versus Paganism. It's irrelevant in the modern world. The world is collapsing unless we all come together and love one another.

I was a hippie during the 60s in London. At about 1968 I heard the Sergeant Pepper's Beatles' album and it blew my mind like it did many hippies and I became involved in my own personal mystic quest. I found that London didn't actually give me what I was looking for so I came to Wiltshire and I went to Stonehenge. There I met up with a group of people who were called the 'Wallys' who had squatted Stonehenge and intended to live there. They intended to put a roof on the place among some of the crazy ideas they had at that time.

Through living with the Wallys I became involved in the festival movement in Britain, which culminated in the Isle of Wight festival and the Stonehenge festival. It was at the Stonehenge festival that I first came into contact with Druids.

The Stonehenge festival was held over the Summer Solstice and we used to wonder who those strange people in white were up at the stones. After seven years of attending Solstice festivals and speaking to Druids I finally decided that I was a Druid.

What is about Druidism that you find attractive?

I think it is twofold. First it is a natural religion or philosophy that has nature as the focal point of its ritual and celebration. Secondly, because it is the old religion of our country I found my own cultural roots in it, something which I didn't know existed before. I think that's what a lot of young people are looking for. I think that has a devastating effect on people when they realize that they actually do have roots in history.

What do you think about Americans, and even those with no

Brythonic or Celtic background, practicing Druidry?

I think it's a system that transcends mere regional boundaries therefore I don't really have a problem with that. I would have thought though that with the Red Indian systems that you've got, that Americans would automatically be drawn to that.

I can also see that it would be difficult being white middle class Anglo Saxons in America. I can see why you would be searching for your roots and then find Druidism because you do come from that stock.

Actually that is what many Indians would say. They see us as Europeans and as invaders, not as Native Americans. They often resent us trying to appropriate their religions so we are sort of stuck in the middle. We feel like Europeans yet we are very attracted to the Native American religions. But we can't claim their ancestors as our ancestors.

I would agree with the Indians. However, you can claim Celtic ancestors if you are from British or Celtic stock.

How is your Order different from the other Orders here in Britain?

We are older than a lot of them. We were founded in 1987. You will find that a lot of them were founded well after that date. We call ourselves The Secular Order and the reason we chose Secular above all other words is because we do not regard ourselves as some sort of Priests wandering around handing out religion to the populace. We do regard ourselves as standing firmly with the populace as a whole who have aspirations for regaining their cultural heritage. We do not stand apart from the people. We stand firmly with the people.

Does 'Secular Order' imply that it is not a religion?

Yes, it does imply that. We don't look at ourselves as Priests; we look at ourselves as operating in a secular world and bringing the word to that secular world.

What is 'the word'?

The word is that the Goddess lives. The word 'secular' means of the outer world and operating in the outer world. We don't cut ourselves off from the outer world. We are not exclusive; we are inclusive of everybody in the world.

It also means a time span. We believe that there is a time span things have to be achieved in. We believe that there is a time span in which we can capture or recapture the Celtic cultural heritage. I am not going to say that it has to be within this period or that. But I believe that if we don't accomplish that within a certain period the world will lapse into the abyss and into chaos.

You don't think we are there already?

No I don't. I think we are on the edges of it.

What do you think are the major issues facing Druidry today?

It depends where you are standing. The environmental issues which are building in the world are definitely within the realms of Druidism. Unless we act together with the environmentally conscious people in this world then all the world will be lost. We must act in whatever way we can do, that's why my Order goes to demonstrations and sits on explosives to stop them from blowing up the country etc.

The second side is to understand the culture and where it came from. You get this fight going on between Wiccans and Christians.

It's not a fight that I get involved in; however, I do get involved in Christianity and sponsor conferences between Pagan and Christian groups.

I was the founder of a conference that took place over five years in a Roman Catholic monastery. It was a Pagan Christian conference. After five years of the Christians being hammered at by Pagans that they were responsible for the deaths of millions of Pagans, the Christians actually did a Mass to which they invited all the Pagans, which was a Requiem Mass for all the millions of Pagans and Witches that had been killed. For me that was the end of the cycle. They had actually admitted their fault.

I have to say, however, that if the media or even some of the Bishops had found out that the Requiem Mass had taken place they probably would have gotten up in arms. There would have been terrible things to pay. Those people were brave to do it. It means that the re-establishment of the Culdee Church is that much nearer.

In England the history of early Christianity, of the Celtic Christian Church, the Culdee Church, is linked with the end of the old Druidic system. But it also heralded the beginning of a new Druidic system. The Druids are the keepers of that history.

If you take the Church of England or the Church of Rome they will never tell people about that history. Therefore it is up to the Druids to tell people where we came from, where the Christian Church came from and how they gained such a hold upon these isles. That is an incredibly difficult task.

I just came from Scotland and while I was there out of the few people I met two of them were doing just that. One was a monk who was actively attempting to revive Culdee Christianity, the other was a minister I met while I was looking at a Pictish stone in a churchyard. He came over and was talking about how the stone had Pictish symbols on one side and a Christian cross on the other and that was the direction that the Christian Church needed to go in the future, that it needed to reclaim its Culdee heritage.

I would say that my own particular Order has been at the forefront of that particular revival. We feel that it is no good for Pagans to just go around slagging off Christians, you just end up in the same cycle over and over again, they will just slag you off. Then we end up in the same old cycle of conflict.

I know that a lot of the early Culdee saints were born and raised as Druids. Do you have any particular favorites?

Obviously the one we all look to is Saint Columba. He was the one who said; 'Jesus is my Druid, he is the one we all listen to.' I have a few favorites; Saint Ninians of Saint Ninians' well in Cornwall was a great Celtic saint. He was beheaded by the Roman authorities and springs gushed forth from where his body lay.

There is Saint Aslhaeph who is local to here; he is the founder of Bath Abbey in the city of Bath. He was 'blood eagled' by the Vikings on one of their many raids of the area. That is where the lungs are ripped out and arranged on either side of the body to look like angel wings. Once again with him springs bubbled up from where his body lay.

The whole idea of the sacred spring and the holy water is a very Celtic idea. As you know there are a lot of sacred springs, usually associated with Goddesses.

And yet, at least in this country we have the names of Christian saints implanted upon those springs. And that means something. That is our heritage and we have to disentangle it through centuries of covering up.

When you look at the sacred spring you are choosing to honor the Christian saint whose name was imposed on the spring whereas a lot of Pagans would look at the spring and would try to honor Brighid or whichever Goddess might have been worshipped there in the past.

Don't get me wrong here. We understand the Pagan symbolism of the Goddess of the spring that is behind all of this. Not all of the Christian saints have been imposed. Sometimes there is a reason why that saint is there. This is exactly the area where you begin to understand roots. You are beginning to understand why that should happen.

You could say that it is the crossover from matriarchy to patriarchy. In this part of the world we have to get over those phrases. We have to put them both behind us and the only way we can do that is to understand why certain things happened in history. Then we won't make those mistakes again.

So we are not saying that we accept the Christian saints and we are overlooking the Goddess. What we are saying is that we understand the Goddess but you must look at why the early Christians did what they did.

They did it because it was incredibly important to them to gain the country. They had to do it. They were absolutely in tune with what they had to do to gain this country. That's what Celtic

Christianity is about, as opposed to Roman Christianity, which was really the reinstating of the second Roman Empire.

The Celtic Christians understood fully that they wouldn't get anywhere unless they understood, took part in, and generally accepted the Celtic festival system. They understood what the Pagan sacred days were and thus celebrated their rites at exactly the same time as the Pagans did. And it worked beautifully until the Church of Rome came up and said; 'I'm sorry, we have to move Easter.' That's when the conflicts came and that was when the Culdee system was persecuted.

From that moment on the Culdee stood with the Pagans, with us, the Druids.

Where would you like to see Druidism move in the future?

America!

We already have Druids in America.

I think it is going along the path it should go along now. I think we are developing beautifully. As far as this country goes, I can't speak for other countries, I would really like the Druids to recapture the Celtic culture and pre-Celtic culture as well, which we mustn't forget.

We have more of a chance of capturing the Celtic culture in understanding that English is a Bardic language. It's not just the Welsh and the Irish and the Scottish. The English are Celts as well. We have it in our blood. If we can just get over those silly labels, which is best described by the label 'Celtic fringe'. If we can understand that we all come from the same source, and it doesn't matter who we are.

We all come from Africa don't we?

Yes. If we can see that then we will have a better view than if we stick in the age-old nationalistic conflicts – I'm Welsh, I'm Irish, I'm American.

When you do 'Druid ritual' what is the main point of your ritual?

There is no form, it is spontaneous. I am eclectic, I love spontaneous ritual. I dislike reading from scripts, I think it looks awkward to people looking on, I think it's calculated.

Give me a group of people doing things spontaneously and I will show you a Druid ritual. I believe that is what it comes down to.

But in order for a spontaneous ritual to be very powerful and effective, don't you have people who know what they are doing? They have to have some kind of background.

You just need one person who is a Druid. It is the true role of the Arch Druid to be a good emcee, a master of ceremonies.

What if you have a group of people who are totally untrained?

It works every time. If you have a good Arch Druid or Druidess who is trained in the art of being the master of ceremonies. As long as he knows what is going on, you can control any form of chaos and anarchy that people can come up with it.

Do you have any kind of a training program?

No. We have no form of training at all other than if you join my Order you generally become a jester first and after a couple of years of jestering, which is not an easy role, you then go into the inner circle.

So how do you become a competent Arch Druid?

You don't. There is no such thing as a competent Arch Druid in this country as you should know from these interviews.

Well, you have all of America listening to you...is there anything you would like to say to them?

Keep the faith. Rock and Roll was probably one of the better ideas that America came up with, so extend that. Music and Bardic arts are the key to it all. Not an Arch Druid standing up and claiming anything.

Artists from all of the disciplines of art coming together in a circle will have more effect than any Arch Druid or any group. The O.T.O.? Forget it. Ordo Templis Orientis, a ritualistic magical group. It's gone. Forget it, it's past, that form of occultism is over. It is up to the artists, together with those working with the natural forces – environmentalists and people who understand tree lore etc.

Although there may be resistance, especially in America, with the Indian, Native American system, the Indians do have to understand that we are Europeans looking for our roots. And we have to understand that they have their roots. Once that bridge is gapped then you will have it. Whatever you do just continue the artistic motivation and it will all come out right in the end. Look to the Rainbow Tribe.

Dylan Ap Thuin
Interviewed August 8, 1996
Via internet

Dylan is the Arch Druid of the Insular Order of Druids, a Bard in the Order of Bards, Ovates and Druids, a member of the Council of British Druid Orders, a member of the Gorsedd of Bards of Caer Abiri, and a third degree Wiccan Priest.

He is co-author with Chris Clayton of Spiral Jibe's *Primal Urge*, a cult book popular with British Druids and distributed through Labyrinth. He is currently writing a book on Druidry called *Druidry into the Light*, which sets modern Druidry in a cosmic and historical context for seekers of the 21st century and which will include a Druidic version of the *Book of Shadows*.

Dylan is a New Age book-shop keeper and a tarot counselor who practices the arts of tattooing and body piercing.

The Insular Order of Druids was founded on Summer Solstice, 1993, at Stonehenge. IOD is one of the three Orders who celebrate the eightfold year at Stonehenge. They recognize three grades of Druid; Bard or Fili, Ovate or Vate, and Druid. Members are encouraged to work on all three grades simultaneously.

The Bardic grade concentrates on visual arts, music, poetry and story-telling. The Ovate grade emphasizes basic ritual techniques, divination, altered states of consciousness, philosophy, law, the movements of the heavens, nature studies, decision-making skills and personal power.

The Order aims to spread and encourage interest in Celticism, to build a society of like-minded friends, to prepare individuals for public and solo ceremonial work, to recreate ancient Celtic ritual in a current century framework of law and ethics, and to re-connect individuals with the natural world.

The IOD believes that new Druidic information is being channeled at the present time and that this should be actively encouraged.

Can you please describe your early religious upbringing?

I am half Welsh; I was brought up by my grandparents, first on the Welsh side, then on the English. If asked they would probably all have called themselves Christian, but I never noticed this at home. At school there was only one option – Christianity was what they meant by religious education. There was no comparative religion and Paganism was never mentioned. Whilst still at school I discovered Paganism and Eastern mysteries for myself.

When and where did you first become aware of Druids?

I had always been a philosopher of sorts. In my teens I studied Kung Fu and this brought Eastern mysteries to my inquiring mind. I also did roleplaying as a hobby and a curious thing happened, my first character was a Druid – and in order to play this character better I began to read everything I could find on 'Celts', 'Witches', and 'Druids'. The strange thing was that I wasn't reading anything new. Most of the concepts were ones I myself had thought of when very young. At last I had some convenient labels for my strange inherent beliefs.

With the above taken as stated, I had no option. I did not so much 'discover the path' as 'discover myself upon it'. This was my first quickening – and I soon found I was not alone.

Can you describe your training?

I self-initiated as a Witch as soon as I knew what one actually was. The 'Walt Disney Fairy Tale' had dissolved to reveal an occult truth. Why had the truth been concealed from me, and by whom was what I most wanted to know. Then I found a ritual magic group practicing in my area and was admitted to training and workings.

I had also discovered that there was a full working Coven of Witches in my home town, and I spent most evenings chatting to the High Priest and High Priestess. The ritual magic group was not 'Pagan', it was purely magical. When it grew too big for the temple the group split. We had all come from different backgrounds and those with Pagan tendencies left to form a new and separate Coven.

The initial Coven was again a training group. We had amongst us Alex Sanders' press secretary, a member of his original Coven. When I was ready initiation was given and eventually I was trained up to High Priest. Several different styled Covens then followed, the original one split as Norse, Celtic and Egyptian interests went their separate ways.

Then I took a break from the Pagan scene for a while and founded a Romano-Celtic living history society. We did re-enactments of battles, gave lectures and learnt a whole lot of useful stuff about the Celts. This too in time split, becoming at least two living history groups and some whose main Celtic interest had always been spiritual. These were my seed group.

Years later whilst on Summer Solstice pilgrimage at Stonehenge, I found members of the C.O.B.D.O. [Council of British Druid Orders] and was invited to the next quarterly meeting. Finding that I met all requirements I founded the Insular Order of Druids.

But I also had a more subtle form of training. In 1987 I had a bad motorcycle accident which blinded me in one eye. This sparked off a slow 'Shamanic' style re-birth experience. I had dreams of dismemberment and of the re-forging of my body by Dwarven smiths in an underground chamber. I would wake and feel things changing inside of me.

And my mind was open to some major consciousness shifts. I received spirit communications from a female guardian spirit at Stonehenge and a whole host of communications in London, from a spirit that referred to itself as 'a Merlin'. I was also taught

Cabala by a magician and studied astrology and tarot with a local society known as MAAT.

Can you describe your rituals? How do you worship?

The Insular Order of Druids meets on a monthly basis for lectures, poetry, storytelling, meditations, and path workings.

We follow the eight-fold festival system. The rituals themselves are a combination of High Ceremony overlaying a Wiccan/Pagan sub strata. They are recognizably similar to Wiccan rituals in theme, but they have a much deeper Celtic overtone. They have as much classical lore and traditional content as 20th century law allows. Other aspects have been borrowed from the working traditions of other Druidic groups dating back several centuries. There are also elements that have been personally channeled or revealed to me.

This year, 1996, I was asked to write and perform the Summer Solstice ceremony for the C.O.B.D.O. on Parliament Hill in London. This was a slightly doctored version of the original Insular Order ceremony and included a masked battle of the kings.[11] We do private ceremonies and public ceremonies, ones where members of other Druid Orders are allowed, and work with Wiccan and Pagan groups. We attend Caer Abiri (Avebury) and other group events we are invited to. We have done ceremonial work for television and radio. We fulfill some of our ancient civic duty by performing opening ceremonies for city councils etc. and I am currently trying to set up an English speaking Eisteddfod with Portsmouth City Council.

How do you personally define Druidism or the Celtic spiritual path?

First of all my answer would be different if I was talking about original or modern-day counterparts. I look on the ancient Druids as a social caste primarily. The ancient Druidic magical secrets were chiefly those that would be termed 'trade secrets' in later days. By this I mean arts and sciences like smithing.

The ancients would closely guard their knowledge, knowledge that would be considered magical by the laity. In a way the Druid caste was a collective of specialists with a deeper knowledge of particular fields than the common man. It was an early trades guild or 'Masonic-style friendly society', containing doctors, lawyers, teachers, historians, skilled gentry and scientists – at this time in human history magic and science were one.

Proven methods were science to the Druid, but magical to those who were not in the know. For example, the skill and knowledge required to take iron ore, a stone, extract the metal content, forge it, and magically produce a sword. Magic to the commoner, but once one is aware of the underlying scientific principles; it is an art that could theoretically be practiced by any with the will to do so.

But modern-day, that's another question. I sometimes define 'the way' as 'the art and science of self-becoming'. But this in itself needs considerable explanation. Other times, when asked to describe the underlying essence, I say that the main principle is to follow the cyclic path set out by nature in her eternal round of season following season. By tuning into the spokes of this apparent wheel – the eight festivals, one is tuning into what Mircea Eliade[12] would call essential facets of mythic time or being. Following the festivals over the years one not only tunes into the prime tides of life, but year by year our understanding of these prime-key-points deepens, bringing us closer to our true Druidic selves and bringing a harmony with the rest of creation.

But other Druids see it differently, and their views are also correct. Anyway the 'Celtic Spiritual Path' is one that changes every day. In order to stay upon it, we too tend to change. To try and chain the path into any one fixed ideal is to lose the path and stagnate. We must go with the flow and become whatever we must become along the way. Wherever we go we will always be, and if we be true to ourselves, we will always be on our own personal path. And at the end is our destiny, which we ourselves have forged by our 'hammer blow steps on the path we have trod', and each person's destiny is theirs alone – therefore each person will find the path differently.

One thing's for sure, the path we tread is a labyrinthine maze, sometimes it will appear to turn back on itself, sometimes we will think we are getting further from our goals – only to find them nearer around the next bend. My best advice to any seeker is; 'To thine own self be true, to others show honor, and be your own keeper rather than your brothers.' If you do all this you are on the path, or not far from it.

One final thing on this one – an outsider looking at Druidry will only see eccentric people in white robes, doing pretty weird stuff. This is all true, but it is like looking at the shell of an egg and thinking that is all the egg is about. We however know that the true value of the egg is the 'spiritual nourishment' contained within.

How do you think Druidism is unique from other Pagan paths such as Wicca?

This is simpler. By their nature other Pagan groups, Wiccans etc., tend to work in secret and at night. Druids on the other hand tend to work by day and openly. This is the chief difference – anything else is political bracken that makes the path harder to see.

Talking from a purely British perspective – up until the Roman conquest there was simply the old religion, which although it had a huge pantheon of 'specialist deities', was principally manifest in everyday society within the family unit – wherein the heads of the household were in a way deified and ancestors were worshipped and communed with.

When the Roman State officially outlawed the Druid caste, like with most illegal things, it did not vanish, but went underground or disguised itself. There were only certain 'shell-like aspects' that could be enforcedly prohibited anyway. And this shell was merely one public face.

When the official religion of Rome's army became Roman Catholicism, female Druids could no longer enter the Church as some had done within the earlier form of Celtic Christianity. Any continued form of 'old religion' worship was done in secret, at night and in much smaller groups than would have previously been the norm – by necessity. And so the basic Wicca structure and ways were born.

Other manifestations were everywhere. Getting away with what they could, Bards and travelling minstrels roamed the land. What remained of the Celtic Christian Church still taught Druidic ideals, hidden under the thinnest veneer of new religion.

The Druid caste continued, but was lost to the eye. The caste functions continued as many necessary trades, and in time all the functions of the Druid were performed by people unaware of their heritage. Assimilated into the new and changing culture, the knowledge survived entirely, not in an intact form, but in hidden fragmented forms. The label of Druid had been lost to antiquity.

Another newer label, that of Witch, was distorted beyond belief by the competition's propaganda. And to the common, Christian-seeking eye, Rome's conquest was complete.

After the repeal of the Witchcraft act in the 1950s, people could effectively attach whatever religious label they liked to themselves. The problem was not attaching it, but getting others to acknowledge it or understand what you meant by it.

Are there any problems within Druidism as it exists today?

The main point I insist on making here is that we Pagans should concentrate on our common concerns and similarities, rather than on our petty political differences. Most Pagans these days seem to be running round fighting and screaming at each other's plans or methods, like children, and over totally idiotic things. What would our beloved mother Goddess say to such children?

We should all remember that once there was simply the Old Religion. And we would not expect every family on our street to be run in the same state-prescribed way. We are all different. We are all practicing our own version of the old, handed down ways.

What is your vision for the future of Druidry? Where would you like to see it develop?

First of all no-one's vision of the future can exist until the above problem is dealt with. Let's face it, although interest in the Pagan revival is growing, we are still very much a minority. Worse, we are a diffracted minority with no unified voice. And we simply do not have the rights that other ethnic minorities take for granted.

Our prime concern should be to make the labels mean what they used to mean. As I said above, most of our ancient functions are now being performed by modern-day professionals – in a much more professional manner than most Pagans seem to be able to do.

WAKE UP PAGANS and realize that really all we have left of our ancient role is a tiny shell fragment of the whole egg we once took for granted. Pagans today are a kind of Priesthood, recognized only by themselves. Most of us do not deserve the labels or titles we hold. In the future, if we are not to become a laughing stock, we must reunify the distant branches of our common Pagan tree. Act as a trunk and not as many twigs.

Our first priority should be to gain the same rights as other minority religions have. Get these rights and make sure we use them. I would like to see state recognition in the validity of what we are. I would like to see official Pagan churches. There is some progress on this front as I write, but we will never pull it off until we can agree about what we are.

Rights are not freely given to all. They must be earned these days. We, the various forms of Pagan Priesthood, must offer the public or the state, things that are of real value or worth to them. Here, in Britain, the native home of Druidry – everyone sits up and listens when the Arch Bishop of 'City X' says something. But when the Arch Druid of 'Whatever-wherever' says something, everybody says 'so what'.

In order to gain respect from the community, we must stop serving ourselves and start serving the community. Start making it want us, need us and value us once again. This is the way we must develop. And it is not easy work. We have been happy being children of the God and Goddess for too long. The future is our coming of age. It's time to grow up and face the harsh reality of the world as adults.

We are not just children of the Gods, we and the Gods are one, so let's act like it. We are the first generation of this 'New Age', this coming Aquarian age – let's make sure we leave something behind that our descendants can safely build upon.

I think Druidry could turn full circle and become popular with the professional classes. We could mature to become the equals of our ancient counterparts. Or we could continue being children of the Gods, playing at being the things we call ourselves.

To be honest, I think that unless everyone can settle their petty political differences – we will simply continue being of value only to ourselves. Until we do, the scene is not what it could be. And being what we are seems more of a curse than a blessing.

As an example of what I mean see if you recognize this scenario; Joe Bloggs meets a Witch who says they are a White Witch. Joe mentions another Witch they have heard of two miles down the road. What does the first Witch say? – 'Oh, you don't want anything to do with them, they are a Black Witch.' Later, Joe Bloggs meets the second Witch and cautiously makes contact. Well, she seems OK. He makes the mistake of mentioning the first Witch, and what does the second Witch say? – 'Ooh, she's a Black Witch – I'm a White Witch.' What difference do the two Witches have? They are essentially the same. Both are trying to gain control of Joe Bloggs. Both fear the growth of personal power of the other Witch, because they are both on power trips. Any power the one Witch has is power the other

Witch cannot have.

The sad truth with this scenario is that the two Witches know each other, they used to be friends – they used to work together. This problem permeates modern Paganism to its core. I have seen it in every facet of Pagan manifestation; Witches, Druids, and New-Agers. This is no Witchcraft, no Pagan craft at all. It is pure bitch-craft, an art that politicians are breast fed upon. Please, please let's not stoop to that level.

It is most refreshing, Ellen, when we see the reverse. You said you respect Dr. Ronald Hutton, and his respect for me gave you enough respect to interview me – even though we have never met. That's all we really need to do, stop bickering and learn to respect each other.

Are there any other 'hot' issues for you, anything that is particularly on your mind these days?

I'd like to go back to my 'Old Religion history lesson'. When the Romans first invaded Britain, they found a fragmented group of people living in various small tribes. As they had done on the continent they played one off against the other and then they crushed or assimilated them one by one.

The only potential political unifying force they found was the Druid caste who could move freely through the squabbling tribes unmolested. This was the power of the Druids. This was what the Romans feared. This was why the Druids had to be crushed, outlawed, and destroyed. This set the scene for the centuries of Pagan persecution yet to come.

Believe it or not there are still Romans out there. You already believe there are Witches, Druids and Pagans. Are we to be played off against each other like the Pagan Celtic tribes? Or can we become the unified force the Romans always feared?

That is what the politicians fear, our unified force. That is why we don't have the rights other minorities are granted. And that is why we must deal with our own problems first. And then see what we can do with the problems of society itself.

Sir Septimus Myriddin Bron Baronet

(December 19, 1928 – November 3, 2015)
Interviewed December, 1996
Via mail

Septimus calls himself quite simply a Celtic Priest, who as the seventh son of a seventh son carries certain privileges and responsibilities. At the age of eighteen, upon the death of his superior officer, he was promoted to sergeant and became the youngest sergeant in the British Army at that time. He has not published because as part of his training he was told to never put certain things in writing. He is a member of the Order of Priests of the Inner Circle and a Companion of the Chalice Well.

Can you please describe your religious upbringing as a child?

When I was born my parents were told that I wouldn't last more than three days. Unknown to my father my mother took me from the hospital two days after I was born and had me baptized in the Roman Catholic church. Three days later I was still alive and she then took me to the Salvation Army, to the Citadel, in London, and had me dedicated under the flag, this again was a type of baptism. She kept doing this in different churches, the Church of England, the Baptist Church. I think the only two she didn't go to were the mosque and the synagogue. I still have the Baptism certificates as proof, but I still wasn't taken to any churches as such for a Christian upbringing.

At the age of three when it again looked like I wasn't going to make it my father decided to do it in the way he thought it should have been done from the beginning. I was then taken to the stones and baptized. Then I was taken to the doctor who declared me fully fit and couldn't understand why the illness that had overcome me had entirely gone from my body. Doctors in those days weren't informed about spiritual medicine which was practiced by the Druids.

It was decided, when it was deemed that I was no longer ill and in danger of dying, that as the fifth generation seventh son, I should be trained as a Priest of the Inner Circle. I started my training at about the age of five. This continued until the war started. I was then enrolled as a boy sailor. The only problem was I didn't have a Christian name and I didn't have a religion. There was no birth certificate; Druids didn't have birth certificates because nothing about Druid families was written down. So I was given a Christian name. It was very strange because when people called to me by my Christian name it took me quite a while before I answered. They thought even then that I was a bit strange. They weren't wrong, mind.

Once on board ship they decided that I had to have a religion and as the only Priest on board the ship was a Roman Catholic Father they decided that I would become Roman Catholic. I had then joined the very people who in the last two thousand years had done more in their way to wipe us out than any other Christian organization. I had my First Communion at the age of fourteen, but as I kissed the Bishop's ring I felt sick to my stomach, I knew that this was not what was intended for me. Three more years to go before I could leave the Navy at seventeen years of age.

Then instead of going aboard ship, because I would have done, I joined the Army. I was in Germany at the age of seventeen and a half. I served in Germany, Korea, Malaysia, British Honduras and Guiana. And after all that, when I finally came home after twelve years, I carried on with my studies and finally gained my Priesthood at the age of thirty eight years. I was anointed once again at the place of my awakening, Stonehenge.

How do you define Druidism?

As a religion. Let's face it, Druidism is a religion. There are some writers today who say there is no way that any of us can possibly follow the religion the way it was done before this century. I think I am a good example that it can be followed. I don't know exactly who was at my baptism at the stones; I know there were at least two of the three Priests of the Inner Circle plus quite a few other people. I've almost got my seventieth birthday coming up and I think that is proof enough that as I was very close to death's door and I've lasted almost seventy years that our religion does work.

My father said that he prayed to Our Lady of Avalon, to the Old Gods and to God Himself, the Supreme God, and this is something we must never forget. There is a Supreme God. There are also lesser Gods. Perhaps our God is the same God as the Christian one who said; 'Thou shalt have no other Gods before me,' and the Christians took Him over. God is God is God. That's the way I have always felt about it.

We were always brought up to look on Christ as a magician, a Magi. The Magi were magicians who could heal people and not just by touch but by thought from a distance or from close up. He was also part of the Druidic religion. Don't forget that by the time the Culdee, the early Irish Church, had arrived, they accepted Druidic Priests into the Christian religion.

Who were your teachers? How were you trained?

I had two main teachers. One was an Irish Druid; I only ever knew his first name. The other one was a French Priest. The first thing I was told was that when you are being told something, no matter what it is, don't just listen with your ears, listen also with your heart. Your ears hear things and then they are gone. If you listen with your heart you will take in what is being told to you and that will stay with you forever.

Are you part of a Grove, do you practice with a group?

No. The Priesthood is not nor ever has been part of any one Grove. I am a member of the Order of the Priests of the Inner

Circle. That is an Order that came from Ireland. We are related to the Ancient Order of Druids. I am probably the last of the old Priests. A Priest of the Inner Circle is part of the whole movement of Druidry. There was a time in the past when if there were any problems in or between any Orders, the Priests would sort them out. Remember that there were twenty one Priests of the Outer Circle. There were seven Priests of the Middle Circle and three Priests of the Inner Circle. The problems, if they were minor ones, could be sorted out by the Outer Circle. If they were a little bit more intense, possibly by the Middle Circle If they were really bad problems they would then be sorted out by the Inner Circle Priests.

In those days Druids were not just Druids, dressed up in black robes for the sake of dressing up. You had carpenters, stone-masons, husbandmen who looked after the cattle, sheep and goats, and chickens. You had writers, artists, teachers, doctors, philosophers. All had their part in the Druidic movement. This seems to have fallen by the wayside now, although it is my hope that one day it will come about again.

My Order is not a modern Order. It was founded in 1497.

Are there any problems among the Druids today?

Yes, there are. Many problems. I cannot see them being sorted out in the foreseeable future. But one day they will learn that what has gone before can be brought back. To this day I do not know of any one Druid or so-called Arch Druid who has sworn loyalty to the Old Ones and to the stones in a manner that was in my teaching. This can only be done in the presence of a Priest of the Middle or Inner Circle and wherever there is a stone circle. I still have faith that one day it will happen again.

I like to go to the Druid assemblies and just stand and listen to what is going on. You hear these little innuendos – that the Druids from the West Country hate the Druids from the South Coast. That the ceremonies should only be run by Druids from the West Country. Ceremonies are run not only by Druids from this country. They used to send Druids from France to be trained over here so they could go back to France and teach the Word over there. Whenever we held big ceremonies, before the war, the Druids would come from all over the world, not just from France but from Germany, from Norway, from Sweden. And they would all take part as equals, not; 'I'm the Governor and you are just one of the lesser Druids'. A Druid is a Druid is a Druid. There are High Druids. But High Druids were taught never to look down on the lesser Druids – if there was such a thing as a lesser Druid. You cannot say; 'I am an Arch Druid and because of that I am your Governor.' There is no such thing in Druidic religion, nothing like that must ever be allowed to take hold. Unfortunately it has been allowed.

As a Priest of the Inner Circle I could give modern-day Druids a lot of advice if they were prepared to take it. If someone doesn't like something that is going on they must go to the camps of the Druids and say they don't think this is right or that is right and can we sort it out? Don't wait until they are in the middle of a sacred circle and then say this person shouldn't do this and that person shouldn't do that. That is just not on.

If that had happened in my father's day those Druids would have been de-frocked. They would never again have been allowed in a circle or at least they would have been banished for one, two, or three years before they were allowed back in. You don't smoke and drink pints of beer in a sacred circle. This is what happens at Avebury. You always get two or three people in the circle who are talking and talking, right through the ceremony.

The last time I went there I thought I would sing the Blessing of the Stones for them, in Gaelic. In olden times when you said you were going to sing something you didn't actually sing it, you recited it as a poem. Two thirds of the way through the ceremony asked if I could sing the Blessing and Bobcat said yes, please. I walked into the middle of the circle and I stood there quietly and

I just looked at everybody. Within half a minute everything had gone quiet in the circle. I did that to bring some kind of order.

My great great-great grandfather came from Ireland, Lord Bron. He married the daughter of a High Druid of the tribe of Whitlock. The name Whitlock means 'the tribe that lived in the circle'. The village that we lived in is only a short way from Stonehenge. The family were the guardians of the stones, warriors, warrior-priests. We were thrown out of the circle two thousand years ago by the Romans and of course the Christians have kept us out ever since. The family history was handed down from father to son, mother to daughter. It was never told to anyone outside the Order of Druids. I am afraid I do not write books, most of my knowledge will stay as it has always stayed, kept from those who would do us harm.

We are not and never will be known as High Priests. There were High Druids, but not High Priests. We will always be just warrior-priests. We defend the right to our religion to any who would join us.

My father and my grandfather were Druids, but we are not allowed to come out into the open. Masons were, so they both joined the Grand Order of Buffaloes and became Masons. As such they could still carry on with their Druidic ceremonies. So Druidism, as it was known in the 1920s and 30s, was really Orders of Masons. It took many years, even after the war, for people to accept the Druidic Pagan way of life again. They no longer wanted to be held to the Christian way of life. They wanted to go their own way.

The Flower People in California are a good example – they wanted to go Pagan. If we had had the same thing over here then perhaps things would have been better, I don't know. All I know is that the group who call themselves New Age wanderers do not in any way shape or form represent New Age Pagans. It just isn't on. I am not saying that they are all tarred with the same brush, but most of them, whenever they go to sacred sites, they destroy rather than uphold our beliefs. It's probably seventy five percent of what they do, which has lost the New Age Pagans and Druids their rights to go into Stonehenge.

It was these New Age Travelers, spraying and painting graffiti on the sarsens and going to the Rollright Stones and leaving disasters. They never tidied up after themselves. They ripped branches off of trees to burn. They took stones to make their fire pits and after they had finished instead of clearing up and putting the stones back where they belonged they just left them there. Let somebody else do it. This is what they do and it is wrong. If they want to become part of the Pagan movement then they are going about it in the wrong way, a very *very* wrong way.

Several Priests have tried to get the Travelers involved in Paganism as we are. But they seem to be intent on doing things their way and only their way. They are not going to have anyone telling them what to do. If they want to call themselves Pagans they must read documents which show what us Pagans do and what we have done in the past. Paganism is still a religion. The Pagan Druids are a religion. I would dearly love to see the New Age Travelers join us so that we could become one. Someone in the distant past said that if you split up an army you can conquer them. If they stay together there is nothing you can do. 'Divide and conquer.' One of the old Romans said that.

At the moment we are divided. Until we become one single powerful group then we will just stay the way we are at the moment. We have asked and asked until we are blue in the face to have Stonehenge back. That is our Temple. We have allowed Muslims, Hindus and Buddhists, you name it, every religious group in the world has been allowed to take and make Temples out of buildings in this country. But when it comes to the original religion of the British People which is Druidism, the government turns a blind eye. They refuse to acknowledge that we are a religion.

I have written so many letters to prime ministers, police chiefs. Don't throw cordons around our Temples. You can only go so far and they just totally ignore you. We can go into Stonehenge and hold ceremonies after the public has gone home. But do we really want this or do we want to be able to perform our ceremonies in Stonehenge with the public looking on? When they hold services in Canterbury Cathedral they don't just hold the ceremony for the Priest and the local people. Everybody, anybody comes in off the street and takes part. If you don't want to take part you just sit on the sidelines and quietly listen to what is going on. This is what should happen at Stonehenge.

How do you worship?

Until the advent of Philip [Shallcrass] and Bobcat [Emma Restall Orr] at Avebury, I did all my worshipping in the woods, wherever I happened to be at the time. Until I went to Avebury I only wore my robes at the most important events and that was rare.

As you know my robes are of the green. This is not only because I am Celt, but because wearing of the green in the woods the Romans could not see it and so we survived.

In my backyard I have a Fairy Ring. The Old Ones knew about Fairy Rings and they passed down a few of their tips to us younger Old Ones. The outer circle of the Fairy Ring is always covered in toadstools, what they call the death cap toadstools. The children were always told that those were the Fairy houses and we must never, ever touch them. I was taught afterwards not to destroy the illusion for children.

Where the outer circle was, was the outer perimeter of the roots of an old oak tree. You only ever get a Fairy Ring where there has been an oak tree. The grass on the inside of the circle is always a different color. The grass on the outside can be dark green or light green, whichever, but the grass on the inside of the Fairy Circle is always a different color. It makes a beautiful picture in the summer.

In English mythology a Fairy Ring is a sacred space. If you want to bless someone, or get a message, or heal somebody from a distance the healing can be sent out from the circle. If you need to pray you pray in a Fairy Ring. If you want to put a curse on somebody you can also use the Fairy Ring. But if you do decide to put a curse on somebody it must never be to harm them. I remember asking one of my teachers what the point was of putting a curse on somebody if you don't intend to harm them. He said you can harm their possessions, but not the body. The body is the body of an animal and it is sacred. If a snake went to bite you, you would not hit it with a stick – you would gently open it's jaws and let it go. You do the same thing with human beings. You never ever harm the person. You can do all this from within the Fairy Ring.

The Fairy Ring is a sacred place that comes from the roots of the sacred oak. At times I go out into the garden and stand in the middle of the circle until my mind has calmed down and then I come back indoors and get into bed and fall asleep immediately. You can lose yourself in the Ring, you can retreat into it. You can meditate in it. Most Fairy Rings are hundreds or sometimes thousands of years old. They have seen the planet grow. They have seen man grow and become strong.

The circle has always been a sacred thing to us. It is the beginning and the end, it is infinite, it is like reincarnation, which is a belief of the Druids. After we drop the overcoat we are in now we put on a new one. We come back.

Some of my teachings were with herbs. We do not disclose our herbal knowledge. I will tell you one thing though about your Native Americans. Their Pipe of Peace was called that because what went into the pipe was a hallucinogenic drug called the Thornapple.[13] The leaves and the roots of the Thornapple were ground up into a powder, put into a pipe and smoked. As it was passed around everybody became happy. This is why it was called the Pipe of Peace. As a Companion of the

Chalice Well, every time I go there I bring home as many bottles of water as I can carry. With that water I start off acorns from the Mother Tree and when the babies are big enough to be taken out they are given, not sent but given, to any organization that might want them for re-planting. Of the hundreds that I have brought up I should think a very small number were put in private gardens, all of the others were put in sacred places. So once again we have the ancient oak trees growing in the sacred places where they were once cut down. This twenty first, the Winter Solstice, I hope to go down to the Stones, to Stonehenge, and if the police haven't put a four-mile exclusion zone around it the way they did at Summer Solstice, then I may be able to perform the ceremony of the Blessing of the Stones, which to my knowledge was last performed in 1938, the year before the war started. Obviously the year the war started nobody was allowed near Salisbury plain because of the military activities there.

I was born within a few miles of Stonehenge. I'm probably the only one who was ever baptized at Stonehenge as a young child. The original Baptism is now being used as a children's blessing in the ceremonies at Avebury by Philip Shallcrass and Emma Restall Orr. This was not intended to be just for children. I have baptized babies and adults with this same baptismal service. It was handed down to me in written form. At the beginning of this century it was decided that it was one of those things that could be written down for other groups if they wished to use it.

The Celtic Baptism

I baptize thee with Mother Earth,
from whose loins we come,
and to whose arms we fly,
when our journey here is over.

I baptize thee with the winds that come from the four corners of the Earth,

the winds that
scatter the seeds of the harvest,
and blow away the snows of winter.

I baptize thee with fire,
so that thy spirit may be cleansed of evil, and thy days be long
and fruitful.

I baptize thee with the waters of life,
the waters that no living thing can do without.

Now give thanks to our
Lady for thy bounteous harvest.

Blessed be as blessed is,
and may we all be blessed.
May the blessings of the Goddess and the Gods be with you,
always.

Scholars and Writers

I've always considered myself a Pagan. I come from ancient and honorable Pagan DNA. I come from the Celts who, as you know, are one of hundreds and hundreds of hill people, mountain people, Earth people, nature people, who tried to build their lives and their families in situations where they were as far away from the political capitols of Rome and London and Paris as they could. And I know that we all share that sense of, we are not mainstream people. I was born in Western New York State. I checked it back, and I was conceived on the day that alcohol was made an illegal drug in this country. I consider that an omen. There was a tendency among the Celts and the Pagans to get involved in intoxicated revels and to get carried away into poetry and declamation and celebration of life.

In Boston, Massachusetts, which was one of the beginnings of white male culture in this continent, there's always been this tradition of the most uptight Calvinist Protestantism. At the same time, in the same place, we had the basic source of American Mysticism where there were people like Ralph Waldo Emerson who was thrown out in 1836 because he said; 'Hey! The God is not in the temple, the God is not in the Unitarian Church, the God is not to be found with ministers and all that. Divinity is within. Divinity is within!

Dr. Timothy Leary, Excerpted by permission from Timothy Leary Live at Starwood' an audio tape from 1992 available from A.C.E. (The Association for Consciousness Exploration)

The Druid (old Irish Drui) was priest, prophet, astrologer, and teacher of the sons of nobles.
Fergus Kelly, *A Guide To Early Irish Law*

Making generalizations is always a dangerous activity but it can perhaps be said that American Druidism as a whole has tended to favor a scholarly bias while British Druidism has leaned more consistently towards the poetic and intuitive spheres. The American bias has been largely fostered by Isaac Bonewits of ADF and continues to some extent in the selection of articles for one of the most widely distributed Druid magazines, The Journal of The Henge of Keltria, of which Tony Taylor is the editor. The British bias seems to stem from the romantic fantasies of Iolo Morganwg and of the Medieval Grail legends, and of the early fraternal, Masonic influenced English Druid Orders.

In this chapter several American Druids argue for the Celtic Reconstructionist view, that in order to practice this religion one must be well acquainted with the literature. While Ronald Hutton is a noted British scholar who has concerned himself with debunking cherished historical myths and assumptions of the Druid and Pagan communities as a whole. Kaledon Naddair contributes an essay in his own inimitable form and Steve Wilson discusses ancient Irish poetic disciplines.

Dr. Ronald Hutton

Interview conducted through the mail
July 16, 1996

Dr. Ronald Hutton is a professor of history at the University of Bristol, England. He is a Doctor of Philosophy, a Fellow of the Royal Historical Society, winner of the Hadley Prize and Blackburne-Daniell Prize of the University of Cambridge, and of the Benjamin Franklin Prize of the Bookseller's Association of America, as well as a member of several Druid Orders. He will not confirm (or deny) that he is himself a Druid, but prefers to be regarded as an academic who understands and defends modern Druidry and is expert in certain aspects of history which are important to it.

Ronald is the author of seven books including *The Pagan Religions of the Ancient British Isles* (Basil Blackwell, 1991), *The Rise and Fall of Merry England* (Oxford University Press, 1994) and *The Stations of the Sun: A History of the Ritual Year in Britain* (Oxford University Press, 1996). He has written a number of pamphlets including The Shamans of Siberia (Isle of Avalon Press, 1993) a popular publication among Pagans, and has authored more than thirty essays, some of which have appeared in *Paganism Today* (eds. Charlotte Hardman and Graham Harvey, Harper-Collins, 1996) and in *The Druid Renaissance* (eds. Philip Carr-Gomm and Dwina Murphy-Gibb, Harper-Collins, 1996). Since 1996, Ronald Hutton has gone on to publish eight more books, of which the most recent is *Pagan Britain* (2013).

Can you please talk about your religious upbringing when you were a child?

I can fairly claim to be a second generation Pagan, as I was brought up by a widowed mother who imbued me with a view of nature as full of immanent divinity and a particular love and respect for the literature of ancient Greece and Rome, which I later supplemented with that of early Ireland.

Hers was a very romantic, unfocused, Edwardian sort of English Paganism, and she did not belong to any formal or initiatory tradition. However, when I encountered Wicca in 1968, I regarded it easily and affectionately enough as a mystery religion, drawing mainly upon Greco-Roman imagery, which took its place very appropriately within the broader Pagan culture to which I belonged.

I have never experienced any sort of conversion experience, and have never had any sort of personal relationship with Christianity, which I have always regarded with benevolent neutrality. My religious 'temperature' had always therefore been lower than that of many of my Pagan friends, and I have long taken for granted assumptions like the divine feminine, which they are often inclined to regard as the end product of a major shift of consciousness.

How did you first hear about Druids? What drew you to them?

I assume this question refers to the modern variety, the ancient kind being a natural component of my British historical heritage. There was very little sense of Druidry on the British Pagan scene in the 1970s and early 1980s, Wicca making most of the running. By the 1980s writers like Caitlin and John Matthews were establishing a distinctive, Celtic, strain of modern British spirituality, but there was nothing distinctively Pagan about it.

Towards the end of that decade I became aware of the appearance of people calling themselves Pagan Druids, but they were confined to the more determinedly 'alternative' ends of British Paganism, being concentrated around Glastonbury or associated with the campaign to reopen Stonehenge at festival times. It was only around 1990, with the success of the re-founded Order of Bards, Ovates and Druids, that Druidry began to make a real impact upon the Pagan mainstream.

What led me to get to know it? I began meeting representatives of OBOD at Pagan Federation local conferences in 1991-2, where we were on the lists of speakers together, and I liked them. In 1993 I met both Philip Carr-Gomm and Philip Shallcrass at a large conference at Avebury, which was the origin of the Gorsedd there, and befriended both; as a result I was invited by both to address events which they organized for Druids, and came to be very fond of their respective Orders.

Over the years 1993-4 I found myself repeatedly in the role of peacemaker between Druidry and Wicca, as the former too often defined itself at the expense of the latter, and the latter reacted angrily. This process meant that I drew a number of leading Druids much closer to the Craft, and felt it only right to show a proportionate closer interest in their ways.

I lent my assistance as an academic expert witness to Arthur Uther Pendragon's case before the European Court of Human Rights to obtain access to worship at Stonehenge, and he knighted me into his Order as a gesture of comradeship in late 1995. Through my frequent appearances as a speaker at Druid events, I have also come to know, and to enjoy friendly relations with all the other British Druid Chiefs.

How would you define Druidism and the Druid path?

I would define it as the means by which certain groups of people have succeeded, at various times over the past two thousand years, in creating a contemporary spirituality which draws upon religious and magical images deriving ultimately from the Iron Age of the British Isles. These movements have been in an important sense cumulative, as each has drawn upon all those which have occurred before, and in their later manifestations they have extended their range of symbols and sacred sites to incorporate those from all the earlier periods of British and Irish prehistory.

In an important sense there can be no 'authentic' Druidism (I prefer from habit the term 'Druidry'), because we shall never know enough about the original Druids to use them as a point of reference. All our earliest records of them were written either by Greek or Roman outsiders bent on demonizing or eulogizing them, or medieval Irish Christians, who in turn regarded them in extended retrospect, either as romanticized magicians or as evil Pagans.

The Bards of medieval Wales and Ireland were, in fact, the sponsors of the first Druidic 'revival'. The Druids are the figures who dominate the spiritual life in the British Isles and neighboring parts of Europe as history begins; they are the obvious symbolic point of reference for those trying to rediscover or re-imagine a spirituality rooted in these particular lands.

You are something of an expert in the area of Pagan history. Can you compare and contrast Druidism and Wicca?

Yes, I can do that, but only for Britain as in the U.S.A. the context is rather different. Druidry made an impression upon the modern Pagan scene in America much earlier, and British Druidry has yet to produce scholars of the weight of Isaac Bonewits and Ceiswr Serith. The number of American Druids who are fluent in Celtic languages (in old or modern forms) still far exceeds that of their counterparts in Britain; and come to think of it, only since 1989 has British Wicca produced writers of the intellectual rigor of Margot Adler or the polemical challenge of Aidan Kelley or (conversely) Don Frew. On the other hand, the U.S.A. still has many more real fundamentalists of both persuasions, with a seemingly limitless credulity for foundation myths, than Britain now harbors.

Here goes. British Wicca is much longer-established than British Druidry, and its identity is far more fixed; conversely, it lacks some of the raw energy of the younger movement, being rather less prone to flexibility, experimentation and adaptation. It is much more strongly a mystery religion, carried on in private and with only initiates present except at specific more open festivals.

Druidry by contrast courts public attention and involvement, holds daylight rituals as prominently as those of night and the tween-times, and (save in the higher grades of the mystic Orders) is much more open to friends and relatives (including children) of members.

Ritual is central to Wicca and peripheral or occasional in some Druid Orders and costume is definitive for most Druids. Wicca normally creates a level of intensity of experience rare in Druidry, and has a more pronounced sense of creating and controlling its sacred space; it is also inclined to be far more risqué and dramatic, incorporating nudity and sexuality and achieving altered states of consciousness in a way which is also unusual among Druids.

Druidry has very little sense of working magic, and energy is only regularly raised through the 'awen' chant: magic and energy raising are integral to Wicca. Druidry is far more concerned with healing the ills of its members, the land, and the planet, and is proportionately now much more mixed up with radical politics than Wicca. It is also more closely allied to 'alternative' lifestyles and the New Age. It is also more concerned to produce literature, art, and music.

Although there is no doubt that Pagan Druidry is non-sexist, its Orders are still overwhelmingly led by men, with women increasingly self-assertive at the second rank. By contrast Wicca is built upon the notion of female power. I find myself constantly refreshed and comforted by Druidry, and constantly exhilarated and challenged by Wicca. The intensity of affection which each produces for fellow group members is the same. If the 'flavor' of Druidry is that of a fine Rhine wine, then that of Wicca is of an old Scotch whisky (and Shamanism of a Bloody Mary).

There are a number of interesting ironies in each. Wicca traditionally claims to be the religion of the peasant masses of Europe, earthy and concerned with folk magic and fertility, but is in essence a refined, Neo-Platonic set of mysteries which draw heavily upon Freemasonry and the Golden Dawn, in very creative and novel ways.

Druidry claims to be the tradition of poets and intellectuals, but its modern membership is often far more rough-edged than Wiccans, and it is far more engaged in environmental issues. Wicca draws its religious imagery from all over ancient Europe, with an especial debt to the Mediterranean and the Near East, but is actually the only religion which England has ever given the world. Druidry claims to be the essentially native, British, tradition, but although its main strength is in England its sources of inspiration are in the other (Celtic) parts of the British Isles, originating in languages which hardly any British Druids either read or speak. Druids name themselves after Iron Age magi, but hardly ever gather at Iron Age monuments; instead they focus overwhelmingly upon Neolithic and early Bronze Age sacred sites which Iron Age farmers cheerfully destroyed. What both clearly have in common is that they tolerate me with remarkable good humor as I point out such problems as these.

How were you trained in Druidry?

In Druidry, only by reading the standard OBOD correspondence course, which is the model of its kind and a monument to the genius of Philip Carr-Gomm; but then there is not much training as such around in the other Druid orders, which just get on with doing things.

Can you describe the work you do with the groups you associate with?

My support for the British Druid Order and the Loyal Arthurian Warband is mostly literary, and I am close friends with OBOD, at both national and local level.

Can you talk a bit about your books and how they relate to

Druidism?

Pagan Religions of the Ancient British Isles was the first attempt in recent decades to synthesize what was thought about the subject by the current academic experts in the different areas of this vast field, and so has an obvious interest for contemporary Druids. I have often quipped that the book takes 100,000 words to explain that we know virtually nothing about the subject. Actually, it originally took over 100,000 more, and even so the amount of compression needed to cover 30,000 years of material resulted in some impoverishment and distortion of that material. In the event, the publishers chopped out much of it in the process of production, in order to keep the original unit costs, and that increased both faults.

It also suffers at times from the obvious difficulties of a non-expert trying to summarize the work of specialists. It often gives an impression of deliberate and heartless iconoclasm, because its whole point was to try to determine what could be said *with absolute certainty* about ancient beliefs and practices, and thus it applied a ruthless testing process to all speculative theories or else showed how they had now been abandoned because of fresh research.

It tried to suggest that the increasing amount of data about the ancient past, coupled with an increasing lack of certainty about the interpretation, actually empowered people like Druids by enlarging the number of possible imaginative reconstructions, but this message apparently got lost at times in transmission. This was largely because it was not written primarily for Pagans, but for educational institutions and their staff, and the non-Pagan educated general reader; but as well as becoming a best-seller among both those groups it also turned into something of a classic among Pagans.

It must be clear from what I have said above that I find several faults with it, and the whole thing now badly needs re-writing, but it is the only work of its kind. Druids may like to save time by looking at the digest of its contents which I provided specially for them in my essay 'Who Possesses the Past?' in *The Druid Renaissance*.

I am more proud and confident of *Stations of the Sun*, which although it still contains quite a large component of synthesis includes the huge mass of original research which made up *The Rise and Fall of Merry England* with an equally large amount of hitherto unused information from folklorists' collections. It provides Druids (and everybody else) with the very first properly researched history of British festivals, from the beginning of history to the present.

At a quarter of a million words, it is my largest book to date, and one of its aims was to provide details of the enactment of calendar rituals (and especially of very old seasonal rites) which would enable people to revive them if they wished. There are scores of songs, poems and ballads associated with the turning of the year, from Hebridean Gaelic 'ranns' to West Country wassails, and I have tried to provide all the known variant forms of the customs instead of choosing one as standard. The theme of the book is the way in which the ritual year has constantly developed over the centuries, and the conclusion contains suggestions of consequence to a range of fields from Celtic studies to modern sociology.

Again, from the perspective of an expert on the history of Paganism can you give your short version of the history of modern Druidism in England?

Its origins lie in the antiquarian rediscovery of ancient monuments in the 17th century, which burgeoned further in the 18th. This raised the profile of the ancient British past in the English imagination, and between 1700 and 1830 Druids and megaliths were constantly being deployed by writers with a range of different purposes and beliefs – often dramatically contrasted. Thus, John Toland used them to promote Deism, William Stukeley to promote orthodox Anglicanism in opposition to Toland.

Even more than in the ancient world Druids were portrayed at one moment as bloodthirsty savages and at the next as enlightened savants. With this high profile, it was inevitable that they would get co-opted into the service of organizations, and did so in two different ways, often over-lapping. One was a renascent Welsh nationalism, the other a working-class radicalism which laid heavy emphasis upon self-education and self-help.

One strand was expressed most strongly in the work of Iolo Morganwg and his allies, the other in the Ancient Order of Druids. The two interacted with each other constantly until they began to run out of steam finally in the mid-20th century. At times they received reinforcement from other impulses, such as the Scottish nationalism of William Sharp and Lewis Spence. In these last two figures, they also combined with the world of the early 20th-century English mystics and occultists, and the last great product of this mélange was Ross Nichols, who survived long enough to link Victorian Druidism to the interests of modern Earth mystics and to inspire Philip Carr-Gomm, leaving the materials for the recent Pagan reconstruction of Druidry.

Is English Druidism experiencing any problems that you are aware of?

It may be entering into a serious schism, resulting from the separate origin of, and natural division between, 'spiritual' and 'political' Pagan Druidry. The former consists of OBOD, the BDO, the Druid groups related to the Fellowship of Isis, and some smaller Orders. It was concerned to establish a distinctive modern Druidical spirituality, and to assist people in personal growth. The latter arose as one expression of England's radical subcultures, and its impulse was to promote alternative, social, religious, and political values. It consists of the Secular and Glastonbury Orders, the Loyal Arthurian Warband, and (again) higher visibility, both at Pagan gatherings and in the national media.

For a time it looked as if they could co-operate with excellent results, most obviously in the Council of British Druid Orders, but this hope foundered on the issue of Stonehenge. To 'spiritual' Druids (and I stress that these terms are matters of different emphasis, not absolute categories) the top priority was to obtain access to the stones for private worship, with the blessing of the quasi-governmental body which manages them. To 'political' Druids, the top priority was to establish a prescriptive right for anybody to enter the stones to worship and celebrate at festival times, as a natural liberty.

This issue brought to the surface natural antipathies; between those who wanted a Druid gathering to be a place where worldly preoccupations could be forgotten and the gates opened to other worlds, and those who wanted it to be essentially a political forum. To 'political' Druids, the other sort could look like complacent bourgeoisie enjoying fancy dress. To 'spiritual' Druids, the other sort could look like thinly-disguised Hell's Angels on a spree. As a result of these latent tensions, the Stonehenge issue resulted in a quarrel which led to the resignation of OBOD and the BDO from the national Council in early 1996, stripping the latter of the support of the overwhelming majority of British Druids.

The rift may widen further, and result in a similar withdrawal from the Avebury Gorsedd,[14] and severe cultural impoverishment of what has become British Druidry's (and increasingly British Paganism's) largest public gathering. Readers may remember that I myself have friends on both 'wings' of Druidry, and regard these developments as a tragedy. Both sorts of Druidry have an important role to play, the 'spiritual' Druids as promoters of a distinctive form of religious and mystical experience, and the 'political' as promoters of civil liberty, through a very effective form of performance art. I hope that history will reveal the present difficulties to have been growing pains rather than suicidal folly.

What in your opinion does Druidry have to offer to society in general, and how would you like to see it evolve in the future?

Much of my reply is suggested above. I would like to see it take its place along with Wicca, Shamanism, Asatru, etc., as one of a very large range of different spiritual experiences, to suit very different human needs, in a new pluralist and privatized world of Western religion, based upon small gathered groups working within specific traditions within an atmosphere of disestablishment and mutual tolerance enforced by a secular state. I would also like to see Arthur Pendragon, Tim Sebastian, Rollo Maughling and others take their place in a pantheon of English folk-heroes who confronted established authority in the name of popular liberties, using motifs drawn from deep in the British folk-memory.

Kaledon Naddair

Interviewed in Am Faoilleach (the Wolf Month), 1996
Via mail

Kaledon Naddair (The Caledonian Adder or The Piktish Serpent) 'was the first to reformulate authentic native Keltic Druidical Shamanism whilst others (who have subsequently masqueraded in this scene) were still Anglo-classicist librarians or pseudo-occultists in London'. He is based in Dinas Eidyn (Edinburgh) where he does research, writes, and practices Shamanism. He and his group also practice in the wilds of Alban and in and around the megalithic sites of Britain though he has 'never been tempted to relocate to England or the US for mere financial gain'.

As a child he had pronounced psychic ability and by the age of sixteen he embarked on an extensive study of many ancient religions, mythologies and wisdom traditions, always retaining his PiktishKeltic essential core.

He has been president of the Keltic Research Society since 1979 and in 1982 he founded The College of Druidism, a Keltic-based initiatory organization with branches in Britain and other countries. Since 1982 he has also run a modern Qabalah group in the Western Occult Tradition. In 1984 he was appointed general secretary of the European Pan-Keltic League.

Kaledon has given workshops and lectures to conferences, groups, and individuals for the last twenty years. His books and talks express his passionate and outspoken commitment to his native Keltic Tradition with comparisons from Indo-European and Semitic lore.

Kaledon's books and publications include: *Druidism Ancient and Modern, Druidism – A Guidebook, Keltic Folk and Fairie Tales (Their Shamanism Explored), Keltic Shamanistic Calendar (two volumes), Storytelling in the Keltic Tradition, Keltic Tree Lore (three volumes), Keltic Bird Lore (Shamanism), Keltic Animal Lore (Shamanism), Petroglyph Sites in Alban, Piktish and Keltic Art*

Symbolism, Keltic Divination Alphabets, Piktish Art: Its Shamanistic Symbolism, Sacred Geometry and Aesthetics, and The Shaman and Ritual Drumming. He is the editor of three magazines; Inner Keltia, The Piktish Shaman, and Awen.

The ancient Druids were Kelts, fact! They only officiated to Keltic folk whilst their rites and rituals were Keltic in nature and were conducted in one of the Keltic languages. Any art, symbolism, music, mythology, or folk customs that were employed were from the Keltic tradition.

After the Roman Empire (military or Church), the greatest amount of destruction inflicted upon the Keltic tradition has undoubtedly been done by the rapacious greed of English colonialism. For over a thousand years the English have sought to ruthlessly eradicate the culture of all the Keltic countries (Alba, Kymru, Eire, Kernow, and Mannin) that were adjacent to them.

Out of 1,001 examples, here are just a few; in Ireland the English discouraged the speaking or writing of Irish, and of the Brogue, Moore described it as 'the ugliest dialect in the world'. Traditional Irish orthography was denied whilst the Ordnance Survey imposed their English Phonetic Anglicized spellings of place names onto maps. One English landlord made a bonfire of precious Irish vellum manuscripts, whilst another ordered his tailors to cut them up for patterns, and for school children to cover their Latin grammars with. The Druids, Bards and Filidh were gradually stripped of all their privileges and forced to work as starving peasants. Millions less would have died in 'The Famine' if wagon-loads of meat, fish, vegetables and fruit had not been shipped under armed guard over to England, or paid as rack-rents to their mainly English landlords. All this was accomplished with thousands of beatings, hangings, and shootings of native folk. Whilst in Scotland after 1745 the English banned the speaking of Gaidhealig, Highland Dress, Clan-customs, seasonal festivals and even the playing of music. The Welsh and Cornish fared little better with vast influxes of Anglo-Saxons seeking to extirpate 'the cursed British tongue' that the Cymry held so dearly. It took until the 1960s and the 1970s for the Welsh to achieve a modicum of media rights for their language within their own country.

After spending many centuries trying to destroy the Keltic culture of their neighbors, strangely at the turn of this century, and more so in the last twenty years, it has become fashionable amongst some of the more trendy English to 'get into' the Celtic scene *maan*. The English who assume all cultures are theirs for the taking, do not seem to think that some 'payback' is required; they wish to avoid any Karmic debts or Ceartas to the native Kelts they have for so long denigrated.

The most obnoxiously arrogant English writers on Keltic topics even go so far as to think that they own the Keltic heritage not their own, and proceed to give it out to other peoples with the abusive sentiment of 'go ahead experiment and play with Celtic things, it is the common property of all' muthafuckers!

Exploiters, (whether English or other foreigners) often say why can't we just shake hands and forget the past. That is easy to say when you are going to lose nothing and gain the rich pickings obtained from ripping-off another people's culture and spirituality. Before there can be forgiveness and reconciliation there must first of all be full acknowledgement of crimes committed and major amounts of recompensing the natives for what has already been stolen or destroyed. One of the simplest things Anglos need to admit is that they are NOT Kelts, and simply living in Britain does NOT entitle you to pillage the Ancient British Cultural Tradition. It needs to be clearly remembered that the lineal descendants of the ancient Britons ARE THE WELSH and some Lowland Scots; NOT, however, the English. And whilst the English have tried to filch King Arthur and associated lore, in reality King Arthur hated the Anglo-Saxons and made it his life's work to try and drive them out of Britain back over the channel to their Low-Deutch home.

It almost beggars belief that I have to re-state the obvious that the only people that have an automatic entitlement to the riches of the Keltic cultural tradition are Kelts! Kelts by race, birth, language and cultural upbringing in the Keltic homelands! Most Americans that have written to me seem to have a small amount of Keltic ancestry that has reached them through a spaghetti-junction of blood-lines; that little connection may help you to re-attune, but remember that you also will have probably suffered from decades of adverse conditioning, which will do as much or more to distort your Keltic quest.

Knights Templar, Rosicrucians, Freemasons, Hermeticists, etc., all have a niche in the Western Occult Tradition, as Wicca, Odinism, Heathenism, and Ostara have a place with modern Neo-Paganism – BUT NONE OF THOSE ARE REMOTELY KELTIC THUS NONE OF THEM CAN BE PROPERLY CALLED DRUIDICAL.

In my various books and magazines I have promoted Keltic things, yes, but with this strong proviso, that it must be shown considerable respect, especially by outsiders – English, Americans, Australians, Dutch, Germans, or whomsoever. To be guided into real Keltic wisdom one has to realize that perhaps the best guides are the few remaining native Keltic masters. For as Americans, if you were stupid enough to follow the writings of the English pseudoCelts that would be the blind leading the blind, or more precisely the ignorant teaching the ignorant of the Waanabee Keltic Tribe.

In summation, outsiders can be adopted into the Keltic Tradition, but that should only happen through the guidance of actual Kelts. The process of assimilation to this culture will require a great deal of effort, training, and re-conditioning; and above all it requires respect in thought, word and deed.

1) Respect the Keltic Tradition's cultural and spiritual ways

and methods (and don't mix with others).

2) Respect the Keltic culture-bearing teacher (if native) as your guide into this.

3) Respect the Keltic language(s) that it was originally formulated in (and don't replace with English).

4) Respect the natural environment and its denizens that you are taught within.

If you adhere to these guidelines then you may well become someone who helps and eventually enriches the Keltic Cultural Tradition; whilst if you go against these principles you may become one of the many who are at present exploiting, distorting, and diluting Keltic culture into an Anglicized hotch-potch. The choice is yours.

Erynn Rowan Laurie
Interviewed July 18, 1996
Via internet

Erynn describes herself as a fili-in-training (a poet). She is the moderator for the Nemeton-L email list for Celtic Pagans and Druids. Her books *include Ogham, Tree-Lore & The Celtic Tree Oracle, Pt 1* (Preppie Biker Press, Seattle, 1992), *The Cauldron of Poesy Lectures* (Preppie Biker Press, Seattle, 1992), *A Circle of Stones: Journeys and Meditations for Modern Celts* (Eschaton, Chicago, 1995) and she is a contributor to *The Druid Renaissance*, edited by Philip Carr-Gomm (HarperCollins, New York, 1996).

She has written articles for Circle Network News, Sagewoman, Fireheart Magazine, Obsidian, and Manteia.

Describe the religion you were raised in. What was it like growing up?

I was raised Christian, nominally Southern Baptist. It was a pretty fearful religion, lots of hellfire and damnation, no sense of humor, and no ritual experience. I accepted it mostly because I didn't know any other way, even though I disagreed with a lot of what they were telling me.

I grew up as a Navy brat, and we moved around the East Coast a lot until we settled in Western Massachusetts after dad retired. I was ten at the time. We lived in one of the Berkshire hill towns on the Deerfield River.

Our neighbors were dairy farmers, and I spent most of my time during the summers out in the woods, down by the brook or over at the farm. In the winter, my grandfather, who lived next door, taught me tracking and how to set traps and skin animals.

He was very abusive, and that has had a big negative impact

in my life. But everyone around us considered him a gentle and very Christian man. There was a conflict in this that I never understood. How could somebody be 'a good Christian' and do those things?

My grandmother was a birdwatcher, and deeply interested in ecology. We spent hours together watching and identifying the birds that would come to her feeders. She seemed to know everything about birds. We would go out to the edge of the apple orchard during the summer and I would do bird imitations for her, and call cardinals and chickadees down close to us in the trees.

The relatives on my mom's side of the family were all very fundamentalist, and I remember there were always a lot of Chick[15] tracts and comics around their houses. One of my uncles still runs a fundamentalist children's telephone ministry near Boston. Mom was always more of an agnostic, and interested in reincarnation and astrology. She sent my brother and I to church because it was 'good' for us.

Dad's relatives were Catholics, but generally I never saw much of Catholicism except for his family's weddings. My father had a parting with the Catholic Church very early in his youth, and still carries a lot of resentment toward the religion.

For two years I went to a Christian private school, which was very Bible-based. But I remember doing a history project where we built a model pyramid, and I got to paint the Gods and hieroglyphs on the inside.

I was fascinated by the Egyptian deities, and for a while I studied the *Egyptian Book of the Dead* and learned how to read hieroglyphs. I also read a bit about Buddhism, which I really liked, and some of the Greek and Norse myths.

I went to week-long Baptist summer camps for several years with my cousins, where I had the life scared out of me by the end-times propaganda movies that they showed before bedtime. I remember having a shouting match with one of the camp counselors about why we had to have chapel services and Bible studies so many times a day, when God was just as much in the trees and the lake as he was in the book. This didn't go over too well.

When I was twelve or thirteen I started studying astrology and tarot, and I remember reading an interview in the local paper with some Witches. I decided then and there that I would be a Witch when I grew up, and indeed I spent some time as a Wiccan, I'm a 2nd degree Alexandrian, among other things. But my grandmother was horrified by my declaration of faith, and because I didn't have access to people or books back in the mid-1970s, I had no way of pursuing my interests.

I remember finding a book on Witchcraft in a used book store and thinking that if I had to have all these tools and fiddly things in order to be a Witch, there would be no way I could hide it from my relatives. I suspect that if there had been books about Druidism at the time, it might have been easier for me, and my path would have been rather different.

When and where did you first hear about Druids? Or Celtic spirituality?

I started practicing as a Pagan in 1984 after I got out of the Navy, and in 1986 I was living in Oregon and taking a correspondence course in Celtic Witta. It was pretty much like all the other Wicca I'd been reading about, but I started learning the stories of some of the Celtic deities.

One of the Goddesses came to me and told me that I had to learn Irish for her, which was something of a departure from my previous experiences with deity.

The more that I studied the material, the less I thought that Celtic religion looked like Wicca, and I decided that I needed to follow my own path rather than blindly follow someone else's.

How were you trained?

Aside from the Celtic Witta course, I've never had any formal training. Pretty much everything I'm doing now has been derived from self-directed study and meditation. I read everything I could get my hands on, no matter how awful a book it was.

I've always been somewhat skeptical, and eventually I started to be able to tell the good stuff from the bullshit.

When I find something interesting, I always want to chase it to the source in folklore or the early texts. So when somebody makes a bald assertion about something Celtic and doesn't give me a source, I wonder about it.

If they got it from one of the tales, or from folklore, that's great. I can look it up somewhere and interpret it for myself. If they got it from a dream or a vision, that's fine too. Some really good stuff has been revealed through personal mystic experiences. I'd just like to know so that I have some idea of how much weight to give it in my own experiments and practice.

How do you define Druidism or Celtic spirituality?

I think that there are several things that make up Celtic spirituality. My path tends toward the Reconstructionist, and I appreciate things based on the old texts and folklore. My definition of Celtic spirituality is fairly complex, but these are some of the aspects that I think are necessary. Reverence for Celtic deities. This is easy, and pretty widespread, even among groups that are not really Celtic in focus. Lots of purely Wiccan groups, for instance, revere Celtic Gods and Goddesses, without necessarily being Celtic Pagan. There's more to it than just plugging a Celtic name into a generic deity slot.

I think also that it's important to recognize the Gods as real entities, not as psychological constructs, although they do have that aspect to them. They have likes and dislikes. They have names and titles. They have places and things with which they are associated. These things need to be recognized and respected. They need to be worked with.

The Gods need to be conversed with and listened to, and in some cases, yes, obeyed. I know this is a distasteful concept for some people. Real deities make real demands, and sometimes it is necessary to do what they ask of you in order for other things to happen.

Ethics are important. Not as the 'Wiccan rede', which has no basis in Celtic tradition, but ethics based on the Brehon laws and the practices of the early Celtic peoples. Some of these ideas need to be modified to fit into modern society, but I think that the Gaulish injunction to worship the Gods, to do no evil, and to exercise strength is crucial, as is the Celtic dedication to the truth and a strong sense of ethics about what is right and what is wrong.

The Celts were not an 'anything goes' kind of people. They had a very complex body of laws governing what was appropriate and what was not. Celtic Pagans need both a strong sense of personal responsibility and a code of personal and social ethics in order to carry the Celtic spirit forward.

Respect for what we can know of the historical practices and knowledge of the Celts should be a part of a Celtic spiritual path. We don't have to duplicate what they were doing down to the last human sacrifice, but we should try to understand why they were doing what they did.

If a practice can be documented, and it isn't harmful to people or the planet, it should be looked at and possibly adopted or adapted, in keeping with a reconstruction and recreation of historical Celtic ways as relevant to modern life. For these purposes, attention to scholarship is important.

Respect for modern Celtic communities and languages are essential. The Celtic people are still under siege in all their remaining lands. Languages are dying, as are traditional practices, songs and stories. Going about trying to recreate something from 2,000 years ago while ignoring the plight of those people's descendants is nothing short of arrogant and disrespectful.

I'm not saying that one must perforce learn a Celtic language, although that's a good idea, rather that we have to acknowledge what is happening, and if we have an opportunity and the ability to resist this ongoing destruction, we have a responsibility to take some action.

In so much of the Pagan movement, the Celts are the new 'noble savages', long dead of course, so we can make up whatever we want and call it Celtic. That just isn't the case, connection with our ancestors, whether they are Celtic or not, and with the land spirits is vital. This point is pretty generic and needs to be taken in combination with several other things, because ancestor worship and reverence for land spirits happens in most old Pagan cultures.

I would suggest that this connection and reverence must happen in a style not unlike that shown in Evans-Wentz's *The Fairy Faith in Celtic Countries* or Carmichael's *Carmina Gadelica* for it to be seen as a continuation of the Celtic spirit. Because so many of us are in the new world, we are adrift between the spirits of the Celtic lands and the spirits of the Americas, or Australia, or New Zealand. We need connections with both places, in a way that respects both traditions, if we are to live our spiritual life fully and effectively.

We need to offer reverence to the pre-Christian Celts as our spiritual ancestors and as potential Otherworldly teachers. In addition to respect for the ancestors, we need to respect and care for our children, to treat them like human beings, not chattel or punching bags or sex objects. And we need to build strong family and tribal connections.

The tuath [tribe] was vitally important to the early Celtic peoples, and without these connections, society crumbles. I'm not talking about 'family values' in a narrow Republican sense. I mean caring for and respecting the people we live with and around, whether we are related by blood or not. I mean helping each other through hard times and celebrating the good times. Giving aid and solace to our friends when they're ill, comforting the dying, being willing to help a friend find work or housing when things get rough.

Sometimes we can't repair relationships with our blood families, but we can build strong chosen families and tribes through our spiritual communities. We can try to stop the cycle of abuse that seems to be endemic in our society. We need to realize that, someday, we will be the ancestors. We should be worthy of respect by future generations.

Poetry is intrinsic to the structure of Celtic magic and religion. I've ranted on poetry a lot over the years. I'm talking about the kind of poetry that stirs up fire in the soul and fire in the head, the kind that speaks words of power in its descriptions and its focus, the sort of poetry that sucks you in and churns your guts. Poetry that shows you the bones of creation and the connecting thread that joins all things in the great web of existence.

Poetry is a sacred dialogue between the fili, nature, and the Gods. It is communion and communication. Poetry should be an ongoing process for the fili. It's part of meditation, because when you meditate, you're in a perfect state for absorbing some aspect of nature, or some insight into the nature of deity or of reality, and translating it into words for the world to hear.

Poetry is an invocation of all that is sacred, and it calls the world and the Otherworlds into being. It's a key that opens gateways that nothing else can touch. It brings things into perfect focus.

In addition to poetry as magic, there was also respect for poetry as a social mechanism; it offered praise for those who were worthy, and satire and scorn for those who were not.

It isn't just the reading of poetry, but the making of poetry that is important. Celtic Pagans must *be* poets, even if they aren't great poets. The classical historians noted that the Celts spoke in riddles and loved to obfuscate. Wordplay and veiled reference were common. This 'language of the poets' was a vital part of the transmission of lore.

I talk a lot about poetry and poetic secrets in my essay in

Philip's book *The Druid Renaissance*. I identify as a fili rather than as a Druid, and because the training of the fili took up to twenty years, I don't consider myself fully worthy of the title yet, so that's why I call myself a fili in training. Maybe in another five or ten years, after I've studied some more and published some poetry, I'll feel more comfortable with it.

Connection with the Celtic past is necessary. The Celts had a reverence for history and tradition, and that reverence is a part of the Celtic spirit, I believe. For some, this connection comes through physical ancestry. For others, it comes through the study of history. Some people get it through connecting with the feeling of the myths. Other folks get it in other ways.

I think that this is why we have such heated debates about the importance (or lack thereof) of sticking to historical fact in the Celtic Pagan community. Celtic Pagans and Druids all recognize that something from the past is speaking to us strongly, but we disagree about the methods of judging its veracity and usefulness.

A sense of early Celtic cosmology is necessary; doing things in terms of the three realms of land, sea and sky, rather than the classical Greek four elements. Using Celtic symbols like triskeles and spirals rather than pentagrams. Celebrating Celtic holidays rather than (or more deeply than) the holidays of other religions. Threes and nines as ritually important and the use of a sacred cosmic tree and well combination. Much of this cosmology has had to be painstakingly reconstructed from fragmentary hints, and it goes back again to the argument that historical research is important to learning about and preserving the Celtic spirit.

I think that inclusiveness is important. We can't rely on genealogy or geography to determine who is 'Celtic'. The historical Celts roamed all over Europe, and lands beyond. Anyone worthy might be taken into the tribe through marriage or adoption.

The Celts are roaming still, moving to America, Australia, and other widely diverse lands. And they're still taking people in through marriage and adoption.

Respect for women was a definite part of the Celtic spirit. While Celtic women didn't have it perfect, they were far better off than their Greek and Roman counterparts. Likewise, respect for and acceptance of gays and lesbians seems important. There is certainly textual evidence for men loving men in early Celtic society. Women were not as often written about, but I think it is safe to assume that women had similar choices open to them.

Personal responsibility and a deep sense of self are a part of the Celtic spirit. Hospitality was sacred, and we should treat it as service to the Gods. Boasting and personal pride are evident in every Celtic tale. Sometimes it went overboard, so of course, we have to be careful not to get too deeply into it. But let's remember that spirited argument was a part of the poet's duty, and was one of the ways in which the younger poets learned from the older. Both tradition and innovation are important. We must face realities that our Celtic forbears never dreamed. We must be flexible, but at the same time we must not bend so far that we break. We need to balance between intuition and research, respecting both, and verifying each with the other.

Can you talk about what you were and are trying to do with your books? And with Nemeton?

The Nemeton was set up on-line to provide a place for learning and dialogue in the Celtic Pagan community, and to foster the growth and depth of Celtic Reconstructionist paths. We're not formally affiliated with any groups, so we provide space for pretty much everyone. We stress civil discourse and reasoned debate, so even when people disagree (as they frequently do), there are ground rules, and I hope that the end result is that people feel safe in posting to the Nemeton. I try to interfere with the list as little as possible, and I usually only step in as moderator if things seem to be getting out of hand.

With my books, I'm just trying to share the information that

I've found and the insights that I've had over the years that I've been reading and meditating on the Celtic material. There's so much crap out there that it's hard for some of the newer folks to tell what's good and what isn't.

The popularity of stuff like *The 21 Lessons of Merlyn* and the *Faery Wicca* books proves the point. Sometimes I think that people are afraid to say that certain books are filled with lies. Maybe they don't want to be perceived as divisive or argumentative. But if we're going to try to honestly examine early Celtic religion, we have to understand Celtic history, and you're not going to find it in most occult books.

There's a myth going around about people with unbroken family traditions back to the Druids, family Celtic Shaman traditions, and Celtic Wiccan traditions founded by the Gods themselves. I just don't think that's possible, given the clearances of the highlands, the persecution of the Irish, the famines, and the pervasive influence of the Christian Church.

The majority of the Druids didn't just give up and convert peacefully. And the Christians didn't preserve the Celtic Pagan religions whole in their writings. Maybe people have fragments of traditions, folkways, but nobody has got a whole and intact Celtic Pagan religion that goes back over 1,500 years.

If you find people claiming this sort of thing, my advice is to run the other way. It's like the Wiccan grandmother stories from the 1960s that everyone laughs about now. What's so different about these Celtic Shaman grandmother stories?

Certainly some strands of the traditions were preserved by the filidh and the Bards, but it's clear that they were affiliated with the Churches and that the vast majority of them considered themselves good Christians, and not worshippers of the Pagan Celtic deities.

In my own work, I try hard to distinguish between what we know, what we can infer from fragments and folklore, and what I've created out of my own visions and meditations. I would have a lot more respect for most of the occult authors if they would be honest about their creations and their sources.

Why is it so evil to admit that you've created something? Are people afraid to be judged on their own merits? Our creativity is a precious gift from the Gods, and meant to be used. But there are a lot of people abusing their creativity by writing these fictions and calling them ancient tradition.

I'm working on a couple of new books, one on a different approach to Ogham and the other a general overview of a modern fili's path, but I'm having trouble writing because I'm in pain so much of the time from my fibromyalgia. It's going very slowly, and I have to admit that the Nemeton list takes up a lot of my available energy for writing.

I've also been working on the poetic aspects of my practice a lot more lately, which also siphons off some of my energy from book and article writing.

Do you have a group now and if so can you please describe it?

I'm not working with a group these days, although I do gather with my friends to celebrate the holy days. My practice over the past few years has been almost entirely solitary due to my disabilities, with a little teaching now and then to pass the knowledge along.

For a while my husband and I were offering a correspondence course, but the tapes started breaking down and we can't copy them anymore. Now I'm trying to compile a lot of that material into a book on modern filidecht, to make it more available to people. I tend to be something of a hermit, a geilt or crazy-woman poet. I have daily practices like making offerings to my deities and burning candles, and I do a lot of meditation. I keep Brighid's flame every twenty days as part of a network of Brighid priestesses.

I think that making an effort toward daily practices, even if we don't actually manage to do them every day, is important. It builds our connections with the Gods, with the land, and with the

Otherworld realms. We need to be open to messages from the Gods and the spirits, and the best way to do that is by practicing our communications skills through poetry, ritual and meditation.

We need to walk the paths between worlds more often than once every six weeks, or every quarter.

My 'ministry', if you will (and I use that word because I can't think of a better one), is online with the Nemeton list and the web page that I've started building to promote the Nemeton and maintain a compilation of some of my more obscure writings.

That's where I offer my service to the community, through providing a forum for discussion and exploration of Celtic Reconstructionist paths. Every couple of years I get together with friends to offer a Celtic-oriented festival, with rituals and a focus on ancestor worship and land spirit work.

I thought for a long time about starting an organization, because none of the existing ones really fit my needs, but I realized that I wasn't interested in doing the paperwork or in the politicking that would be necessary for building a group. And I didn't want to be seen as yet more competition for the existing groups.

What's important to me is sharing information, and fortunately I can do that without a group or an organization. Although I'll admit that sometimes I get a little lonely as a hermit. I'm lucky to have some very good friends, and they help keep me from getting too crazy.

Where would you like to see Druidism and Celtic spirituality go in future?

I would like to see more attention to Celtic historical study, more poetry, more frequent community practice, and more communication among groups and individuals. It's through these connections that we'll be able to build up a strong community of Celtic Pagans.

I'd like to see people be a lot more critical of what they read. We don't have to accept things as gospel just because someone wrote them down. The Gods are in the details of things as well as in the broad brushstrokes of comparative studies.

It would be good to have Celtic Pagans earning degrees in Celtic studies as a resource for the community to turn to when they have questions about the historical aspects of modern practices. Likewise, I think we need philosophers and theologians to explore both the old mythologies and people's new visions more thoroughly. Not so that they can tell us what to do, but so that we can look more deeply at the implications of these things for our practice and for our community.

We need mystics to plumb the depths of the Celtic corpus and the spirit realms, and share their visions with us, to walk the mists and bring back mysteries. The Gods and spirits have not stopped speaking to us, it's just that so many of us have forgotten how to listen. And often when we do listen, we've forgotten how to be discerning.

I think it would be good for us to develop relationships with traditional communities of Celtic people in Europe, and to be involved with their struggles to maintain their rights, their languages and their cultures. Otherwise the whole process of Celtic Paganism strikes me as being similar to the theft of Native American ways by the New Age.

The Celts aren't dead! They are struggling for cultural survival on the fringes of Europe. There's so much they could teach us, if we were willing to act in a respectful manner and to work with them in their efforts to continue their ways of life.

I think also that more involvement with the environmental movement is desperately important. How can we connect to land that's poisoned and dead, to forests of stumps? What does it say about our relationship to animal spirits if we don't fight to save the animals from extinction?

When we become more aware of the Earth and the land spirits through our ritual, meditations, and poetry, one inescapable part of that connection is that we begin to feel the pain of the world.

We need to bear that pain, and then we need to do something concrete to ease the world's suffering.

Doing magic and writing poems about it are important, but they aren't enough. We need to take direct action, whether that means writing to legislators, or voting, or running for office, or chaining yourself in front of the bulldozers. Practice civil disobedience, because so many of the laws and so much of what is happening is unjust.

Satire and ridicule were important tools of social control for the filidh among the ancient Celts. I think we need to use these powerful techniques against the Earth-raping corporations and politicians. We are being led into death and disaster by unfit rulers, and the Earth, as Celtic tradition has told us, is expressing her displeasure by becoming the Wasteland. We need to speak out against the fools in office and the fools in office buildings through our art and our actions.

Let's not be afraid to curse those who truly deserve the cursing, for traditional satire is the art of cursing, make no mistake. These arts and actions are a part of our service to the Gods and the greater community. Taking real action brings us back into a place of power in ourselves and our communities. It puts us into a right relationship with the Goddesses of the land.

We need to be aware of the consequences of our personal choices in life, and the things we buy and do. Recycling is nice, and donating money to environmental organizations is a cosmic good, but it isn't enough. There are a lot of places you can go and books you can read to learn how to take positive action. Doing something in the mundane world helps to combat the frustration and depression that can come with deeply connecting with the world's pain.

Cailte said that what maintained the Fianna was, 'truth in our hearts, strength in our arms and fulfillment in our tongues'. We need to practice a little strength and fulfillment in our lives, to walk our talk.

What do you think Celtic spirituality has to offer the world? The Pagan community in general?

Celtic spirituality, if it's done right, can offer the world a model of sanity in an insane time. It can offer a way of looking at the world through poetry and beauty, a way of harmony and right relationship with the land and its spirits.

The Celtic way is one of respect for intellectual achievement and the work of the scholar and the artist. There's too little of that in secular American culture. We're lost in the adoration of consumer goods, while the world-changing work of mystics and the voice of poets go unheard.

Our society worships science and thinks that it isn't missing anything. But we can't offer the world anything at all until we start being honest with ourselves and others about our origins and our work.

Are Druidism and Celtic spirituality experiencing any problems that you know of? Locally? Nationally?

I've already talked about dishonesty in the community, and passing off fiction as history. Some people will say anything they think you want to hear to gain power and authority over others, or to get sex from admirers.

Not all Pagans are nice people, our community is just like every other. There are some really slimy individuals in the Pagan community. Unfortunately, calling attention to this sort of thing usually just gets you keelhauled. You get accused of starting 'Witch wars'. They'll say you're a rumor-monger, or you're told that 'it's just a personality conflict'.

Well, sometimes real problems do exist. And some of the problems are serious. Pagan child abusers and rapists and wife beaters and thieves and con men and psychotics are out there ruining people's lives. Gullibility is another problem that strikes me as something we'll have to face before we come of age. Liars are supported by people who unknowingly accept whatever is told to them. I think we'd have less of a problem with fictional histories and traditions if people would just take the time to do some reading and checking around. We would have less of a problem with abuse in the community if people would listen to each other and check into stories about abuses rather than trying to bury them under the sod.

It would be nice if we could trust everyone to be who and what they say, but unfortunately we can't. I'm not suggesting that we run around being paranoid about everyone we meet, but some networking and a little bit of care in our relationships with other people could go a long way toward pointing out the problematic individuals and groups.

Is there anything else you want to add?

Pursue the Salmon of Wisdom. Let it lead you to the Well. Be prepared to sacrifice everything for the gift that the Gods have waiting. It is worth your life.

Cathbad
Interviewed July 7, 1996
Via internet

Cathbad is presently involved in the creation of a new Celtic Pagan group. The email list-serv called Imbas-L is in the process of incorporating as a tribal Celtic organization loosely based on the idea of the old Celtic clans, with individual tribes or Groves that operate fairly autonomously and a Council to oversee administration. He is currently on the steering committee, which is composed of members living in several different states, provinces and countries.

Cathbad refers to himself as a 'Celtic Pagan' because he feels the title of 'Druid' is a recognition of achievement and responsibility that he has not yet earned, though he hopes to one day.

His publications include: When All the World is Asleep in Crossroads, a Pagan journal based in Milwaukee, Wisconsin, Visions of a Better Way in 'Focus' (University of Guelph Press, 1993), The Solitary Practitioner's Frequently Asked Questions on Druidism, and The Ethics of Druidism, published on the internet.

Can you please describe your religious upbringing as a child?

My family is Roman Catholic, in the Irish style of Catholicism brought to Canada by my father, who was born in Ireland. I was an altar boy for six years, the longest run in the parish at the time. I think the record still stands, an irony that tends to amuse me. I am the only member of my family to change my religion, with the exception of my mom, who converted from the United Church to Catholicism in order to marry Dad. I attended a Catholic school until the end of grade eight.

Having been born in Ireland, my dad had grown up

surrounded by the folklore, mythology, and legends of the Irish people. He gave these to my sisters and I as bedtime stories and rainy day entertainments, but certainly never as religious instruction – that he left to the school and the parish. But he did impart to us something valuable to Paganism, which perhaps he shares, and that is a sense of the magical, the sacred, and the sublime in all things around us. My sisters and I consequently lived in an imaginative world.

I don't think that the Catholic instruction and ritual dampened this at all, it was given to us as a kind of framework by which we could understand anything we didn't understand as yet. It was the simple faith of a simple child, who created his world in the image of legends, Christian and Pagan.

I didn't realize until much later that the idea of the sacred environment could be further enhanced by the Druidic idea of land spirits, well-spirits, tree spirits, and so on. That came around high school, when I started learning more about Paganism. It gave one more thing to my sense of the sacred environment, and that was the identity and individuality of the things around me. It brought them closer to me, I think, because I could empathize easier with something that had feelings and thoughts like I do.

In the Christianity of my youth, the sacred land had the same identity, that of God, spread throughout. That can be comforting, I suppose, because you can never be alone that way, but I eventually thought that nothing was special or unique.

How did you first find out about Druids, what drew you to that particular path?

Upon returning from a vacation in Ireland, my Dad brought home with him a stack of books, mostly about Irish history and mythology. These I devoured, for I discovered the stories he gave to my sisters and I as bedtime tales were in fact part of a larger, integrated, and beautiful literature. But for those years it was as an entertainment rather than a philosophical seeking of any kind.

In high school one of my best friends introduced me to the possibility that the world-view and lifestyle and religion described by the old legends need not remain confined to the legends. I began to ask, what can I accept into my life now, and what not? And is not the Catholic Christianity of my youth also a mythology that refused to die? If that is all it is, what from it should I accept, and what not? Questions tend to lead to other questions, until the point where one questions absolutely everything. I was imagining myself as Descartes, who questioned even his own existence.

It was a lonely time, but a good time for thinking. At first, as is natural, I sought to integrate the Paganism I was discovering into Catholicism. I found a good vehicle for just such a union in Culdee Christianity, the Celtic Church of Columba, (Colum Cille) and others.

Catholicism believes that God, who is one, is also three...then why not four, of five, or twenty, to account for all the Gods of all the religions in the rest of the world? As a thought experiment, I began to direct my prayers to Gaia instead of to Jesus, and found no diminishment in the love and attention that She gave me.

Questions lead to further questions. In Paganism there is no separation of men and women, no concept of original sin, and no clerical intermediary between humans and the divine. One by one, I was throwing out things which I had held to be the foundations of the universe. It is not an easy thing to do, to rewrite an entire metaphysical paradigm. I also had few friends at the time, being something of a loner and recluse. I had to make the discovery process alone. I still am a bit reclusive, and I am still discovering things.

As with all living things, I guess I latched on to that which gave me the greatest spiritual fulfillment, the greatest inner peace. I found in Druidism a way to make my artistic pursuits into spiritual pursuits as well. I do not regret my time as a

Catholic, for if it were not the Catholic insistence that myth is truth, Druidism would not have become so alive for me, nor the other religions of the world in general. Actually, I think I have a greater appreciation of how integrated Catholic thought is. But knowing what I know now, about the Druid's vision of the world and humanity's place in it, I cannot return.

Thus it came to be, that I embraced Celtic Paganism whole-heartedly and completely. And thus it came to be, that I feared my family, and what they would do if they found out.

Two weeks after leaving home and moving into an apartment of my own, I told my family about the decision I had made. I had to wait a year or two before telling them, because I didn't want to be living with them when I told them. That way, they could take no retribution. They probably would not have done anything, but I didn't want to take any chances.

In the two and a half years since then, there have been numerous debates, arguments, appeals to my past, appeals to friends, appeals to hellfire and damnation, all to get me to come back. Now I think we have it down to a kind of amicable opposition, like two boxers who beat each other senseless in the ring and then go out for a beer together. It was a long time coming, but it is a good relationship we have now.

How were you trained in Celtic spirituality?

I am primarily self-taught. Though good teachers have passed in and out of my life, I tend to choose books for my teachers, and meditations and practices and experiences that happen around me. I choose books that are not written by Pagan authors, but rather by academics because academia tends to give more than just a passing nod to history. But of course they say little about how to put it into practice.

I consider my training still in progress. At the moment, I'm pursuing an undergraduate degree in philosophy, which I think is consistent with the kind of training the ancient Druids received. I'm only 22 years old, after all. I have been seeking the

Druids for less than a decade. I am in no hurry; the universe is under no obligation to offer me enlightenment at a drive through pace.

How do you define Druidism as a path?

As a modern thing. I try not to define it, usually. It's just something I do. Otherwise, the historical definition seems most applicable: Druidism was, and is, the indigenous religion of the Celtic people prior to the introduction of Christianity.

Are you in a group, a Grove, are you solitary, or what?

I practice alone. I think I'd like to work with a group of some kind though. Religion is about community just as much as it is about individuality. Community is one of the things I admit I miss, having left Catholicism.

You wrote a wonderful essay on Druid ethics, which you posted to the internet. Would you mind going over some of the main points you touched on? It was rather interesting.

I'd be happy to talk about it. I was thinking about publishing it in a journal, in fact I did submit it to the journal of The Henge of Keltria for that purpose. They rejected it on the grounds that it was too long, which I think is reasonable. Maybe later I'll break it into sections.

I'm going to work on it a bit more because, for one thing, I did not satisfactorily tackle the problem of evil. I think I know why too: the myths don't deal with that problem, at least not explicitly. In the Fenian myths the problem of evil is fairly simple to infer from the known facts, it is the failure to uphold the heroic code of the warriors, which occurs because that heroic code is not easy to maintain. The benefits for actually sticking to the path are also clear, and pleasantly enough, available for enjoyment in the here-and-now so we don't have to wait for an afterlife to enjoy them. But in Druidic mysticism I don't think it's quite so easy to figure out so I think I'll be scratching my head over this one for many years.

I have a triad which I wrote myself, which goes as follows:

Three elements to Druidry in the modern age: history, poetry, mystery. The history third represents the study of that which is known to professional historians in the academic world. To that end, as I have mentioned, I am pursuing an undergraduate degree in philosophy. Poetry deals with the study of the literature of the Celtic people through the ages; for example I consider Yeats to be a great influence in my spirituality. Even though the man was not a Druid he was certainly very spiritual. Mystery deals with applying the other two elements to my daily life.

There is no question that the path is not easy. By taking that which is known from history and poetry and using it as a focus for meditations, prayers, rituals, lifestyle, etc., I think we can come close to finding answers to the various philosophical questions that cause people to turn to religion in the first place.

The mystery is also the challenge because it takes a lot of courage to keep the spirit alive, when surrounded by the unknown.

It's dangerous and even a little frightening. I'll give you an example of what I mean by from a popular science fiction film; there was a great Druid named Spock who while on a mission to save the planet yet one more time gave up the logical discipline of Kohlinar and found his answers by confronting an enemy and discovering that his enemy was as empty of answers as himself.

His questions summed up what I think was going on: 'Each one of us at some time in our lives comes to a father, a brother, a God and asks; 'Why am I here? What was I meant to be? Is this all that I am? Is there nothing more?"

The writing in that film was quite brilliant. The acting... well...let me say that the writing made up for that.

Maybe the problem of evil rests in giving up the search, closing our minds to the sacredness and magic of the universe and not treating all beings as if they were sacred and not treating all the universe as sacred space and not treating yourself as though you are one of the many irreplaceable parts of this great big thing called life.

That was lovely, thank you. What are your current projects?

I'm continuing to publish on the internet as well as in Crossroads and any other journals that will accept my work. I might seek out a group to join sometime, but I'm not in any great hurry. As a career goal, I'd like to become a playwright.

Druidism has given me a means to make my artistic pursuits into spiritual ones as well. A lot of the things I wrote in high school were about the process of changing one's mind and in so doing, risking madness. I'd like to keep on writing plays and working in the theater, doing what I do best.

Since you are on a Celtic oriented path, and since you are Canadian, what do you think it means to be a 'Celt' in modern times?

There is a certain nostalgia which many modern people attach to the 'old ways'. The image conjured to the mind is that of a quieter, simpler, easier life. With the old ways, people can enjoy leisure and pleasure at any time, where the daily chores of survival such as preparing food are in and of themselves pleasurable, and there is no crime or hatred of any kind. It is this kind of harmless fantasy that leads people to explore and investigate these old ways, sometimes with a kind of escapism from modern life's pressures, or to acquire the necessary knowledge before emulation of the old ways begins.

In a religious sense the old ways refer to a kind of primal, uncorrupted spirituality which time and vice have transformed into something no longer pure, and on that basis it is believed that a return to the old ways would eliminate some of the problems that religion has today, such as the abuse of power by Church leaders or the hypocrisy of certain dogmatic religious positions. A Celt living today who wishes to revive the old ways in her life finds herself in an interesting position because the old ways of the Celts can occasionally be as undesirable as modern ways; the Celts were headhunters and cattle rustlers for example, and clearly the practice of headhunting and cattle rustling is not something we want to practice today. The dilemma is, what do we emulate from the past, and what do we ignore?

I think part of the answer to the problem of the old ways can be found, ironically, in the modern ways. The old ways are more than just a certain spiritual disposition, but also a complete set of folklore. It is possible to discover the Celtic spirit by listening to modern Celtic music for example, or by listening to the chants of children growing up in Celtic countries, and the stories their parents tell to them to put them to sleep. Investigating these pieces of culture can indicate the paradigm by which the Celt understands the workings of the world.

For those who wish to build their spirituality into a Celtic one, I think it best to examine certain myths, legends and folktales that have made the greatest impact upon the Celtic consciousness.

One that intrigues me is the concept of the 'sacred king'. In the old days, kings were required to be without physical blemish in order to be acceptable to the Land Goddess to whom they were ritually married. The rite of succession to kingship was a ritual one which secured the link between the king and the health of the land he ruled, and the people who lived on that land. It was a sexual union, a spiritual union, a total union. I think this connection with the land is an important part of the Celtic way of thinking about things, because it demonstrates quite clearly how inseparable we are from our environment. And what is more, if we are truly at one with our environment, it seems only natural to take care of the world, which is what we are. With this connection to the world our self does not end at our skin but encompasses much more. I think this is part of what the poet Amergin was getting at when he gave his famous poem that begins; 'I am a wave of the sea...' I think that is also the reason why so many of the Celtic people displaced out of their homes due to famine or war, always feel a longing to go back to the 'old country', even when they have made the new country into a comfortable refuge. The Celt has an appreciation for the beauty of the world, wherever she is, and takes pleasure in that beauty.

There is also the sense of the inspirational in what is Celtic. The old Druids of Irish myth used to use poetry to construct their magical spells and in fact called their magic poems 'the fire in the head', because that was what it felt like to be inspired. Brighid becomes an important Goddess because that inspirational flame is Her gift. The myths are clear that both men and women were capable of this 'imbas' or sacred inspiration, which is another unique feature of Celtic thought.

In modern Celtic nations one can attend a session, or a ceilidh [dance], where the pipes and fiddles play those complicated jigs and reels. I have found that the contemplation of these tunes has an effect on my feelings, perhaps because a piece of the old Druid magic remains in the sound, as though the vibrations carry its spirit. The experience has all the more impact because it's shared. Even if one is not a poet, musician, writer or dancer, I think cultivating an appreciation of these things is important. It happens that Ireland has produced no less than four Nobel-prize winners for literature; I think that is because the culture places a strong value on the work of creative and thoughtful people.

What else? The Celts were a tribal people, so perhaps in modern times it would be appropriate for a Celt to keep good relations within her family. It is a hard thing to do for one who would be a Druid, when doing things like worshipping the old Gods looks suspiciously like a crazy cult. Another virtue to the old Celts was the unspoken, unwritten, warrior's honor code. But that can also occasionally conflict with modern life because behaving in such ways forces one to be a bit more individualistic, as opposed to the good citizen who has a regular job, pays his taxes, purchases his needs, and in general assumes that such is the good life and doesn't question that assumption. The warrior of honor, however, is no such gear in a great impersonal machine like the global market. The Celt finds her inspiration, be it artistic or spiritual, in the land and among other things, and not exclusively in the mere acquisition of property.

However, I observe that many of the Celts I know spend exorbitant amounts of money on CDs and works of art, and I am no exception. My point is not to criticize the modern economy, but to show how different a Celt is from what society considers normal, and to show that being a little different is a desirable thing to be. I find the pleasures of meditating on inspiration, or the beauty of the land, sea, and sky, more worthwhile and longer lasting than other pleasures. Perhaps that is because as a Celtic Pagan I affirm that these things are sacred and special. Through them we can know important things like what divinity is, how to join with the Gods, and how to find peace.

I am simply using the techniques of the Celtic people to do what people all around the world and at all times have been doing. The Celts saw that their world was composed of three realms: Land, sea, and sky, and proceeded to build their understanding of the world accordingly. Thus it is that we swear oaths on the realms today and conceive of them as possessing spiritual force in addition to physical location. They saw that within the realms things were composed of circles and spirals, like the sun and the moon, the circumference of trees, and hills, and currents of water, and so built their monuments and forts in the form of circles, and held their sacred ceremonies in circles. They saw that between any two things was another place, and by seeking that third space they could achieve inspiration, and so enter the Otherworld and learn great wisdom from the Gods. They saw a third space even between life and death. To me this seems the most natural way to go about doing things. I attempt to conduct my life accordingly. And that is what I think it means to be a Celt.

Druidism is often thought of as the Celtic Reconstructionist religion. Where do you think Druidism is headed now?

I have no idea where Druidism is headed. I think it will share whatever fate befalls the other varieties of Paganism in our search for acceptance among world religions and western society. I have observed that one gets a lot less hostile reaction when one says, 'I am a Druid'; as compared to, 'I am a Pagan'. There is something of a mystique surrounding Celtic matters.

Celtic culture is growing in popularity among the mainstream culture, particularly Celtic art and music. One Celtic festival that I attend every year is only four years old and draws crowds of thousands. It is a good sign.

Where would you like to see things go in the future?

I think I'd like to see Druidism become re-introduced into Celtic culture once again, not to usurp but to coexist with Christianity, for both have contributed greatly to the modern Celtic spirit.

Many of the world's religions are doing ecumenism now, trying to reconcile their differences by asserting their similarities. I have a rather Zen-like approach to Celtic magic, thinking it has more to do with personal transformation than outward activism; the similarities between Druidism and certain Eastern mystic paths like Taoism greatly interest me.

I'd like to see Druid magic in literature and philosophy once again. The Irish Literary Revival created by Yeats and others is close to what I mean, and it's something I'd like to see carried on. Yeats' writings remain an important source of wisdom for me. As an aspiring playwright, that is part of what I hope to achieve in my own writing as well. I'd like to create a world in my drama that is something like the magical world of legends, but with the dramatic tragedy still there.

I'd also like to see Druidism become a force for the healing of this island Earth and the people on it...but I suppose that's a given.

Are there any problems within Druidism that you are aware of?

Well, one problem is probably obvious. The Celtic culture is a subculture in Canada, and in the USA as well, and Celtic Paganism is a subculture even within that. It would be helpful for Paganism if it became integrated into acceptability, but to achieve its aims it doesn't have to be. It has more to do with personal reform than social reform.

Do you have any particular bones to pick? Axes to grind?

I've observed a trend in the re-creation of Druidism according to the imaginative desires of people who seek to cash in on the popularity of Celtic culture. There's been much published material on Druidism that owes more to fraternal-Order styles of Paganism, Witchcraft, New Age, and assorted cross-cultural weirdness than to Celtic culture as it existed historically, or as it continues to exist today in Scotland, Ireland, and other Celtic nations.

I don't think religion can be taken out of its culture, and I don't want that to happen to Druidism. I understand many natives feel the same way, when white people appropriate their wisdom without acknowledging the people who lived it; it is a kind of theft.

We need to make peace with our own past before we can fiddle with someone else's past. For those who would reconstruct the learned class of the Celtic people, it would seem reasonable to go about it in a learned way, and it annoys me when the search for money or recognition overrides the search for knowledge.

Naturally, there is no good reason to stop people from doing that which brings them spiritual peace. On the other hand, mysticism is not a quick-fix. It is a process, and an effort, and it is ongoing.

I fear that commercialism will kill it.

Isaac Bonewits (October 1, 1949 – August 12, 2010)

Interviewed July 25, 1996
Starwood Festival, Sherman, New York

Isaac was Arch Druid Emeritus of ADF (*Ar nDraiocht Fein*), a third Order Druid in The Reformed Druids of North America, a member of OBOD and of The Henge of Keltria, a Third Degree Gardnerian Witch, and had a bachelor's degree in Magic from the University of California, Berkeley, class of 1970. His book *Real Magic* (Samuel Weiser, York Beach Maine 1989) is something of a Pagan classic.

He was responsible for perpetrating various schismatic offshoots of The Reformed Druids of North America in the 1970s, including The Schismatic Druids of North America, The New Reformed Druids of North America, and The Hasidic Druids of North America, which he believed was in many ways the best experiment they did (his favorite offshoot was actually started by Robert Anton Wilson who called his The Reformed Non-Aristotelian Druids of North America, the RNADNA).

He wrote a book called *Authentic Thaumaturgy* (Steve Jackson Games, 1996), which is on magic systems for players of fantasy role playing games and at the time of this interview was writing a book on liturgy, a book on the history of Druidism, and a book on Neo-Pagan poly-theology.

ADF began in 1983 as a network of scholars interested in researching Druids and Indo-European history. Today it is one of the larger groups in America. It continues its tradition of scholarship and seeks to expose groups and individuals it considers fraudulent or dangerous.

Despite the Gaelic name members of ADF come from many

ancestral roots including European, Asian, Native American and African. They eschew cultural and racial bigotry and seek to honor in ritual and in scholarly investigation all Indo-European Deities, ancestors and Nature Spirits.

ADF Druids are forbidden to practice animal or human sacrifice, but are encouraged to make offerings of flowers, oil, wine, incense, music, song, drama, prayer and love. They celebrate the eight festivals of the Earth year based on astronomical research, meaning a few days before or after most other neo-Pagans celebrate.

An ADF Grove consists of three or more members in a common geographic area who meet twice a month for fellowship and worship. ADF recognizes three 'circles' of advancement, and has a demanding study program that seeks to prepare candidates for the Druid ministry.

Can you talk about your childhood? What religion were you raised in?

I was raised Roman Catholic. My mother was a devout Roman Catholic and my father was a Presbyterian Atheist. I was Catholic until I was twelve or so. When I was thirteen I went to a high school seminary in southern California. At the end of that year I decided that while I had a vocation to be a Priest it wasn't in their religion. From that point on I started doing a lot of exploration into different religious and magical systems.

When I was thirteen I met a woman from New Orleans who was into Voodoo who showed me few things that were pretty remarkable. That was when I learned that, yes, Magic really does work if you do it right. I watched her spells work on a few people who had no idea that a spell was being cast. I was lucky that my first exposure to Magic was through a working folk tradition and not through a left brain, highly abstracted, theoretical system. I was also lucky in that she made it clear to me that it doesn't work all the time. That Magic is something like poetry or music, when it works it's great, when it doesn't work it doesn't work.

So I investigated a lot of Magical systems, I read a lot of anthropology, comparative religion and para-psychology. I joined several groups and got thrown out of them for heresy. One was the Nichiren Shoshu pseudo-Buddhist group who kicked me out for asking awkward questions, like where was all the money going? They were collecting a lot of money and it turned out it was going to support this ultra-right-wing political party in Japan. I was also saying that everyone sits in front of this Magic scroll and recites this mantra, and I understand that's how the Magic works, but exactly how does the energy go? What are the details of what is happening? They didn't want to deal with questions about the Magical technology of what they were doing because they didn't want to admit that it was Magic.

That was an attitude I had run into before, talking to Catholics about praying to the saints. They are not supposed to admit that what they are doing is casting Magic spells.

I was recruited by and then had a run-in with Anton LaVey's Church of Satan. I published an article about that called 'My Satanic Adventure' in Earth Religion News and in Gnostica, which are both long defunct. I was at the University of California at Berkeley and there was a corner of the campus where Telegraph Avenue meets Bancroft that was the traditional soap-box corner. Various Evangelists would stand there and attempt to evangelize the students going in and out of the university.

One year I decided it would be fun to confront them with something they hadn't been confronted with yet. That is to say that heckling Evangelists was one of the major forms of amusement in those days. I decided to do something a bit different from the usual heckling. I dressed myself all in black and came out and did an Evangelical lecture on behalf of the Devil, using all of the standard clichés of Southern Baptist Evangelical preaching.

I talked about how wonderful the Devil was and how the students ought to be ashamed of themselves for not being more sinful. The looks of horror and astonishment on the faces of the Christian Evangelists was truly heart-warming to behold.

I started doing that regularly, several times a week. I talked about why people should be more actively involved in leading sinful lives. I was promoting what I now refer to as left-wing Luciferian philosophy. That's the approach to Satanism that treats Lucifer as the intellectual rebel fighting against tyranny. It's a very popular version of Satanism among teenagers and college students because they are in the rebellion stage themselves.

I got recruited one day by a very attractive young lady from Anton LaVey's Church of Satan. She said; 'Hi I'm a Witch,' and I said; 'That's nice.' I had already done quite a bit of reading about Witchcraft at that point so I wondered what flavor of Witch she was. She said she was with the Church of Satan. I said; 'What's that?' And she said it was an organization of people promoting the Devil. So I said; 'OK, that sounds like fun.'

She invited me to meet the great man himself. So I met him and he invited me to join the Church of Satan for free, which was quite a change in his day. I started attending Church of Satan activities and they gave me a bunch of literature to hand out just like all the other Evangelists had.

I had a lot of fun for several months, mostly because we got to dress up in costume and do ritual. I became one of the Satanic altar boys, assisting with the ritual, including occasionally faking some Enochian language to impress the rubes. Eventually I started noticing that everybody else in this organization was extremely right-wing and middle aged and not very well educated and I watched LaVey playing his crowd like a musician playing an instrument and I began asking awkward questions there.

Members of the church started coming to me for advice about how to do spell-casting, which I thought was kind of strange because at seventeen it turned out I knew more about Magic than

Mr. LaVey did, who was in his thirties or forties at the time. He had a huge Occult library, but he hadn't actually read most of the books.

I think the fact that people were coming to me for advice on spell-casting plus the fact that I was a long-haired Hippie-Commie pervert weirdo combined with the fact that LaVey was very upset that I was flirting with his daughter was what got me in trouble.

It was hysterically funny, he was trying to protect his daughter's virtue, this Priest of Satan.

You mean she hadn't been used as an altar?

Not yet. She wouldn't give me the time of day, but it was really amusing that he was so paranoid about his daughter.

So at any event I got kicked out. I went back to campus and continued on my merry way and a short while after that I made the acquaintance of a Druid, Robert Larson. He was a graduate of Carleton College in Northfield, Minnesota, and had been one of the early members of The Reformed Druids of North America, which was founded by David Fisher and Norman Johnson in 1963. When Bob Larson mentioned that he was a Druid some sort of bell went off in my head and I said; 'Tell me more,' and he did. And I said; 'OK, I want to do this.' He initiated me into the RDNA and we started off with a Grove in Berkeley.

Why were you attracted to Druidism? You could have become a Witch or other things.

At first I didn't know what it was. It was the word 'Druid' itself that had some sort of very powerful effect on me at a very deep level that I was never really able to analyze. I just knew that this was something I wanted to investigate and participate in. And the more I researched about the Druids the more it seemed to me that here was a group of people who did very valuable things for their community, had a strong effect on the world around them, and who valued things that I valued; reverence for nature, respect for the intellect, the active use of the arts in their work, and the public service aspect. All those things fit together for me to say this was something I wanted to be involved in.

When you say public service are you referring to Druids who belong to groups that resemble the Rotarians? I don't notice that Druids are doing a lot of public service.

Actually, all of the local ADF Groves are required to do a public service project every fiscal quarter. That wasn't exactly what I meant by public service though. I meant providing religious and counseling and teaching services to a community. The RDNA was providing religious services, open ceremonies that anyone could attend if they wanted to. At that point that was all it was.

I almost immediately saw where it could go and I proceeded to do historical research into the origins of the RDNA, I edited what they had in the way of scriptures and historical material at the time, wrote a bunch of new material and then Robert Larson and I printed it out as *The Druid Chronicles (Evolved)*.

I did not understand completely at the time, on an emotional level, how committed many of the early RDNA members were to anarchy, to not being members of any particular religion. They had the common meso-Pagan idea that Druidism wasn't a religion, that Druidism was a philosophy that you could apply to any religion.

Can you explain what you mean by meso-Pagan for those who may not have heard the term?

Paganism is a term for nature-based, polytheistic religion, wherever and whenever practiced. Paleo-Paganism refers to these religions whenever and wherever they were practiced before the arrival of Christianity, Judaism or Islam into their communities. That is to say, Africa before the slave-trade, North and South America before the arrival of Columbus, Taoism, Hinduism before Islam came into India, and obviously what all our ancestors were doing in Europe, BC.

Meso-Paganism is a term that refers to groups that began as

attempts to revive, reinvent, or perpetuate what they thought the paleo-Pagan ways of their ancestors were, but which happened in a social situation where there was information and attitudes from monotheistic religions coming in. So what you got was a blend of Paganism and, usually, Christianity. So you get things like the Rosicrucians, a mix of Pagan and Christian, and the Theosophists whose system was a mix of very badly garbled Buddhism and Hinduism with a heavy overlay of icky-sticky-sweet Victorian Christianity.

I have read the Ancient Order of Druids' lesson plans and they are almost pure Theosophy.

I am not surprised. Other meso-Pagan groups would be the Sikhs who are a blend of Hinduism and Islam, and Aleister Crowley's Thelemic religion, which is a mix of badly garbled Egyptian religion with his Fundamentalist Christian upbringing. The various fraternal movements in England are by and large meso-Pagan. They are doing essentially Christian mysticism with a Pagan overlay. There are exceptions now, but that is the way it has been until recently.

Neo-Pagan religions are the ones started over the last forty or fifty years as efforts to revive what they thought paleo-Paganism was, but done under social circumstances where it wasn't necessary to inject Christian theology into it. It was possible to avoid monotheistic patterns and therefore construct something that was more 'New Age' than Christian. Neo-Pagan religious movements are paying conscious attention to where their ideas are coming from when they mix them into what they are doing.

These are not air-tight pigeon holes. They are not hard and fast, rigid definitions. There is often a time period of decades to centuries where a given religious tradition is shifting from paleo to meso and then into neo. Neo-Pagan and meso-Pagan religions are now communicating thanks to modern technology in ways that they never could before so we are seeing meso-Pagan groups such as OBOD shifting over to becoming neo-Pagan as they analyze their materials and realize which parts were authentically Druid and which parts were Christian window dressing applied to prevent persecution a hundred years ago. The Reformed Druids of North America was a meso-Pagan group and a lot of their meditation books and materials for rituals included quotes from Oriental mysticism.

So, at any rate, it seemed obvious to me that if we had a bunch of people going out into the woods, singing hymns of praise to the Earth Mother and invoking various Celtic Gods and Goddesses then what we were doing was a neo-Pagan religion. That apparently for some reason wasn't quite so obvious to the other members of the RDNA. There was a great deal of resentment for the fact that I was declaring it to be a neo-Pagan religion.

So over the course of a decade or so as I moved to different parts of the country pursuing mundane employment, I started up local Groves of what we began calling The New Reformed Druids of North America. At one point we called it The Schismatic Druids of North America because I said, fine, we'll make a schism in the RDNA. Our group will be the one that says we are actually Pagan.

The best experiment I did in those days was The Hasidic Druids of North America. The HDNA started off with a couple of college students from Saint Louis, Missouri, who came to my house in Minneapolis and said that they loved the RDNA theology and that they also loved their childhood upbringing as Jews but they couldn't stand the Jewish theology. So they said is it possible to take the life-style aspects that Judaism has, which are so rich and life-affirming, and mix that with neo-Pagan theology? So I said, well sure, why not?

So that gave us a chance to experiment with creating neo-Paganism as a way of life rather than as a hobby or as something you put on and take off like a hat or a coat. So we created the HDNA based on the classic Jewish tradition.

First we produced the sacred scriptures, we sat down and brainstormed for a few days and wrote the Mish Mash of Hasidic Druidism.

It was a collection of laws and wise sayings about what it meant to be a Hasidic Druid. Then we made Xeroxes and mailed them around to various Pagan friends who had been born and raised Jewish and we said we needed commentary on the Law, just like in Judaism there is the Mishna and then you have the commentary on it, which is the Gemara.

We didn't have quite enough people commenting on every single line so I invented four or five other personalities, Ancients of Blessed Memory, and wrote various arguments and discussions about them. When you study the Talmud there are commentaries on Torah and on the sayings of previous generations of Rabbis, and arguments. So we published it all together and called in The Temara. I think there were about twelve people involved in this activity. We told people they should never study the Mish Mash as if there were no Temara.

Then we put together a set of Hasidic Druid prayers that we called Considdur the Alternatives. A Siddur is a Jewish prayer book. Basically we invented a whole bunch of customs and things for people to do, taking off from Orthodox and Hasidic Jewish Customs like hair length and special hats that you wore and a ritual meal every Friday night. Friday night at sunset began the special period known as 'Weekend'. We would lay out the table in a fancy manner and have a meal and discuss theology.

Isn't Friday night reserved for the women? They act as Priestess in the home at that time.

Well, yeah, but we didn't want to be sexist about that. I don't think we made a big deal over who was doing the actual lighting of the candles.

How many people are still practicing Hasidic Druidism?

I have no idea, probably none. People constantly ask me for copies of the material so it may well be that there are people out there practicing Hasidic Druidism that I simply don't know about. It was always difficult to organize anything in the Reformed Druid movements or any of their offshoots because most of the people involved were anarchists. They didn't like organizations, they didn't like having to report to a central body and they forgot to send in changes of address every time they moved. So the over-all national structure for the Reformed Druid movement fell apart four or five years after it was instituted.

There are Reformed Druid Groves in different parts of the United States. There is an NRDNA (New Reformed Druids of North America) Grove in Seattle run by Cindy Sallee that has about seventy regular members. There are one or two NRDNA Groves in the San Francisco area, of less than a dozen members each. There is a Grove in Ann Arbor, which is the old-line RDNA with no changed initials. They have about a dozen people. There may be others scattered around the country, but there is no way of knowing because those RDNA groups who don't think of themselves as Pagan have no communication with the Pagan community.

So how did ADF happen?

ADF evolved out of what I was doing with the NRDNA. I have been going through lots of old papers in my library recently and there are bits and pieces of what was to become ADF going as far back as 1980, and some liturgical material that goes all the way back to the original RDNA. And I suspect that some of that material goes back to the United Ancient Order of Druids. So ADF was actually a continuing evolution.

Yes, a lot of people tend to forget that. They think that ADF just sprang out of your head like Athena out of the head of Zeus. I try to remind them that there were precedents, liturgy and symbols, that came before.

Quite a bit came from the RDNA.

And from England. People have no sense of that. Can you talk about the things that came from the older English tradition?

Well, some of the style of language in the liturgy came from England. It is a very formal style that was popular among British Druids. Some of it I can't talk about because it is secret initiatory material. It's not secret in ADF, but it is secret in the United Ancient Order of Druids and some of the other Druidic groups. I have collected literature from Druid groups for twenty five years now and some of the stuff I have is stuff that was scripts for initiation rituals for British Druid groups.

Do you mean you took their secret stuff and put it in the ADF liturgy?

No, but the stuff I got out of Reformed Druidism, some of it is from the secret material of the British Druids.

How did they manage to do that?

My guess is that David Fisher who is the founder of the RDNA, who said that he was a Druid already when he got there, did it. It is often the case when people are inventing new religions that they claim they are not inventing anything new, that they are perpetuating something old. But a lot of the earliest versions of the Reformed Druid liturgy and some of the language that he used looks like it could have been lifted straight out of the fraternal Druid movements. Minnesota was still a rural state and The United Ancient Order of Druids was very popular in rural America for two hundred years. I suspect that a father or an uncle or somebody in his family was a member of the UAOD or one of the other fraternal Druid movements in the United States and that he had exposure to it from his family. Makes him kind of a 'Fam. Trad.' Druid I suppose!

At any event, the point I am making is that ADF was an evolution out of the earlier available meso-Pagan Druid material in this country plus my personal experiences and the research that I was doing. ADF officially started in 1983, around Samhain, when I met a Pagan from Oklahoma who was attending an Irish language class in New York City. I happened to mention some things to him that a previous Irish teacher, Dr. Jim Duran, had told me.

Jim had told me about the apparent survivals of paleo-Pagan religious practices in the Baltic territories after World War II. He said that if we were to take the materials from the *Carmina Gadelica*, the Vedic materials and the materials from the surviving Lithuanian Pagan groups, that we would actually be able to combine that with what was already known about the Druids and produce about eighty per-cent accuracy in our picture of what the actual Druids were really doing way back when. So it was Jim who gave me the Indo-European connection. He has a PhD. in linguistics and he is also a scholar in Celtic studies. He is also the one who told me about Dumezil.

The Indo-European connection is very important to me because I believe that for a Druid organization to succeed in fulfilling all it has potential, it has to be bigger than just Celtic, because although there are a lot of people in this country with Celtic ancestry there are an awful lot who don't have Celtic ancestry or for whom the Celtic part of their family background is minority. But if we work with Indo-European basis we will pretty much cover eighty per-cent of the population of the US and Canada. I believe Paganism should become a mainstream religion. You don't become a mainstream religion by keeping people out.

So, this particular Pagan and I were sitting around discussing Druidism and Indo-European studies and so forth. I told him what Jim Duran had said about how it would be possible to reconstruct what the old religion really was in ancient Europe and he said; 'Let's do it!' And I said; 'Absolutely not!' But as has often happened in the past with me, whenever I try to get away from Druidism, I wind up being picked up by the scruff of the neck and dragged kicking and screaming. So I said; 'Alright, this time if we are going to start a Druid organization we are going to give it a name that has no connection to any other Druid organization. I am tired of wasting my psychic energy fighting with people because they think I hi-jacked their organization.' So I said, OK, we'll call it 'Our Own Druidism' and we translated it into Irish which became *Ar nDraiocht Fein.*

You realize, of course that Our Own Druidism, OOD is almost the same as Ancient Order of Druids, AOD?

SHHHHHH! Yes! The Fein part I got from Sin Fein, which is ourselves alone, or ourselves together against the world. I was thinking also of the fact that it made an interesting bi-lingual pun. It makes a pun in Irish – *Ar nDraiocht Fein,* depending on exactly how you pronounce it can either be Our Own Druidism or Our Own Kingdom, Our Own Land.

So I said let's start our own neo-Pagan tradition that has a commitment to excellence from the beginning. Let's start by putting up a network of people in the Pagan community who are scholars, real scholars who actually have some background and some training and who are more scholarly than romantic.

There are a number of Druid Orders, mostly in Britain, who believe that extensive book-learning can act as a barrier between having a genuine living experience of encounter with the Deities and the spirits of nature. While you are on the subject of scholarship would you please explain the rationale for putting the emphasis on scholarship? That is something that you really brought to Druidism, especially to ADF, which is somewhat unique as an emphasis. I don't see it as much in the other Orders.

Well, I think you see it in The Henge of Keltria.

I think Keltria puts half of its emphasis on scholarship and the other half on intuitive exploration. Visions and poetry are just as important to us as scholarship.

Well, I had several motivations for founding a Druid organization that put an emphasis on scholarship. One motivation was the fact that the paleo-Pagan Druids, the people we are patterning ourselves after, were the intellectuals and the scholars of their tribes. They were the entire social class of people who worked with their heads. They would not have been as tolerant of romantic nonsense as a lot of modern-day Druids are. They would have insisted that there is knowledge that is determinable, that is testable and verifiable and that the Gods pretty much expect us to use our intellect as well as our intuition.

The emphasis on scholarship was also there because 99.9 per cent of what had been done in the world of Druid revivalism for the last three hundred years had been intensely romantic and fantasy driven rather than scholarly. While I believe that vision and divine inspiration are absolutely crucial to the creation and perpetuation of modern-day Druidism, I also believe that we don't do the Gods and Goddesses any favors by telling lies about ourselves or about them. That we owe it out of respect, both to the ancient Druids and to the Deities, that we do the hard work to dig out what is actually known about them on the Earth-plane level of scholarship so that we find out what their proper names were, how they were pronounced, the sorts of things that are critical in ritual like what their favorite colors are, what the traditional musical tones and rhythms would be for invoking them, and all the sorts of things that can be done if you do enough hard scholarship.

Obviously you have to plant your seeds in the soil of good scholarship. You can mix a little B.S. in with it, but you need to be aware of it when you are doing it.

There is one criticism that I have heard about you, which is that people feel your approach is lacking in spirituality.

Well, I don't brag about how spiritual I am. I've always thought that was pretty much a sign of people who weren't very spiritual. For me the path of the scholar is the way that I practice my faith. I believe that the Gods want us to learn about them and want us to learn about them from legitimate sources rather than things people made up out of whole cloth because it sounded nice. I believe we have an obligation to the Gods to tell the truth as best we as fallible mortals can do so.

There are lots of people being spiritual in the Druid

community, in the Christian concept of what spirituality is. And I suspect that a sizeable number of those who criticize me for not being spiritual enough are indeed thinking in terms of Judea-Christian ideas of what constitutes spirituality i.e. 'Otherworldliness'.

Christian theology makes a sharp, clear-cut dividing line between this world and the Otherworld, between mundane Earth-plane level activity and spiritual activity. I don't believe the ancient Druids or any of the other Indo-Europeans believed that. In fact most Pagans around the planet don't believe that. Most Pagans believe that this world fades imperceptibly into other worlds, that there are no sharp dividing lines.

So the criticisms of me as a scholar are not made by scholars. The anti-scholarship attitude within the Druid family as a whole is partly people fearing that if good scholarship was done, many of their cherished beliefs and practices would be shown to be historically inaccurate. It's people who don't personally want to do the kind of hard work that scholarship requires. It's people who don't want to get involved in long, detailed scholarly arguments because they feel it takes away some of the fun and the romance of what they are doing. And a lot of it is Christian dualism, the belief that inspiration and trances and guided meditation works for me so therefore anything that is different from that won't work and it is a bad thing.

Meso-Pagan Druidism tends to be stuck in Christian dualism just like every other meso-Pagan group happens to be. So it's easy to slip into that attitude of thinking that what you use as your method of spirituality, because it works for you, is the only correct way to do it. We have in ADF, and I believe in Keltria, and other neo-Pagan Druid groups around the country, people who are both scholarly and deeply religious. For them scholarship is their ritual. It's the way they honor the Gods, by searching out lost information and bringing it back to the rest of the community.

Keepers of lore.

Yes, somebody has to keep that lore and keep it going. If you knew that a bunch of people were making up herbal information out of thin air and teaching it to themselves and to each other, wouldn't you as a professional herbalist feel a little concerned that maybe they should do some real scholarship and actually learn botany?

Well, maybe not botany, but they should at least learn the tradition. What has worked for thousands of years is probably going to work now.

But the point is that when you talk about herbs, for most people who are total space cadets, you need to make it clear that herbs can be dangerous if you use them incorrectly. And if you want to get the maximum value out of using herbs for healing you need to study what the mundane world has to say about herbs as much or more than what there might be in the way of fantasy, folklore, and romance.

The information about who the Druids were and what they actually did and what Indo-European cosmology actually was, is information that is just as critical for doing powerful and effective ritual as the information about folk traditions connected with herbs and medicinal uses of herbs is to using herbs as part of your path.

Magic can be dangerous if done really clumsily by people who don't know what they are doing, but more important for the Druid community, because the Druid community is fairly conservative about how they do Magic, is having accurate knowledge about what Druidism was, about what Magic is, about what the cosmology and mythology and theology of our ancestors was. Having that accurate information gives you more tools with which to practice your path.

Ralph Blum is the man who made Rune stones popular among the New Agers. Rather than doing research among the many available sources on the meanings of the Runes he simply made them up out of thin air. He meditated and looked for signs around him in his life and basically 'channeled' all this information about Runes, which he proceeded to publish.

And it worked.

Yes, it worked. Any system of divination works; however, it doesn't work as well as Rune systems that are based on the actual traditions of the Rune Masters. I've seen people using his attributions for spell-casting and I've seen people use the real, researched meanings of the Runes. Especially if you use Runes to cast spells or to invoke Deity it is a really good idea to know what the actual meaning of the Runes are rather than the stuff that Ralph Blum, who is a New Ager, made up out of thin air. For personal Runes about am I going to meet a cute guy at the dance Saturday night, Ralph Blum's Runes will work just fine.

The originator of the Runes, who was Odin, hung upside down from an ash tree and intuited the Runes. So how is that any different from what Ralph Blum did?

For one thing you are mixing the planes here. The story about Odin coming up with them is not a historical statement about where the Runes came from. You are comparing apples and oranges there. However, somebody, at some point, adapted the Roman alphabet to create what we now call Runes. That is the current opinion among most Rune scholars, except for the Scandinavian Rune scholars who insist that they invented them out of thin air. Kind of like the Hindu archaeologists who insist that the Indo-European people started in India and went West, or the German archaeologists who insist that Germans and Celts were dramatically different tribes. None of the non-German archaeologists say that.

The point is that almost every custom in a religion starts out intuitively, but there is a difference between an intuition that somebody had a few thousand years ago that was then handed down, taught, elaborated and handed on, building up power in the collective unconscious, building up a Magical current around it, and something that somebody intuited last week.

It may very well be that people are having legitimate intuitions, even today. I think they are. But that is a different thing. That's an intuition that is brand new, that doesn't have a lot of psychic energy invested in it yet. The original meanings of the Ogham or of the Runes have been there for hundreds or thousands of years so they have much more Magical power connected to them.

I think that a problem that the New Agers have, and many of the fraternal Orders in England are essentially New Age groups, is in thinking of Magic as real. Of thinking that psychic energy physically exists and that there can be statements made about it that are true or false. If there are no rules and Magic is just something you make up to make yourself feel better then of course you can do everything intuitively.

But if you think in terms of the Collective Unconscious, and that there are such things as Magical currents, that certain objects or symbols really do have power, then you have to start paying attention to the traditions. Because the traditions are the originators and perfectors and perpetrators of that Magical current. To simply ignore them because you are too lazy to do scholarly work and make up new ones for yourself means not that you are going to get yourself in trouble, but that you are abandoning large chunks of the tradition that are available to you to make your work more meaningful and more powerful.

So, looking at the Druid community now, where do you think it is headed? And where would you like to see it go?

I think the American Druid community is headed pretty much in the direction that I foresaw ten years ago. We are having an increasing number of Druid Groves planted in more and more cities around the US and Canada. We are seeing more people, not just from the already committed Pagan community joining, but also people from the outside coming in, attending Druid activities and becoming part of the Pagan community. In many ways this is boosting the growth of the Pagan community as a whole.

I am seeing more work being done in terms of liturgical experimentation and design and more connecting with the mainstream
religious community. Some of our people belong to their local
interfaith councils and we are seeing Druids pop up in the local
newspapers at times other than Beltaine and Samhain.

What we are seeing is that when you open up a publicly open
Pagan group of any sort, Druidic or non-Druidic, that more and
more people start coming because there is an enormous hunger
in Western civilization right now for meaningful religion, and
they are not getting it from the monotheistic mainstream.

The Neo-Pagan Druids, by and large, have the most effective
liturgical design and tradition for large scale public ritual. I see a
lot of Wiccan groups that are doing public ritual by borrowing
our techniques and our methods. I am seeing a continuing
amount of overlap between the Druid community and other
branches of Paganism including Wicca and Asatru. I see more
research and publishing being done. All in all I'd say we are
growing at a fairly steady rate.

We are also having more interaction with Druid groups in
other countries, exchanging newsletters and things of that sort.
More really good Celtic material is being published, both by
people who think of themselves as Pagan and by scholars who
are finding they have an audience. By and large the Druid
movement is just percolating along.

What I foresee is that within twenty years or so there will be
public Pagan celebrations led primarily by Druids in most places,
in every major and minor town in America. I see us doing
publicly televised ritual on the Pagan holidays. I see us having a
very strong impact on the environmental movement and vice
versa. If anybody are the appropriate chaplains for the environmental movement it is going to be the Druids.

I have noticed more and more people in the Druid movement
quietly joining the Sierra club and the World Wildlife Federation
and putting their time and money where their mouths are,

something I'd like to see more of in the general Pagan community.

You are an Arch Druid emeritus and a Third Degree Wiccan Priest. Could you compare and contrast those two traditions?

OK, the differences between neo-Pagan Druidism and neo-Pagan Witchcraft basically fall into two categories, theological and liturgical. The primary differences are that Wicca is, by and large, duo-theistic. That is to say that all Goddesses are seen as the faces or aspects of a single Goddess and all Gods are seen as faces or aspects of a single male Deity. The Feminist Witches or the separatists are completely monotheistic, they see all Deity as aspects of or faces of The Goddess. So what you get are these giant marshmallow puff Deities where everything has been blurred together.

Central Wiccan theology comes out of Dian Fortune's book *Applied Occultism,* in a chapter called Isis and Osiris, which starts out with the phrase; 'All Gods are one God and all Goddesses are one Goddess and there is one initiator.' The rest of that chapter then goes on to essentially give ninety five per-cent of what turned into Wiccan theology. The emphasis is very much in terms of seeing the universe as an interplay between Yin and Yang, between giant polarity forces of male and female.

Neo-Pagan Druidism on the other hand is polytheistic. It places emphasis on interacting with each God or Goddess as the unique individual that He or She was originally worshipped as. This doesn't mean that we don't see the very clear-cut and obvious IndoEuropean similarities between the Daghda and Thor for example. It is very clear that they fulfill very similar roles in their respective religions. But when we are invoking the Daghda we don't mention Thor. When we are invoking Brighid we don't mention Cerridwen or Dana or any of the other Goddesses from the IndoEuropean pantheon. We invoke Brighid as Brighid. We treat each Deity with respect as a unique individual.

These two approaches are not contradictory. I drink coffee, but I also drink tea. There is nothing in the essence of coffee that would prevent me from drinking tea. I probably would not mix them together in the same cup because it wouldn't taste very good.

So theologically the difference between Wicca and Druidism is that Wicca is duo or occasionally monotheistic and Druidism is polytheistic, that is to say, neo-Pagan Druidism as practiced in North America.

There are people, like Morgan Llewellyn, who claim that the ancient sources imply that the Druids were monotheistic.

That's hogwash. That was invented by Iolo Morganwg. Iolo was an early agitator for the Unitarian movement.

Are you saying there were no Greek or Roman references to monotheistic Druids as Llewelyn claims?

No, I am saying that the Greek and Roman references to the Druids don't say they are monotheists. There are occasional references to the having a high God, but most Pagan polytheistic systems have a high God. The idea of the ancient Druids being monotheists was invented by the fraternal Druid movement, specifically by Iolo Morganwg when he was forging his 'ancient Welsh' manuscripts. He was an early promoter of Unitarianism in England, back when that was a form of liberal Christianity and by an amazing coincidence it turned out that all the ancient Druids he wrote about were also Unitarians. In fact he said that the pre-Christian Christians were just sitting around waiting for the baby Jesus to be born so they could all run out and convert to Christianity.

Frankly, I have seen nothing in the historical record to indicate that the ancient Druids were anything other than polytheists. To try to take modern ideas of monotheism and put them into the mouths of the ancient Druids is actually doing them a severe disservice. A lot of the fraternal, meso-Pagan Druids are monotheists because they got the idea from monotheism. But the neo-Pagan Druids in North America are definitely polytheists. Whether or not some of them also have a high God or Supreme Deity figure in their pantheon will vary from individual to individual.

I have always taken the general Pagan attitude that a supreme being is pretty much irrelevant. That whoever, or whatever, he, she, or it, or they might be, they have no impact on our day-to-day lives. They are not going to be humanoid enough that anything that would be spoken in the human language about them would be anything other than outrageously incorrect.

So the other major category is in group structure, focus, and liturgy. Wicca is small group oriented, private, exclusive, and closed in its activities. None of those are negative terms. Neo-Pagan Druidism on the other hand tends to be medium to large group oriented, public, inclusionary and open.

That is an emphasis that ADF happens to have, not all Druid groups are that public. In fact in the United States I don't think there is another Druid group that has that as a major emphasis. Keltria welcomes newcomers into its rituals, but there is no mandate that a Grove has to do that. In fact, for us the emphasis is on building kinship bonds. We think of it as the clan system. Our public service emphasis is in our publications and our correspondence course, both of which require a lot of time and effort and which have a great reputation as far as dependability and depth.

The neo-Pagan members of the RDNA have the emphasis on public ritual. ADF which came out of the RDNA has the emphasis on providing publically accessible worship and other religious services to the community. Keltria had a very Wiccan-based orientation when it branched off from ADF. They wanted to have closed meetings for the Groves.

It's not that meetings are closed. I think our feeling is that if you are constantly bringing in new people to worship you have a different quality of ritual than when you work with a group of people over time, constantly building on your knowledge and, over time, constantly building on your intimacy. But anyone can approach us and ask to join.

It's not an either/or situation. For example, in some of the larger ADF Groves we also have small closed groups.

Our groups are not closed. If someone calls us and says they would like to come to a ritual then the Grove might have a policy that anyone can come at any time, or they might have to check it out with everybody else. It's not closed in the way a Coven is closed. We just don't have the emphasis on advertising to the general public who know nothing about us.

So far the ADF Groves haven't been buying ads on the radio or putting ads in local newspapers. But they do promote in occult bookstores.

In my area the ADF Grove advertises regularly in the local Wiccan paper. Every issue they have several invitations, for every single ceremony. Speaking for myself, I have been at this for a while, and in order to feel really satisfied I want to do ceremony with experienced people, at least some of the time.

There is a certain level of intensity that you want that is easier to do with people who are at the same level of development.

Or even when I work by myself, I am going back to that more and more. I find that constantly working with new people is a different kind of mission.

In the mainstream churches you will often see that even though they have a Sunday morning congregation who come in to do the standard public ceremony, they also have religious retreats, special prayer group circles, Bible study groups, and smaller groups that are focused on a particular kind of activity. That is a normal human pattern. We are seeing that in the larger ADF Groves.

Our emphasis is on doing both, being publically accessible Pagans for those people who want and need us and simultaneously doing the things in small groups that are best done in small groups.

It doesn't have to be an either-or, black-white choice.

The original Druids did rituals to which the entire tribe was invited. In fact, to be excluded from the public rituals was considered a form of punishment. I have always felt that Druids have an obligation to provide publically accessible open worship for the people.

So you are regarding the entire United States as your tribe?

Yeah. Why not? There are people who haven't joined our tribe yet but would if they knew we were here. The experience that a lot of ADF Groves have had and that various splinter groups have had is that as soon as you start letting people know you have open available ritual you have a dozen people at your first ritual and six weeks later you have two dozen and six weeks later you have fifty people. A year later you have a hundred people showing up. If you make Paganism accessible to the general public, the general public will show up, or at least that segment of it that is hungry for a new religion that has some real value to it.

This is one reason why the study program in ADF makes a distinction between the congregational ministry and the other forms of ministry that religious leadership can engage in. Some of our people really feel that calling to run a public Pagan church.

Can you talk a bit about your upcoming books?

The books I am working on now include a book on Pagan polytheology, analyzing various traditional theological issues from a polytheistic perspective. Pagans have a great deal more in common in their beliefs than even they are aware of so what I am doing is an analysis of what Pagan theology is.

I am working on a book on the history of Druidism, both ancient and modern, which will include a lot of the Indo-European research I've done on the similarities in the clergy class of different cultures.

I am working on a book on liturgical design; preparation, and performance, how to do public ritual for worship purposes effectively. That is something that even the mainstream doesn't have much on. The neo-Pagan community by and large has been attempting to adapt Wiccan liturgical design to large-scale public ritual and finding that it doesn't really adapt very well. Based on the experimentation I have done over the last twenty five years and the experiences that ADF and other groups have had with doing large-scale public ritual, I am doing a book on how to create those rituals, how to perform them, and step by step walk-throughs.

Are there any hot-button issues, axes to grind, or things you are particularly fired up about in Druidism these days?

A hot issue for me that has to do with the Pagan community in general, is that it's time for us to finish up our adolescent rebellion phase already and go on to being adult. I think it's very important that the neo-Pagan community start planning for the future in terms of giving us buildings so we can have ritual when the weather is lousy, making arrangements for long-term care for our elderly, paying attention to the needs of our community in a social-work sense, and becoming part of the fabric of religion in the Western world rather than keeping ourselves separated and isolated form that fabric. I think it's time to start planning ahead decades at a time rather than just the next festival season.

Gordon Cooper (Lorax)

Interviewed August 12, 1996
Via internet

Lorax has a BA with a dual major in Turkish Language Studies and Anthropology, a minor in natural sciences and is a *sam duan* (instructor-level) martial arts practitioner with more than three decades of experience in the *Hsin Lu Tao* school. He is a General Class amateur radio operator (callsign KE7RYM) with a keen interest in using FM radio to observe meteor showers, following the effects the Sun has on our magnetic field, and in listening to the radio heartbeats of the Earth.

He was co-moderator of the Nemeton-L list, an early internet forum for discussion around sacred Irish poetry, word-craft, and related matters. He was active on GEnie and Delphi bulletin boards in the 1990s, often posting on filidecht, history, and modern approaches to poetry as a sacred art. The term 'Celtic Reconstructionist' was first used in the house he shared with his wife at the time, Erynn Rowan Laurie. More than a few of the paradigms in CR were explored, developed or co-created by him in public forums, festivals and phone calls from 1991-2001. He was a founding member of Seattle Pagan Scholars in the mid-1990s. He has published in journals as varied as The Georgian Newsletter and Gnosis. He is an OBOD Mt. Haemus Scholar, and has supplied materials and editing for OBOD's current Bardic *Gwers*. He is on the Grand Grove of the Ancient Order of Druids in America (AODA) where he sits in the Comfy Northern Chair as Archdruid of Fire, having joined AODA in 2003, and appointed to the Grand Grove in 2005. A Bishop in the Gnostic Celtic Church (GCC), he has been writing on the subtle interplay and manifestations over the past centuries of what might be described as the Cryptic Interdependent Sacramental Movement in Western Culture. He is working on several projects, including a manual of tools for Druid Comrades and a workbook on esoteric physical culture, including German and American influences on yoga in the 1890s. He is an avid film shooter and darkroom photo-chemist, working in 35mm, medium or large format black and white or color, and produces large-format platinum or gold prints from time to time.

Can you please describe the religion you were raised in? What was it like for you growing up?

My maternal grandfather was a Brethren (Mennonite, not Amish) minister, whose 'turf' included a goodly chunk of a Midwestern state. Until we moved to the Deep South, I spent a great deal of time with him. He had been born in a sod house on the prairie, and the experience of being in touch with the soil was a truth that he lived.

Following time as a non-combatant in the US during the First World War, he became a schoolteacher for a few years. After that, he felt the call to minister, went to seminary, and ended up as a pastor until the end of his life.

I remember sitting outside with him in the hot Midwest summers at night, and having him quiz me on my knowledge of star types, constellations, and how close together one should plant corn and strawberries. Plants and science mattered as much to him as theology or Old Testament genealogies did.

It has been intimated to me by other relatives that he was grooming me and one of my cousins for the ministry. The closeness of the extended family and being raised in a kinship group that went out to third cousins was a generally wonderful experience. The downside was that he and my grandmother were affectionate, but sometimes distant, and did not tolerate failure or a perceived lack of discipline on the part of a child, no matter how young.

My grandfather died not long after we moved to the Deep South. It is a loss I still feel to this day. I am certain that he would most vigorously oppose my choices in spirituality, but would respect it. My father's parents were members of a Congregationalist Church that was quite progressive in its theology and more than a little Universalist in doctrine.

I attended churches sporadically after moving to New Orleans, where my father worked for Gulf Oil. I attended Ben Franklin High School in New Orleans, and along with the bulk of those students, I left conventional religion.

The next move as an oil company brat was to Houston. On a clear night, just before Easter in 1974, I was running my usual ten miles near the subdivision we lived in, and spotted an illuminated sign for an Easter sunrise service through the trees. As I ran farther, I got angry that the Christian church had co-opted the name and many of the symbols of this non-Christian holiday. After a few more miles of running down a road that was bounded on both sides by nothing but stands of slash pines (cut down a few years later in the name of progress), it felt as if I was moving between rows and patterns of trees that were dancing with me. I remembered that in pre-Christian times Easter was celebrated in holy places in nature, on the tops of hills or in groves. I felt the trees whispering to me that I would never be complete as a person until I found these people who had their fellowship with nature and spirit, though at the time I assumed that all such folk had died out long ago. I decided to follow that path, wherever it would take me.

The only book that I could find on Neo-Paganism was *The New Pagans* by Hans Holzer. The shock it caused to my sixteen-year-old self was enough to put me off of initiation or ritual until I was in my twenties. The sections on The Church of All Worlds and the posturings I found from the public teachers of the initiatory Craft traditions left me very cold. Of course, that was the impression my sixteen-year-old self had.

So when and where did you first hear about Druids and about Celtic spirituality in general?

The Friday preceding the weekend nearest Fall Equinox, 1976, at about 8pm, in Monterey, California. I had enlisted in the military, and was sent to the Defense Language Institute for a year of living, sleeping, and breathing in the Turkish language. Right after I was assigned quarters I met my first and best Craft teacher, and two persons who would become Coven brothers.

My teacher was an elder of the Welsh Tradition of New York by then, and was corresponding with Gwydion Penderwyn. My memory is that Gwydion said that there was an awful lot of folklore and other materials out there, but that each person needed to do their own research and meditations in order to comprehend what Druidry might have been, and could be. And, that the Celtic languages were vitally important to this process.

Outside of the twenty or so self-identified Neo-Pagans (and hundred or so magicians) that I met at DLI, I didn't meet any other folks interested in such things until I returned from my two and a half years overseas. Southern Spain was not the sort of place that one could find kindred spirits.

And how were you trained in your tradition?

My teacher in the Craft and I were roommates, in language school and overseas. My apprenticeship lasted almost six years. We studied the traditional ballads, English and Celtic folklore, Mircea Eliade's writings, Joseph Campbell's works, and examined *The White Goddess* (and found it magnificent poetry, but academically poor in places). We studied menhirs, stone circles and the Morris dances, the usual stuff that Euro-Pagans read, just in greater depth.

I would say that after Ashe, my Craft teacher, the person who contributed most to my understanding is Murtadgh an Doyle, a New England Craft elder who has summered in California for the past few decades. His cogent observations on Irish culture, the Gods and not-Gods, the super-*Sidhe* and the *Sidhe*, to use his terms, his willingness to call a spade a spade and his capacity to explain how to internalize a Celtic cosmology and make it sing are inspiring, cogent, and spur me to further research and self-development.

In the mid 1990s I spent a great deal of time reading primary textual materials, preferably in facing page translation. Unlike Erynn Laurie to whom I was married to in the 1990s, I don't read modern or Old Irish, but I am enough of a linguist to spend time puzzling out the meaning of a critical phrase or word.

One of the enormous stumbling blocks that we moderns have is that we have a society with high literacy, and we attempt to evaluate extant materials from previous cultures as if their modes of communication were primarily written. This was not the case in 6th or 7th century Ireland, when the Filidh in the monasteries began writing down the stories.

When an oral tradition is written down, its entire character changes. Albert B. Lord explored this topic quite thoroughly in his critically important book *The Singer of Tales*.

A story could now be longer than the vocal endurance of a *Seanachie* or *Filidh* , but with a rendering of speeches, commentaries and stories into written compilations (like the *Tain*), a body of work is created, an original that is unlike its component parts.

This translation into text explains the mysterious deaths and reappearances of major characters, and some of the conflicting genealogies.

Within oral epics, there is never an exact repetition of a tale. When Lord and Parry did their research on oral tradition in Bosnia in the 1930s, they discovered that even when the storyteller and the audience insisted the story had been told exactly the same way on two evenings, length, emphasis, and details varied greatly.

Contrary to the insistence of earlier folklorists, the singer/storyteller within a living oral tradition does *not* function as an organic digital tape recorder. Incidents, phrasing, emphasis and length of tale are modified on the spot for the audience and the circumstances of the performance. Lord says that each performance must be regarded as a unique creation, even if the elements are common to a region or group of storytellers.

It is in light of this information that we must examine the surviving and accessible texts and inscriptions that we have. There are no pre-Christian sources for the Irish and Scottish corpus, and next to nothing of Gaulish or Iberian Celtic materials survived. We do have some decent archaeological data, which is reinterpreted every fifteen or so years to fit a new paradigm, like name lists of rivers, hills and other spots that appear to be sacred to someone.

How do you define Druidism or Celtic spirituality as it is practiced today?

The most accurate answer is also flippant – those who self-identify as Druids, Filidh, or Celtic Neo-Pagans are best known by what they do or do not do. There is no official body besides the *Eisteddfodds* of Cornwall or Wales that bestow status as a Druid. By the standards of most of academia, we are just people playing games in our spare time. Hopefully we do not want to become the Druids who faced Caesar across a river or who sacrificed people for crimes that today would be regarded as minor!

What is needed now – as in each generation that faces massive change – is to live the truth of Druid ontology, a vision where nature is sacred, where each place glows with an expression of life and spirit all its own. Especially in the cities.

Since most of us probably will continue to live in urban areas, it should be one of our tasks to green the cities. To work with the parks department to assure the continued existence of green spaces. To plant appropriate native species of trees, grasses and flowers. To engage in what Gwen Thompson called 'guerrilla gardening'; planting appropriate wild flowers and grasses in bare sidewalk borders, working to preserve the increasingly rare traditional varieties of food plants by putting them in gardens and sharing them with friends, and by joining Seed Exchanges. I urge people to build rooftop gardens, grow some portion of their own food, and given the bee die-off and its consequences, to establish bee colonies wherever feasible.

There are 20th century poets who are propagating and extending the Celtic tradition, and it is in our best interest, and theirs, to purchase and appreciate their works.

The short list would include Vernon Watkins, David Gascoyne and Kathleen Raine. In my opinion, Kathleen Raine is a legitimate inheritor of the Celtic poetic tradition and qualifies as a *Filidh*.

She puts words to the spirits of nature with a powerful almost classical style. Musicians like Azam Ali are bringing *Sufi* ideas and songs to the West. Their message of tolerance, joy and sharing needs to be spread as far and wide as possible. Understanding the wisdom stories, poems and songs of the Islamic East certainly is better than water-boarding teenagers who happened to be in the wrong place at the wrong time.

If we really do intend to create Druidry as a 21st century religion we shall need a powerful tradition of storytelling, and I do not see that happening within Euro-Paganism. I would suggest that folks find a local storytelling society and learn how to work magic orally. Robin Williamson is a fine *Seanachie* who is worthy of our support and appreciation.

Gaelic poets writing in English, Irish or Scots Gaelic need to be supported. There is the very real chance that one or more Celtic languages may disappear from their homelands within our lifetime. This would be tragic. Thomas Kinsella, *Nuala Ni Dhomhnaill* and Seamus Heaney are good poets to sample. Kinsella's rendition of the *Tain* is the finest on the market, in my opinion.

Can you talk about what you have been trying to do with your books? And other projects such as the Nemeton list on the internet?

What I have tried to do with my writings is to provide a voice that recognizes the power of inspiration, with its roots in the reality of the Celtic historical and archaeological past, to the best of our abilities. There are no easy answers or a quick path to illusory power, ideas change in response to our needs today. *The Candle of Vision* by George William Russell is as applicable and vibrant as it was a century ago.

The hope is to get people sufficiently inspired to pick up the source materials and at least ask the *Sidhe*, the Faery, what they think of the stories that the texts tell about them. Please disagree. But at least read and think about the primary texts and extend them to your own life in a useful fashion.

The actual source materials for Celtic Paganism and the Matter of Britain are more exciting and richer than the pabulum that the major occult publishers want their readership to find. Reading *The Fairy-Faith in Celtic Countries* is more enriching than a book by an author who 'borrowed' a wholly invented Craft Faery tradition from their teacher, claims lineage from the *Tuatha De Danaan*, then declares themselves an *Ollamh* (poetic master) after a few months.

The nature of the materials available to the religious reconstructionist suggest to me that the ancient Celts of any era or place did not have a systematized religion. There was enormous variation between regions. Customs and festival dates often differed. Even something as seemingly simple as distinguishing between the 'good' deities and the 'bad' deities is complex and regionalized.

As an example, the peoples in the North of Ireland are said to be descended from Balor, who is generally demonized in the stories. The natives of Tory Island, Balor's home, viewed him as a generous deity who was killed by that irrational upstart, Lugh. Any attempt to fit the Irish deities into a Dumezilian tripartite system ultimately fails, since many of the deities fill all three functions. Or niches outside of a tripartite scheme!

There was no caste system in Ireland, Scotland or Wales. Anyone could become a *Filidh* with enough talent, study, and demonstration of talents. While not easy, the training was widely available. With many kings, nobles, scattered populations and few cities in Insular Celtdom throughout much of its history, employment opportunities would have been good.

Filidh were employed in monasteries as scribes, and the system of training and status of *Filidh* in their multi-colored cloaks, harpers, and *Seanachies* seems to have continued up to the time of Elizabeth, with some survivals into almost modern times. Women keened at funerals in Ireland in a fashion that Caesar would have recognized into the early years of the 20th century.

An Earth-centered spirituality should honor and respect the Earth here and now, and not just some hypothesized ancient Ireland or Wales. When is it Beltane in Seattle? Not hard – when the hawthorn tree blooms. What is the bile, and where does it live? Not hard – a cedar in Schmitz Park.

Nature is the preserving shrine, and I would rather not see my temple shrink in size. Yet the mythic, Otherworldly, primeval Ireland or Wales does exist, and for many of us it provides an idyllic anchor, a remembrance of what we should strive for in the here and now.

I guess the only way to evaluate the success of modern Druidry would be by the stories that our children, grandchildren and spiritual descendants will tell about us. What deeds do we want to do and what legacy shall we leave to them? [See additional note 1 at the end of this chapter.]

Are you working with a group or Grove at the moment?

I have a devotional practice, and try to spend time with the trees and listen to the *Sidhe*.

I have come to realize that Neo-Pagan organizations and groups generally spend more time on getting out newsletters, election protocols and politics than they do on their spiritual practices. Far better to hold a picnic and help restore a salmon habitat or plant a few trees than plan for the colonization of Mars by Neo-Pagans.

If I do decide to teach a course or have a formal group again, it will be outside in an old growth forest area, where the spirits are more visible.

Where would you like to see Druidism and Celtic spirituality go in future?

I would like it to have a future. I am not at all certain that this latest wave of Earth-centered spirituality will remain viable. After all, the Open-Air Camping movement in England and Europe in the 1920s that combined gymnosophy, nature religion, Pagan revivalism, the women's rights movement, sexual liberation and pacifism did not survive into WWII as a force for change, despite its bright promise. If some of us are right and these things do come in waves, a lot of the folks who are committed Neo-Pagans should live just long enough to be around for the next wave. I expect to see something of a slowing in growth, and then a decline in numbers, along with broader and broader application of the term 'Neo-Pagan'.

The definition of Neo-Pagan is and has always been something of a moving target, but when Klingon Wicca[16] rituals are featured prominently in a major festival, then I would say that the fantasy elements are starting to take over, and this is not the movement that I entered in 1976.

I have heard groups and the leaders of groups insist that magic cannot happen, ritual is simply psychodrama, that deities merely exist within one's own head, and saddest of all that there are no ethics, rules or common standards of behavior possible within Neo-Paganism.

If the current movement does survive, I would expect the establishment of rural and urban shrines, retreats, and learning centers. I have a fantasy of seeing clear-cuts replanted by Neo-Pagans, and having those trees bear silent witness to our commitment to our spirituality.

I think that paid clergy are an unlikely prospect in the Neo-Pagan movement. In Seattle, people complain about being asked for a dollar or two to help cover the site fee for public rituals, and I would expect that paid clergy would not find gainful employment in the Pacific Northwest. Nor do I see that they fill a need. Anyone can serve as a minister and perform weddings in the state of Washington.

Religious discrimination is an issue that rears its ugly head, especially in child custody and welfare cases, and the best that the community can do is to educate the welfare system about ourselves, to reassure them that we as a community will not threaten the welfare, safety, or emotional well-being of a previously abused or vulnerable child. Some of the Neo-Pagan groups in Seattle have spent time talking to Child Protective Services about these issues, and have at least made some CPS workers doubt the Satanic Mass Kidnapping/Generational Child Abuse stories that some sections of the Religious Right have been spreading.[17]

What do you think Druidism and Celtic spirituality has to offer the world? What does it have to offer the Pagan community in general?

To the world in and of itself? Allies for native peoples and threatened habitats around the world. A vision of what can be. A way to spirituality that does not need to borrow slavishly and automatically from whatever tribe or group makes the cover of Shaman's Drum this month. As North Americans or Europeans, we have vast political and economic power over the destiny of people that we have never met. We should exercise that power consciously.

I do not think that there is a single Pagan community. There seem to be many. In the best of all possible worlds, we could walk our talk with grace, dignity, and a certain amount of fun along the way, and serve as good role models.

Is Druidism experiencing any problems that you know of? Locally or nationally?

We are flesh and blood persons, raised within a fairly sick society that is undergoing radical changes every decade. Many of us got into Neo-Paganism to fill a void in our lives, and then ran full tilt into some of the same emotionally abusive situations that we had hoped to leave. The community has its share of abusive leaders, sexual predators, and hosts of compliant folks who don't want to rock the boat.

The two organizational models that seem to pervade Neo-Paganism are still that of the autocratic lodge and the collectivist group which would rather suicide than admit it has a leader. There is this disturbing trend for groups to churchify and merchandise themselves, complete with bumper stickers, shirts, and pleas for money and the hope of expansion. Just like big business or the Reverend Falwell.

Most of the major Neo-Pagan organizations seem to model themselves on a western church, ceremonial magic lodge, or commune. These are not the only options nor are they the best choice. Persons with a calling towards a single deity, like the Daughters of the Flame who are devoted to *Brighid*, could form loose affiliations, sharing poetry, visions, music and fellowship. I would like to see more discussion of householder Paganism for those persons who are not doing ritual primarily for others, but for themselves.

In my meditations I return repeatedly to Chretien's story, the first known Grail text, where progress towards finding the Grail comes through the actions of Feirefiz, a Moslem and the half-brother of Parzival. Only when the brothers unite can the Grail be found. I think this is a message that both East and West would do well to consider and then take appropriate action. [See additional note 2 at the end of this chapter.]

The music within Neo-Paganism is thankfully no longer stuck in a filksong mode.[18] I would hope to see powerful music and movement developed for festivals and small groups, rather than yet another spiral dance and eight hundred verses of 'Gimme That Old Time Religion' trotted out at festivals. There are entire traditions, like Shape Note Singing and Plainsong that have yet to be tapped within English.

Seeing the explosion of home computer-facilitated studios

with musicians like Damh the Bard producing and directly selling their own works is a hopeful sign. The rise of YouTube puts songs and music videos like Suvetar by Gjallarhorn on our phones, tablets and TV screens. It is up to an appreciative audience to support these groups by buying their albums, funding their projects, and otherwise allowing them to keep creating.

There are a plethora of existing non-profit organizations doing ecological direct action or conservation work. We should not reinvent the wheel. And, unlike some Neo-Pagan organizations, environmental groups have financial records that are open. By and large these groups are efficient, and if someone has the financial or personal resources to commit to a cause, there are ample opportunities out there, waiting for that person's time and energies. In passing I'll mention the Xerxes Society (dedicated to understanding and preserving invertebrates) and the Lady Bird Johnson Wildflower Center as groups doing important work.

Our community has outright frauds selling books by the caseload, while good ritual designer/authors like Ian Corrigan don't get exposure or credit in the community for their contributions over the years. Or, as happened to some of the few folks doing decent, original work, they have had their materials lifted, freely adapted and published in mass-market books or used without attribution online. If the notion of *filidecht* retains any respect, authors and sources should be celebrated and cited.

Neo-Paganism on the internet and blogosphere varies wildly in expression and quality. Something that disturbs me is anything written before X Day (the day that Compuserve and AOL joined the internet community) is generally ignored. Many researchers, authors and fine artists are not participating in Facebook, or elsewhere on the internet. There isn't enough time or energy in a day to create and look at cat videos.

Philip Carr-Gomm expressed to me that he felt the best Druidry was yet to come. I will second that hope.

Additional Notes

1) The Nemeton list was a safe, flame-free enclave for discussion of Celtic Neo-Paganism period. Discussions of Atlantis, generic Paganism, Native American Shamanism, Satanism and other non-pertinent items were not allowed. Traffic on the list varied quite a bit, but there were generally at least two or three fruitful topic threads open at any given time.

   There were poets, linguists, historians, fiber artists, computer programmers and even Arch Druids on the list. It was an exciting, sometimes warm, but hopefully never hostile place for quality discussions.

2) The text has Feirfaz convert before he can see the Grail. Jews in Chretien are similarly portrayed in a less than favorable manner. As an oral storyteller, I choose to tell this portion of the story a bit differently.

Michel-Gerald Boutet

Interviewed August 30, 1996

The Third Annual Druid Summit, Western Massachusetts

Michel-Gerald whose bardic name was *Uindoderuogenos* (son of white oak) later received the name *Boutios* when he was accepted in the KGH (*Kredenn Geltiek Hollvedel*). He has a background in graphic arts and art history and works as an art teacher in Quebec. He is the author of *The Celtic Connection,* a collection of essays on Ogham, Native American rock art, zodiacal interpretations, Celtic inscriptions in Japan and the Americas, and other Epigraphic problems. He is a *Cobios Druuis* (a helpful Druid, assistant to the *Ariaxs*) of *Druuidica Comardia Eriutalamonos,* (DCA), a Canadian branch of the Breton *Comardia Druidiacta Armorica* (CDA) (A. Le Goff *Commana*, 29237, Brittany, France). He is active in ecumenical outreach to Druid groups in America and Europe including the *College Des Druides des Gaules,* the Council of British Druid Orders, and The Henge of Keltria.

As Boutet explains;

The CDA was founded in 1936 by five initiates of the Breton Gorsedd which is affiliated to the Welsh *Gorsedd.* The CDA is a splinter group of the *Kredenn Geltiek,* the first truly Pagan Druidical organizations in the world as the other Meso-Druidical groups of the time were all pseudo-Pagan, Masonic and Christian based 'Grail religion' type groups.

Can you please talk about your childhood, how you were raised and your religious upbringing?

I am French-Canadian from a very Catholic family; my

mother was most concerned with the religious aspect. My grand-father was more of a traditional male and he was interested in story-telling, folktales and provincial kinds of things such as painting and traditional music. People like him maintained the traditions of the French in Canada. The elders had lots of conversations with the Indians. If they didn't go to Mass for seven years they were cursed by the parish priest as being 'Warlocks' or 'Werewolves'.

There was a Werewolf society in Quebec called *Loup-garous* in French. What they were doing was they had contact with the Scottish Masonic lodges and the Algonquin *Midewiwin* (Medicine Societies). The *Midewiwin* were what I would call a Masonic lodge within Indian society. They were like the Druids, they were the gurus, the ones who had the responsibility of transmitting information or initiation or science or herbology, astrology, all these things, to the next generations.

In the French-Canadian society, because of the parish priest and the strong Catholic influence, this was seen through very bad eyes. Once you were sent from the church after seven years for not having done your Easter or Christmas devotions, they would curse you in the parish and call you a Werewolf. After you had been cursed as a Werewolf you couldn't go back to the church for at least seven years.

Was your father a Werewolf?

No, that was in the older generations. This was a symbolic totem animal because of the myths and legends of the French-Canadians. What they were in fact were pre-Christian Celtic folklorists. They didn't call themselves Druids because they had lost contact with all of that and because the Druid craft which was priestly had been wiped out of Europe.

The word 'Pagan' means 'peasant' and these were true peasants who were living their natural mysticism. Everything went around the forge, the smith, horseshoes and horses and whatnot. All these things went together like herbal medicine and whatnot. This is what it was all about.

How did you become involved in Druidism as a path?

I went to a Catholic college. In the first year the brothers initiated me into *The War of the Gauls*[19] by Julius Caesar. The image of the Druids struck my imagination so powerfully; it reminded me of some of the people I had known as a youth in rural French Canada. It was almost the same. Then they said that these Gauls were us at some point in time and we had changed because of the Romanization and Christianization and that we were not like that anymore. Of course the parish priests were very careful to tell us that these things didn't happen anymore.

Then I went on a trip to England and I discovered the Order of Bards, Ovates and Druids. I went to a Toc-H club, this was a club for foreign students in London. I wanted to go to Stonehenge and I was talking with a Mr. Brittian who was a Welshman running the club. I wanted to know more about the Druids and he said to get Stewart Piggott's book on the Druids,[20] he said it was the best book to buy, that was way back when. He wouldn't tell me much more. So I read the book and from there on it was just like stepping stones. I learned later that the Toc-H club had associations with the Order of Bards, Ovates and Druids.

What I learned was that the Druid lodges met in the forests and observed the Equinoctial and Solstitial events. They were devoted to the study of stars, science, astronomy, and all natural sciences, under the guidance of the Druid masters.

Your group has a rather unique understanding of Druidism. Could you please explain the underlying beliefs of the CDA?

Well, French scholars had gone to India and they discovered a lineage there that claimed to be of Celtic origin. There were Indians wearing kilts and playing bag-pipes, which the English assumed was due to their readiness in assimilating British culture. Further inquiry revealed that around the year 600 CE, as Christianity gained ascendancy, Druid records in Europe were burned and destroyed or buried. This was why the Coligny calendar was found broken in pieces and buried for example, and many Druids fled Europe at the time travelling from Scythia to Persia and finally to India, integrating what was then known as the *Kumara* lineage. Nimbarka was its prime Indian teacher.

There are still Gurus in India who are the direct descendants of the initiates of these Druids. *Uindia*, (Gaelic *Findias*), was one of the sacred mythical lands of the Aryans, the *Arioi*, 'Free People', ranchers of noble birth, and it is believed to be in the Himalayas. Other *Uindias* are found in the Baltic areas.

India is a place where almost every religion on Earth has been honored and respected and kept alive so it is not unusual that the Druid religion would be kept alive there too. It is somewhat ironic that descendants of the Gaulish Celts went back to India and rediscovered the religion of their ancestors. Afterwards a Breton scholar, Morvan Marchal, decided to restore the original Druidic religion of the Four Druid Master's lineage.

The *Kumara* lineage of India is also based on the Four Masters. This includes the Three Primordial Druids and the Four Sons of the *Daghda/Dagodeuos* and the Triple Goddess who were also referred to as the four poets or the four youths. The Three Masters are the resident masters of the etheric plane who manage the destiny of humanity and who are Avatars of the Triple Godhead. They are of the First Noble Class (*Brahmins*) and they preside over the teachings of morals and religion and over the three functions of priest, warrior, and producers.

The Four Masters or Four *Kumaras* cover the four directions, tend over the destinies of men, and over the affiliations of Druids. They govern science, astrology, astronomy, natural sciences, philosophy and genealogy. They have power over everything which is material and spiritual.

Are you saying that they actively influence people? For example if somebody is studying astrology would the Kumara who is in charge of astrology actively influence the learning and the progress of that astrologer?

Absolutely. The first disciple of the *Kumara* in charge of astrology is *Prinnionos*. Within the Druid caste there was a devotional caste as well called the *Ceiilioi Deui*, Companions of the Gods. These were the ones who maintained devotions to particular Gods, tribal Gods, family Gods, masculine and feminine, active and passive, along with the neutral forces. These Druids attended to the sacrifices that the Gods demanded from the people.

The Triple Godhead and the Triple Goddess, for example *Brighid/Brigantia*, were usually worshipped by the priests and priestesses of the Druids. Other Deities were reserved for the warriors and the farmers.

These things get very complicated. We are in the age of *Kali* in India and for the Celts the age of *Mile*, the 'age of havoc', which still has three hundred years to go. At this time religion is becoming much degenerated; there is a loss of the knowledge of who our ancestors were, a loss of our own spiritual legacy and origin.

The next age is supposed to be a return of the Golden Age which the Indians understood as the *Krita* age, the Celtic – *Aes Prinniios*, the Age of Astrology, the first Golden Age, the *Uidia*, from which *Druuidia*, Druidism, comes. Dru means true, *uidia* means science, the seer's craft.

It also means strong, as an oak.

Yes, that would be a Bardic word-play for tree, *'uidu'*, and *'deru'*, oak tree. The *Uidic* faith is the western branch of the Vedic faith. It dates to about the same time.

My understanding is that the Vedas are 8,000 years old. Are we talking about that time?

Oh yes. At the time of the Indo-European migrations.

That was about the time when the oak tree was the dominant tree in the Indo-European homeland.

Yes. We are the Danubian Aryans. There are Lower Danubian

Aryans, and there are Elbian Aryans. Those who were at the source of the Danube went southeast and became the Hittites, the Hyksos, and other tribes in Persia and India known as the Aryans or Indo Iranians.

You don't think they came from the Caucasus mountains?

Oh no, those were held by tribes of non-Indo-European peoples similar to the Basques, Finno-Ugric peoples, the Old Europeans. There is an argument over this because the Aryans in India say that the Aryans started in the Himalayas and migrated to the Danube. The Danubians maintain that they migrated to the Himalayas from the Danube.

So how did they get to the Danube? Did they come from Africa?

According to the myths we are from the Northern Islands of the Sea, in the Northern World, and that our souls originated in the constellation of the Great Bear. Then we migrated to the Pleiades and from there, after millions of years, we migrated to this constellation, into Ice Age Europe.

When you say 'we' are you distinguishing us from the Native Americans? The Anishinaabe[21] say that they came from the Star Nations too.

Of course. The Algonquin have a similar tradition. They also have the same origin.

So did we come from the same stars? Or did we come in different waves and from different planetary systems?

We came from different stars at different times. In Africa there is a tradition of coming from Sirius, the *Dogons* have that. The ethnologists will maintain that this was brought in by colonial French missionaries who told them about these things. But I think that even if that is true this still has a deep resonance with these people because it speaks to them of what they know already. The Algonquians have a saying that; 'The salmon always goes back to the fountainhead.' The Druids have the same saying. So speculation has it now that we projected ourselves into the Earth plane, *Magosia* (plain), and we projected our thought forms into the bodies of the anthropoids that were living here – the Neanderthals. This was a fairly late time because most of the people from the other constellations had already projected themselves into humanoids.

So you are saying the Arioi[22] were relative late-comers?

Yes.

Where does this information come from?

The myths, these are motifs typical to all of the Indo-European myths. They are also present in the *Algonquian* myths. These motifs were analyzed by ethnographers. Of course the different branches of the Vedic teachings have always maintained these things and they taught these things in their esoterica. The Gurus in India still teach this to their disciples.

Can you recommend a book? This is all new to me.

I think the best one to my knowledge is written by Raimonde Reiznikov who is Russian-French. She wrote a book entitled *Les Celtes et le Druidisme* published in France by the Editions Daugles. But I received most of this through verbal initiation, through my teachers. This is the type of stuff that comes when you are initiated into an affiliated Order of the Four Masters.

The instructions we were given when we came here was to keep the yoke. The holy yoke. Yoke as in Yoga, *Iugon*, yoke. It is present in all the Indo-European languages. The practice of Yoga was part of the Indo-European religion.

The yoke is a spiritual string from the Fountainhead, the seventh chakra on top of your head. This is from where the *Kundalini* snake ejects itself. It's like a silver filament. It swims back into the ethers and goes back to the ethereal plane.

So our job is to do what?

Our job is to maintain that light, as in sunlight, as in *Brighid*, as in *Lugh*, as in all that is light. *Brighid* is the fire that comes out of matter and returns through the wisdom of craft and creativity and arts and poetry and medicine and *Lugh* is the cosmic light.

The Algonquin say that we are the people of the fire and that our problem is we got carried away with it, we lost the balance.

That's for sure. We blew a bomb, right? So we have to go back to the original fire which is the fire within. The fire within is the fire in the mind, the fire in the head. This is the thing that animates the soul. We have to remember what we were supposed to be doing in the first place. We are supposed to be working on ourselves to try to re-discover who we are and where we are supposed to go back to.

And where are we supposed to go back to?

To the Pleiades, and then to the Ursa Major constellation.

Are we supposed to do that physically with spaceships or are we supposed to be able to do that with our consciousness?

Both.

So that's why we have this drive to do technology.

That's it. Once we get to the Pleiades there is a whole new world waiting for us because the old world has been destroyed and re-created.

And will it be better than this one?

No, it will be the same, but on a different level. Instead of being at the third level we will be at the fifth level. We are still evolving. But spiritually we do these things now, we go back to Arcturus once in a while when we dream and when we die.

I had a kabbalah teacher many years ago who said we were supposed to meditate on Arcturus. He said to go out at night and focus on Arcturus. Does that make sense to you?

Of course. Arcturus is the Bear Watcher, *Artaios* or Arthur, he watches over the Bear. The seven stars of Ursa Major are the Seven Sages. The Triple Godhead engendered the other souls which were the seven master souls, the *Ashvins* in Vedic, or *Equites* in Latin, *Eporedoi* in Celtic, and the Horsemen in English. Arcturus is in Bootes which is the constellation of the *Arioi*, the Cow-keepers.

The Pleiades are the Seven Sisters which are under the seven fates. These are the Fate Faeries, the *Coiliacas* or *Cailleach*. The seven stars of Ursa Major are their husbands. This tends to prove that our souls, in our Yin and Yang, *Couocanton* and *Couiocanton*, plenty and void, are tied to these constellations in a sense. Arcturus is watching over all of this. So the first pit stop after the moon and different planets, after we have ejected ourselves from Pluto, is to go on to Arcturus.

This sounds like Theosophy.

Yes it does. But it's all present in Vedic religion, that's where Theosophy got it from.

Most of the Druid Orders that I am aware of today seem to be inventing things as they go along. I just wondered what you think about most of the modern Druid Orders. Are there any problems or issues that you have around that?

I don't have any problem with it. What I see is a cry, an urge, a wish to re-establish what is really innate and inward and to make it manifest and have it come out. The thing is that once this is initiated, because of the ethers and the *Akashas*, because of dreams and connectedness and because of the 'Salmon of Wisdom' that we were speaking of before, inevitably the Four Masters, and these have no sex, they are not old men with beards, they are just neutral souls, are re-invited to manifest themselves to inspire and bring back the Fates, the Faery. Through the Faery who are the Muses in modern language, people become creative.

There is no problem with being creative; man is always creating and re-creating things. Inevitably the Four Masters will be there to re-inspire the light, the fire, and the nuts of wisdom. So it doesn't matter if it's coming from an ancient tradition or a modern tradition because the well of inspiration is coming from within each individual.

It's coming from the old ones who haven't died because they continue through us. It's coming from the heart of the man, the man who began through the woman. The fire is burning inside the heart hearth.

The Fire Altar within.

That's it. And this is the true sacrificial altar. That's where the true sacrifice starts. This is another thing that is very interesting about the ethnological side of things. It was said that when the Druids removed the actual teachings from the western world they removed all these teachings to the *Akasha* where they were kept for the coming age. When the Piscean age would be over and the Aquarian age would be initiated they would be able to retrieve those teachings and bring them back to Earth. And exactly where it is brought back is into the heart of people. Aquarius is the 'Cauldron of Plenty'.

Do you think that's what is happening now?

Yes. That's it.

Where would you like to see Druidism move in the future? Do you have a vision for that?

Yes, as a true fellowship and brotherhood as it was meant to be from the first, all over the world. That the people who truly belong to it, truly recognize their own self. I find Shakespeare's Polonius to be quite silly but he said; 'To thine own self be true.' But how can you be true to a swine when you are supposed to be boar? The boar is research. The boar is cunningness, getting to the root, digging for things.

Steve Wilson
Interviewed June 16, 1996
The Bull and Last, Parliament Hill, London

Steve has been a member of the Fellowship of Isis (FOI) since 1981 and was ordained as a Priest in 1984. He helped organize the first FOI convention in 1990 which has been an annual event ever since. He has been central to the establishment of the Druid Clan of Dana and the Noble Order of Tara, an environmental group within FOI.

Steve is the author of *Robin Hood, Spirit of the Forest,* and *Chaos Ritual,* both from Neptune Press, London. He organized the first Chaos Magic conventions in England. He is President of the Council of British Druid Orders and the Council's representative to the Pagan Federation. He publishes Aisling, the magazine of the Druid Clan of Dana. The Druid Clan of Dana was founded by Lady Olivia Robertson and the late Baron Strathlock, Lawrence Durdin-Robertson. It is a group that celebrates Goddess-based Druidry.

The Irish Druid tradition has always been Goddess-based. The Tuatha de Danaan, for example, are descended from the Goddess Danu and the great Irish hero, Finn MacCumhail, was trained by two women, one a Druidess, the other a warrior. The greatest Irish warrior, Cuchulain, was also trained by a woman warrior.

Finn MacCumhail was also trained as a Bard and the Irish Bardic tradition lasted longer than any other. It was dissolved only after the Cromwellian invasions, four hundred years after the collapse of the Welsh tradition. As the tradition still continues today in some ways it can be said that it never really died.

Steve, can you please discuss your religious upbringing as a child and how you first discovered Druidry? What drew you to it?

I was interested in mythology from age eight and in non-Christian religions from age ten. By twelve I was calling myself a Buddhist, at age thirteen a Taoist, the typical 60s thing. Being half Indian, but brought up in an Anglo-Afro-Caribbean family, I spent much of the 1970s involved in Eastern mysticism and only really began exploring the Western Pagan heritage in the 1980s. I didn't specifically call myself a Druid first, as opposed to Pagan first, Druid second, until I had joined the Druid Clan of Dana and read Ross Nichols' *The Book of Druidry*. Then I realized that Druidry combined both my general Pagan interests and my interest in Earth Mysteries.

How were you trained as a Druid?

It was general Pagan training until I joined the Clan, via the Fellowship of Isis, and in investigating Irish Druidry I discovered the Filidh. When I began investigating them I realized that the training was the Druidic training in disguise. I also realized that the Filidh have faded rather than completely died out. From their establishment, after the decline of the Irish University system about 1000 CE until Cromwell's invasion of Ireland, there was a continuous development. And then the Four Masters of Irish poetry simply fled to France, and the Filidh returned to Ireland thirty years later. Even in the 1890s an Irish professor toured the coast of Ireland in a boat, declaiming Filidhic poetry in the harbor. Huge crowds went to hear him.

I began practicing Filidhic poetry after I read a Gaelic Literature survey published in 1928. It had all the rules of Gaelic poetry and its composition and I recognized a similarity with Zen poetry such as the Haiku, I saw it was a spiritual system. I adapted the rules for English rather than Gaelic. The trouble is that this book was published in the same year as W.B. Yeats' *A Vision*, which most spiritual Westerners would have read at the time. The Gaelic Literature Survey was ignored, the title didn't hint at the spiritual content.

The Druids memorized verses for twenty years according to

Caesar, and the Filidh did the same. Originally Ireland had a Bardic caste just like the Welsh and the ancient Britons but then Ireland's world-famous university system began to collapse around 1000 CE, probably because of the Vikings who occupied Dublin, which stopped foreign students from travelling to Ireland. The Bards gave way to the Filidh.

All their poetry was written in winter, when they spent the entire day in a windowless bothy, a sort of turf hut. They only emerged at night. But the poetry was written about subjects that were investigated during the summer, when they were forbidden to write poetry. I realized this was a sort of fermentation process.

It was also probably so they could take time to work in the fields.

Right! There was no longer a state-sanctioned Druidry due to the Church; the Filidh had to go down-market. When there weren't enough Kings and Lords to listen to stories from the Ulster cycle, the Filidh began developing poetry about the Fenians under Finn MacCumhail, because those were the stories the peasants wanted to hear. I don't believe that it was a full-time twenty-year course, not under Christianity. They must have had to support themselves while they were learning.

What I do in my training course is to change the twenty years into months. In the first section the Deibhdinhe style of poetry is used and it is fairly complicated. There are internal rhymes, alliterations and a strict number of syllables per line. The subject of the poetry is nature, just as in the original Filidh course. The halves of the year become the halves of the month. Each month you spend two weeks visiting and being in a particular place as often as possible, such as the highest hill visible from your house, or the nearest group of trees, and then you avoid it for two weeks while practicing the poetic form on other subjects. Finally you compose the poem in a single sitting, and this is assessed. I don't believe in non-assessed courses.

Then there is a whole aspect of the work running parallel with this work, where you learn the history and geography of your local area. You investigate your own home, determining which direction the water flows in from, where light enters, where the heating is, that sort of thing, so you attune your everyday life with the elements.

The second six months, followed by initiation as a Faidh, is to do with mythology and magic, and will end with a poem that summons up a vision of the Goddess of Sovereignty, the Aisling, which is Gaelic for Vision. You also start to get used to spontaneous verses, dictated by the unconscious, that act as prophesies. They have to come true though!

The final six months is about justice and law. How justice is more important than laws. You have to find out, for example, just who has the right to break into your home when you are not there, usually far more people than you would expect! This ends with initiation as a Druid.

My attitude towards Druidry is to ask – what would it be like now if Druidry hadn't been abolished? That is what I am guessing at, and it's only a guess, but it's a very educated one.

What do you think it would be like now if it hadn't been abolished?

Only the training of Priests would still be the old-fashioned way. The content and mode of poetry would be the means by which it was learned. I don't think secular science would still be learnt by memorizing verses.

There is a school of Druidry that believes you should be Celtic Reconstructionist. That you should do good scholarship, you should go back and read the best authors and get a good literary and historic background. There is another school that encourages understanding through intuition. What do you think about those two approaches?

How many Christians can speak the Greek that the New Testament was written in? Or the Hebrew of the Old Testament? You don't have to do that to be a Christian and you don't have to do that to be a Christian Priest. So why have to do it now to be a Druid?

The fact is that if you want to know about a tree you can read as much as you like from books, which I insist on, but to understand, say, a Birch, you also need to actually be with a Birch. So the Irish poetical method of allowing something to ferment and then having to use these strict rules to express yourself forces you to reach into your depths and come out with things that you didn't even know were there beforehand.

If we knew all the ins and outs of Druidry as it was in the year 1 CE we might not like it. It wouldn't be 20th century Druidry it would be Iron Age Druidry where people were quite happy to sacrifice animals because people had to kill animals anyway so they certainly didn't see killing an animal as such a terrible thing. And I have no intention of chewing raw dog meat to obtain the Imbas, although it probably has certain effects. Raw carnivore meat certainly does. So it is definitely outdated.

Learning Gaelic is certainly not going to make you a better person. The IRA speak Gaelic. I think you are better off relying on intuition because there isn't enough left, there just isn't enough in the books.

I don't see the ancient Druids as a Priesthood because we know that the same organizational structures existed in non-Druidic Celtic countries. I think that Druidry was something that was very bound in with the Celtic social structure. They were people who were experts at law and magic. It was certainly different from ordinary worship. But I also believe it was pre-Celtic. Druidry actually goes back before the Celts.

There is a very slight indication in the structure of Gaelic that it is actually a mixture of an Indo-European and a non-Indo-European language. There are aspects of grammar in Gaelic that you don't find in any other Indo-European language. There are two verbs for 'to be'. There is one that means 'is' and one that means 'is at'. In Gaelic they far prefer to say; 'It is I at the plow in the field,' rather than; 'I am plowing the field.'

I believe that Welsh is a dialect that came out of Roman

Britain.

I am not sure that the Celts ever existed as a single culture. Most of the so-called P-Celtic words can be explained by the fact that the Roman soldiers spoke Greek, not Latin, except for the formal administration of the country. So the ordinary soldier would, for example, have said 'ippos' for horse, not 'equus', and 'pente' for five, not 'quinque'. The rest was Gaelic, and some Latin. Officially the Latin words in Welsh like 'fenestra' for window, came from France via Brittany, which was settled by Britons just after the collapse of Roman Britain. Nineteenth century Anglo-Saxon scholars hated the idea that the Welsh were the true British so they made up this sort of nonsense, as though the British didn't have any windows or need a word for them until 400 CE.

Who do you think the Picts were?

I think the Picts were Celto-Germanic. That would certainly explain why the language disappeared, because I don't think it did. I think Pictish is still there today. It's called lowland Scots. It doesn't make sense that a people who weren't even defeated in battle have dropped their language and only speak Gaelic in a few hundred years. Language just doesn't die out like that.

Old languages are dying out all over the place because English has been imposed on them.

Yet the Picts were supposed to have changed their language twice in two centuries.

Everybody spoke Gaelic in Ireland and it took only a few centuries to practically wipe it out.

Whereas in Wales they had to fight for their language. For the Irish their language is a drag. Every young Irishman is forced to learn the language in school. It's so sad.

How did the Druid Clan of Dana get started?

The first Grove of the Druid Clan of Dana met at the old abbey which is part of the castle at Clonegal where Olivia and Lawrence Robinson lived. Olivia and Lawrence worked with Ross Nichols during the 1960s when he was doing his research.

Can you discuss Goddess-based Druidism?

Druidry is still shaking off the patriarchal nature of the 18th century revival. The Fellowship of Isis developed the Clan to recognize the importance of Goddesses, especially Dana, to the Gaels and other Pagans of these isles. *The Book of Invasions*, where Goddesses are euhemerized, made into human Queens, shows how central Goddesses were to Druid beliefs.

You have been doing research into the relationship between Gerald Gardner and Ross Nichols, can you talk about that a bit?

It started off with a story that began emerging that there was a connection with the origins of Wicca and a particular group of people who were working with the Cross Quarters including Ross Nichols.

We published a letter that had been discovered in a copy of the biography of Gerald Gardner, which was authenticated. It was a typewritten letter from Gerald Gardner to Ross Nichols suggesting a rather humorous way of dealing with the 'problem of the Welsh'. The Welsh Gorsedd was founded by David Samwell and Iolo Morganwg in London. There was a powerful Welsh society of one name or another throughout 18th century London and Iolo's ceremonies were added to the Eisteddfod. Now the Welsh refuse to allow the existence of Druidry outside the 'Celtic Fringe', although none of the Gaelic countries have a Gorsedd.

We realized then that Ross Nichols was given a very special thanks at the beginning of Gerald Gardner's book *Witchcraft Today*. And subsequently we began finding, through research, the origins of the New Forest Coven, which Gardnerian Witchcraft is derived from, in an organization called The Order of Woodcraft Chivalry.

It was an organization based on Ernest Thompson Seton's Woodcraft Indians of America later called The Woodcraft League of America. There is actually a village named after him somewhere in Arizona. He was more or less the founding father of American Naturalism (not Naturism, which is the English euphemism for nudism!). His sketches and descriptions of animal and bird behavior in Canada and the northern USA are recognized as the first accurate descriptions on record. He also published the first book of Native American lore that was approved by the Native American Chieftains and Shamans themselves, *Gospel of the Redman*, in 1916.

He started an organization in New York which was open to the local children. In 1903 Lord Baden Powell went to America to learn about the Woodcraft movement, but ended up forming the Boy Scouts instead. As it became more and more militaristic a splinter group called the Kibbo Kift was founded by one of his disciples, John Hargreave, who subsequently went to Canada. He died in 1983.

The Order of Woodcraft Chivalry was ostensibly a Quaker organization founded by a father and son, Ernest and Aubrey Westlake. It was based at their ancestral home delightfully named Sandy Balls. There are huge circular hills there that have been formed by the action of the river that flows through the New Forest.

Ernest Westlake had actually converted to Paganism as he described it in 1924. At the same time John Hargrave objected to the word 'Pagan' to describe what the Kibo Kift were about, in favor of the 'New Barbarism', which I quite like as well.

The Woodcraft Movement is very occult oriented. I went to their seventy fifth anniversary Fire Lighting Ceremony in the New Forest in which the quarters are called. They actually started in the North rather than the East. Each quarter was called by somebody wearing a different colored robe.

They showed me some old magazines and in 1923 or 24 there was an article about the development of the color symbolism of the Woodcraft Chivalry, by Ernest Westlake. I turned to it and it was a whole table of correspondences of the seven planets, the colors. On the back of the magazine there are stories to be read out to the six-year-olds at a campfire as well.

By 1926 they had adopted nudity and Paganism. Every morning they did an Indian call to the Sun Mother at which point they would all zoom to bathe stark naked in the local river. There are fortunately photographs by a local newspaper.

In 1927 they abandoned nudity and Paganism for a spiritual group led by Harry Byngham who had the nickname 'Dian' which was short for Dionysus. He was very much dedicated to Dionysus, Pan and Artemis, in other words a Horned God and a Moon Goddess.

Throughout the 1930s he wrote articles for nudist magazines and then he turns up in the 1950s writing an article for the Occult Observer, the editor of which was Ross Nichols who at the time was working with Gerald Gardner and of course Gerald Gardner was actually a member of the Ancient Druid Order.

It was always said that he was a member of OBOD, but it has recently been realized he would have died shortly before OBOD split from the ADO. He signed the certificate that recognized Hugh MacGregor as Chosen Chief.

When MacGregor Reid senior died in 1945 somebody called Smith was elected Chosen Chief, but he immediately started taking it in a direction they really didn't like. So the vast majority split away, recognized MacGregor Reid Jr. and amongst the signatures on the certificate recognizing him as Chosen Chief was Gerald Gardner's as well as Ross Nichols'.

What we have realized is that in the 1950s they developed the concept of the 'Wheel of the Year' for which there isn't really any ancient proof. There are lots of bits and pieces, but the idea of a unified system that both the Celtic and the pre-Celtic people used doesn't seem to hold out. Basically what we have realized is that Ross Nichols and Gerald Gardner realized there was a need for a regular ritual structure.

We published our preliminary research in October last year,

the last time Aisling actually came out. We have since discovered when Vera Chapman died, that she was the founder of the Tolkien Society, she was also Pendragon of the Order of Bards, Ovates and Druids and she was also on the council of the Kibo Kift back in the 1920s.

So this connection between modern Paganism and these Woodcraft-based groups goes back to the 20s. The furore hasn't died down yet.

So where do you see Druidry heading in the future?

It's becoming more and more popular. The ecology movement has adopted Druidry, Paganism in general too, but Druidry because of trees. The Irish Tree Alphabet is also linked into the twenty months of my course. I only work with the twenty consonants; I don't count the five vowels.

As a press officer I take a very active approach rather than a reactive one. We've found that the word Druid is considered harmless and eccentric, whereas the words 'Pagan' and 'Witch' frighten people. They shouldn't, of course, but we manage to get much more positive press coverage. We are much more prepared to go public as a result.

Is there anything in particular that you would like to communicate to American Druids?

Yes. You will find us on the net. The Druid Clan of Dana's page in the Fellowship of Isis' website on the internet.

Musicians, Artists and Poets

If you are chief poets versed in the arts,
relate the high mysteries
to the people of the wide world.
Taliesin Pen Beirdd, The Three Fountains

I am a Bard and harper,
I am a piper and crwth-player, of sevenscore singers,
the very best enchanter.
From the lime of competition
I take my winged ascent.
Taliesin Pen Beirdd, Death Song of Uther Pendragon

The Bardic arts have flourished in a continuous stream from the Bronze Age of the Celts to the Bardic schools of the 1700s to the oral traditions of the Celtic countries to the present re-flowering of the Celtic spirit. Celtic tradition has influenced rock bands such as The Incredible String Band, Wolfstone, and Steel Eye Span, folk-rock groups such as Pentangle and Fairport Convention and a myriad traditionally inspired groups such as Solas, Silly Wizard, Altan, The Battlefield Band and Rare Air.

In this chapter, harpists Prydwyn Olvardil Piper and Ann Heymann discuss the Celtic inspiration for their music and Shaman's fiddle player, 'Brahm' Stuart De Usoz, discusses the influence of the Irish nature spirits on his playing. Illustrator Bryan Perrin shows how Celtic Reconstructionist religion has penetrated the visual arts, poet Searles O'Dubhain exemplifies the path of a modern-day Fili (Master Poet) and William Shaw gives a fascinating overview of the ancient role of the storyteller.

Prydwyn Olvardil Piper

Interviewed July 25, 1996
Starwood Festival, Brushwood Folklore Centre, Sherman, NY

Michael (Prydwyn Olvardil Piper) is a Ph.D. candidate in the Department of Celtic Languages and Literatures at Harvard University with an M.A.in Celtic Studies from the University of Edinburgh, Scotland. He is the author of *Renaissance Songbook: The First Part of Songs or Ayres* a collection of Jacobean and Elizabethan lute songs transcribed in both modern notation and guitar tablature, and has become a familiar figure at Pagan festivals and Renaissance fairs where he performs and offers rare and hard to find scholarly books on Celtic and Pagan studies along with harps for sale.

His recordings include At the Feet of Mary Mooncoin, harp and voice in English and Scottish Gaelic, Buried All Me Beforn, a collection of magical songs and ballads from the British Isles accompanied by harp, The Last of the Troubadours, a selection of 17th century songs by Thomas Campion (1567-1620), Live at Pantheocon, featuring Todd Alan and Quest Quintet with Michael on harp and cittern, The Bazuk Brothers – While It Lasts, Prydwyn Olvardil Piper and Dennis Shearin performing songs and instrumentals from the mysterious land of Bazukia on zuk, mandolin and viola, The Bazuk Brothers – Fyne Companions, Michael and Dennis again playing Celtic tunes on harp and Hammered dulcimer, and the newest release, The Witch in the Well, featuring Michael on harp with cello, vocal and percussive backup.

Can you describe you religious education as a child? How you were raised?

I was raised as a good Italian peasant Catholic. My great grandparents, most of them, came from Italy. It was kind of a nice Catholicism. Some people have all sorts of horror stories about being raised Catholic, I never had really big problems with it.

It was a combination of real peasant superstition and magic, the side of Catholicism that you don't always see at the higher levels. The people on the ground were doing the things they had done forever.

It didn't quite make it to my mother's generation. When I got it, it was all 'quaint things grandma does'. You know, the evil eye and wearing the things that look like hot peppers around your neck.

The horns?

Yes. And when I would stay with my grandmother there was this whole going to bed ritual, it was praying. You said a couple of the standard prayers, but then we would go through the ancestors. It was sort of as if they were angels and intercessors. We would go through the close people to us who had died. I had an older sister who died of leukemia when I was young and she was always there. We would do it to try and keep in touch with them and also so they would look out for us and put in a good word with God. It was a kind of angelic protection.

Every kid in the family got a picture of a guardian angel to put over the bed. Looking back on it now it was very magical with lots of spirits around. It was definitely unorthodox by strict Church doctrine, somewhere across the heresy boundary.

A lot of the times we used to go to church were really weird, like Saint Blaise Day. That was one of my favorites. He is the patron saint of throats, if you have throat problems you go to him. On Saint Blaise's Day we would always go to church and they had this ritual where they would bless everyone's throat. There were big lines up to the altar and when you got there the Priest said a prayer and held crossed candles across your throat. You had to move your hair out of the way because the candles were lit. That was supposed to keep you from getting throat ailments for the next year.

Did it work?

It worked for me. Or at least I didn't get throat ailments. We also had 'blessings of the pets' where everyone went to get their pets blessed.

The area I grew up in was still enough of an immigrant community that it wasn't cynical American Catholicism yet. The Priest was a kind of magician you would go to if you needed something fixed on a spiritual plane. There was a prayer or some kind of ritual you could do or you could light candles for this person who died or for a problem in your life. You would meditate on the problem and ask to get help in getting it resolved. It was sort of a magical act.

Was there a lot of emphasis on the Virgin Mary?

Yes, especially with my grandmother. It was the name you heard the most. I think my grandmother felt more comfortable with that.

So you are an Italian from Brooklyn, New York?

I'm half Italian. My mother's mother was Italian and my father's father was Italian. But my mother's father was German-Irish and my father's mother was Breton. The only folk customs that came down from them were food rituals. Things would get made on certain days that would come from one area or another.

So when did you first hear about Druids or when did you first find out about Celtic spirituality and what attracted you to that?

I probably knew about Druids in a vague sense from being interested in history from at least the first year or two of high school. I was probably nineteen or twenty when I realized there were people out there who were calling themselves Druids and doing Druid things today, that it wasn't just something from the past that was over and done with.

I had a friend named Ed. Our relationship over the years has been one where he gets into something and passes it on to me and then he goes off to the next thing and I end up stuck with what he was doing for the rest of my life. He turned me on to traditional music.

He had very unpleasant high school years with bad, weird girlfriends. His life was a disaster, but one of his girlfriends had a mother who was a Pagan and a Witch. She was being raised that way and so he came to know about the whole scene that was out there. I found out about it through him and then, inevitably, he went off and did something else and I'm still here.

Once you heard about Druids and Celtic spirituality, did you work with any groups or get any kind of training?

I read some books. The next thing that really put me in touch was that I lived for two years with a woman named Pam who was all over the Pagan scene. I met her at the Renaissance Festival in New York. She had come to Starwood[23] for years, she had gone to Rites of Spring[24] and had been to women's spirituality gatherings. Hearing her stories made me realize that there was a lot more out there than I had thought.

What was it about the Celtic path in particular that drew you in?

It was the music connection that got me into the spirituality. Part of it goes back to Ed again, he was raised very Irish and he went through a period where he was fed up with having Irish culture stuffed down his throat. Then he grew out of that and found good traditional music as opposed to 'green beer music'. He passed that along to me and he gave me my first pennywhistle.

I was living in Nashville while I was going to college. I came back to New York for my sister's confirmation and then I went back to Nashville and got very depressed. At that time of my life when I would get depressed I would go to used record stores and spend a lot of money. I saw this album with a very intriguing cover and I looked at it and at the credits on the back, took a chance and paid the five bucks. It was an Incredible String Band album.

That just blew all my circuits. I heard it the first time and it was weird but it was interesting enough that I listened to it again. Then the second time it was even more interesting. By the third time I decided I liked it. It was the time of the 60s folk revival. Then I was introduced to a lot of other musicians and I started to realize that the old stuff had a lot of magic and mystery to it.

The Incredible String Band are obviously influenced by traditional music, but they are not strictly traditional. Were there any traditional musicians that influenced you?

I liked the Chieftains and Silly Wizard. They affected the way I looked at music more than being spiritual influences. I don't think I ever did and I am coming less and less to think of myself as a 'traditional' musician. I've learned a lot from strictly traditional music, but it's not really my focus.

You work with magic and music. What do you call yourself? You don't call yourself a Druid.

I call myself a musician. I think that, in and of itself if it is done right, is a magical path. It's a discipline where you are dealing with magical energy and you are channeling things. Celtic is probably my dominant paradigm, but not the only one.

How do you combine Celtic music and magic?

It might go back to praying with Grandma. The things I really feel spiritually connected to are the Earth and nature and the sky, but the ancestors are also very important to me, all the thousands of years of genetics. I have lots of Romans in me too. I have lots of wars taking place inside my genes I am sure.

I like doing traditional material and drawing inspiration from it because it's a connection back through time. There are a lot of pretty songs, but there is also material with a lot of magic and mystery condensed. I was thinking yesterday about the time when everything had to go in your head and be remembered there. People couldn't afford to explain things in a thousand pages and try to stuff that in their heads.

I think it was very important to be able to take sacred, spiritual information and compress it in a way that everything was there, but contained in a very small packet. Like those computer programs that take acres of information and do some kind of magic and go poof, poof, poof and you suddenly have all the information in one hundredth the space. Then you hit a button and it goes 'Whoosh!' and it blows up and it's all back again. Compressed files.

That's what I like about the traditional repertoire. It takes tons and tons of people's energy and feelings and experiences and lessons they want to pass on, and puts it in a very compressed, powerful format. It kind of sneaks in your ear rather than your eye and once it's in your brain it blows up, and even without your realizing it consciously all the information unfolds.

I do a workshop where I talk about music as a magical path, about what it means to be a Bard in modern times. I begin by asking what we mean by the word 'Bard'? There are very strict technical meanings if you want to get back to what the people who were called Bards were in different societies in different times. It is a word that has come into English parlance these days as a somewhat romanticized, somewhat mystical, Troubadoury, performer. In the Irish context it was a lower grade of poet that was called a Bard. There were different levels of training with the Ollamh at the top. The Bard was connected with panegyric, praise-poetry, at least in the Scottish context.

I've always read that it degenerated into that, but that in the beginning the Bards were more powerful magically, that in later times they were hired by lords to compose praise-poetry.

I don't think you could prove that. I used to hate praise-poetry, but now I have found out that most of what we have is actually praise-poetry. Having been forced to work with it at certain points I've seen that it's a lot more than kissing the lord's butt.

If you look at the way people wrote these things there was a code. You weren't so much praising this person as creating a paradigm of the ideal leader. If you read the stuff they aren't talking about this physical person sitting at the end of the hall who is half drunk and carousing with his buddies. It sets up the ideal lord and the ideal lord's wife. There are also a lot of cultural values, notions of what a good leader is and the place of the warrior in society.

There is a very good article by John Maciness in the Transactions of the Gaelic Society of Inverness, Volume 50. He looked at lots of Scottish Gaelic praise-poetry and found that they were dealing with issues of the tribe and the outside, and the leader's role in that. They were dealing with family, blood-ties and their importance, the issues of leadership and gender roles. A lot of the poems hardly exist on the present, physical reality-plane.

All our evidence for Celtic poets, as far back as you can take it and actually be dealing on firm solid ground, is that their main occupation was writing praise-poetry and taking care of genealogies. You can go back to the earliest Welsh poetry we've got, The Gododdin, which describes a battle at a place called Cartraeth. I would describe it as the Welsh Charge of the Light Brigade because there were three hundred British based up somewhere near Edinburgh when that was still a British speaking area rather than an English or Gaelic speaking area. They rode jollily off to war with their trumpets blazing and their best armor on and all that, against the Northumbrians and were just decimated.

Two or three people out of the three hundred got away and one of them, if the story is accurate, was a poet who wrote the poem. It was definitely a prestige-piece, a Bardic competition piece. People added verses and it's been mutated over time.

These days there just aren't the patrons out there who are going to pay a Bard to write praise-poems. Without that bread-and-butter necessity I don't think many people are particularly inclined to write praise-poetry.

So what is a Bard these days? A modern Bard?

In the process of writing praise-poems for someone they may

or may not have liked, the Bards were reinforcing and preserving and passing on the values of the society and of the tribe. That function is part of being a Bard. I don't know what Bards are trying to do today, but it's what I am trying to do today.

You and Robin Williamson are the only two Bards I have met. I don't know any others.

I am definitely a Bard in training. This is a work in progress.

Even though we have books I think that something in your head that you pass along by mouth is valuable. It might change, but that is a beautiful thing, because it grows with the times.

I've come up with a nice triad, the three qualities you need as raw material to build a Bard. Memory is the first, to be willing and able to commit important lessons and information from the past into your head and transmit it to the future. That gets into the whole ancestors' connection.

The second one is voice; my personal tastes are not for strictly instrumental music. I don't think playing music without words is a Bardic activity. That can be part of a larger performance, it can be very profound and spiritual, but it's not the way I think of the practice of Bardism where what you have in your memory is expressed through your voice.

I do have an anti-literate streak, which is kind of funny given what I do most of the time. I think important, sacred spiritual information is better entrusted to people's heads than to books. Once things are in books they tend to take on a rigidity. The three great mono-theisms for example are called 'The People of the Book'. I think when those big books appeared it was a very radical thing, everything was in there and it was handed down from God and it should never change.

We have very little, if any, liturgical literature surviving from the classical world. Meanwhile we know that every major temple had a choir with singers and dancers and a lot of ritual. It's not until the late classical world that you get the idea of putting these things in books, which then makes them immutable and unchangeable.

What I like about the oral process is the way things subtly change. People will swear to you that they do something the same way each time they do it, but you can record them a week apart and the thing will have changed drastically depending on the audience. That type of presentation deals more with the energies that are present at the time than books can.

The third part of the triad is inspiration, which is the thing that allows you to take what is in your memory, what you would like to express with your voice and make that into something powerful and magical.

Imbas, that's what you are talking about isn't it?

Yes, it's the weird intangible thing that inspires. The other part of all this is the idea of the Bard as the 'pontifex' – the bridge builder. That's where we get the word Pontiff from – the High Priest of Rome, the Pontifex Maximus, the greatest of all bridge builders. Some people say it's because they charged large tolls to get over the Tiber River, but I don't believe that. I think it's the idea of somebody who puts bridges between the worlds, between the divine powers and the people.

The stuff I really like in old material is ballads and songs that involve encounters with the Otherworld. I think they place road-maps. They give you hints as to what's there in case you suddenly find yourself in it. They tell you things to be careful of and things not to do.

Jack Rowland is one that does that. Tam Lin and Thomas the Rhymer do it. *The Mabinogion* is another example. Taking the first branch of it, Pwyll goes off and meets the King of the Otherworld. One of the big lessons that I have gotten from it and from these other stories is that the Otherworld isn't somewhere else, it's just a question of looking at what is around you in a slightly different way. The Otherworld is here and we are in it, it's around us.

There is also the idea that you have to deal honorably with

what you encounter in the Otherworld, the importance of giving your word and keeping it and honorable relations. It's not just a Celtic idea, but it's the idea that proper relations with the Otherworld are essential to creating peace and harmony for the tribe or the social unit. All the stuff about kingship and the geasa that were put on kings and even the word Sidhe, which means Faery or the Faery Hill, and which also means peace as opposed to war. The reason they are the same word is that dealing properly with the Sidhe creates the conditions for peace, Otherwordly bliss for the tribe. If your sacred leaders were dealing honorably with the Otherworld the crops would grow and there wouldn't be war. Words were considered very powerful, the honor and truth of someone's word.

Another thing I think Bards did in transmitting stories and songs was to keep alive the concept of the hero. When they would tell stories of the heroes of the past, besides just being entertaining, they presented everybody in the group with the picture of the hero as an ideal. When you had to go off and do something unpleasant like go off to battle you would have that picture in your head, that intangible morale thing in warfare. You can have all the best guns and all the best plans laid out, but the personal energy of where people are at can completely overturn everyone's expectations in a battle. The concept of the hero allowed you to do something that you maybe didn't want to do. It encouraged you and gave you the energy to do it.

There is a song called The Burning Times by Charlie Murphy. It's a big Pagan anthem that takes the Medieval Witch hunts and connects them to what we are doing to the Earth today. We are treating the Earth like they used to treat the Witches. From a historical point of view the song is a disaster, but it's still a very powerful piece. I get charged up from it, it makes me want to go out and do something.

I think that today's Bards can still present pictures of heroes overcoming obstacles, of dealing with the warrior energy, which we still need. It's not necessarily to go off to the next tribe and cut their heads off and take their cows, but there is a lot of work that needs to get done. Promoting a heroic ideal and getting people fired up in that way is an important part of being a Bard these days.

'Brahm' Stuart De Usoz from Shaman is very good at that. He's dealing in a Celtic idiom, he could play fiddle tunes for two days without having to repeat himself, but what he actually does in a performance is to try and create something that will get people to go out and do something. I think doing that today is the equivalent of the old days when the pipes and songs were there to stir people up because the tribe needed to be defended or they needed to go next door and grab some cows because their kids were starving.

It's the idea of the three levels of society with the farmers who grow the food and the warriors and those who pray at the top, the Priests. Most of Indo-European societies seem to have had that three level concept.

They never mention the fourth function, which is the slaves or the untouchables. I see that reflected in our culture today in the way we ignore the homeless, as if they weren't important. They don't exist for us because in our minds we have never recognized the fourth function. They are something you are not supposed to touch or think about or associate with. You are supposed to act as if they don't exist unless you need them to do something. We have millions of homeless people in the United States and we act as if they don't exist. In India they act as if the Untouchables are an acceptable facet of society.

In the Middle Ages the serfs and quasi-slaves would have been considered part of those who grow the food. I think the most useful parallel is the warrior paradigm where you confront what needs to be confronted and protect what needs to be protected. That is something we still need as Pagans and in creating a new humanity who can live on the planet without killing themselves.

Somebody who is a powerful and magical performer could still go out and put energy directly into other things, but by performing he is bringing in a lot more energy because he is connected to the Otherworld. In a good Bardic performance you can bring that energy to a thousand people and you now have that many people who are inspired. Part of what a Bard should be doing is dropping some pretty unsubtle hints about taking the energy and doing something with it.

I think the Bard is like a crystal or a magic wand, something that focuses power that people can use. Performance can be a ritual where people can draw power through the lens of the Bard who is trained to do that.

What about the role of poetry in all this?

In Green Egg they recently had a readers' poll. One of the questions was what sort of skills do you have? Something like seventy or eighty percent of the people said they were poets. And I am sure that seventy or eighty percent of the Green Egg readership are not *good* poets.

It seems that in the last two hundred years Paganism in general has evolved the idea of the natural poet who sits in the woods and stuff just spouts out of them and its beautiful and wonderful. Except when you look at the people who were spreading this idea, like the Beat poets who said; 'You gotta let it flow, man!', you find that they were immersed in English poetry, at least back to the late 16th century. They had read it and re-read it and they tried to imitate it. They learned the art of writing poetry.

They had the meter in their heads.

Yes, and having that meter in their head they could go out in the woods and get crazy and things would come out that resembled poetry.

The ancient Irish poets worked within very strict forms. Those guys were kind of like jazz musicians, they were playing off the form.

Yes, I think it was Charlie Parker who said the first thing you have to do is learn the rules, then you have to learn how to break them. But the technical side of things has to be inside you before you can deviate. A lot of things get published as poetry in magazines, with good intentions, with a good message. What they are saying is good, but it's not poetry.

So what would be good poetry?

I like things to be sung. I'd rather hear poetry in the context of music. I've never been able to get into reading poetry, until I hear it in the air it doesn't do too much for me.

You play the harp. Can you talk about that as a magical instrument? Do you ever work with it to send magical energy?

If I'm performing well that's what I am trying to do. The harp is a very magical thing; I can't tell you logically what about the harp as opposed to the guitar or something makes it that way. Part of it is that it has this long association with Bards of the past.

Playing the harp is a very visual thing for me. If I have been busy and I haven't played the harp for a week I'll sit down and it's like another person of me who plays the harp. I'm always amazed when I sit down and music comes out. I sort of watch my hands, they are on auto-pilot.

Do you feel like the spirits can work through you? That they can express something through you and you become an instrument?

I like to think that. I've never had a harp teacher. I went out and decided I wanted to play the harp after seeing a Robin Williamson concert. I still think of myself as messing with the harp, it kind of tells me what to do. If there's a song I want to learn part of it is hard work and part of it is a trance state. The way the song should be played will emerge. I've been trained to read music and to think of musical theory, but when I am playing the harp I don't sit down with staff paper and write out parts and think of harmonies. It just falls into place.

It sounds like the harp is playing you?

I do feel that way. There is no other instrument that I play that I react with the way I do with a harp. It's a strange, wonderful, weird and bizarre thing.

Does your harp have a name?

We are working on that, me and the harp. The last album I recorded, the Mary Mooncoin part is the name I have used for the harp. It's the public name that she doesn't mind being spread around.

So she has a magical name that probably shouldn't be revealed?

I haven't quite gotten that yet so we are working on it. Mary Mooncoin is the exoteric name; we are waiting for her esoteric name. I have heard ten-minute explications of all the things you can get out of Mary Mooncoin. Mooncoin is actually a place in Ireland, it's an Anglicization. There's a song called The Mooncoin Jig and I'm, pretty sure that's an Anglicization of a Gaelic place name. I'm sure the Gaelic spelling has nothing to do with the moon or with coins.

I was driving in my car one day and I had written on a tape box 'Baby Mary Mooncoin'. I used to play with a group called Baby Mary in Nashville. We had a live tape with the Mooncoin Jig on it so I had written that on the box.

It's definitely a Goddess image.

Oh yes, definitely. It has the Goddess and the moon is there. And it has Mary who you were obviously surrounded by as a child. It resonated, it works.

There's a guy I know from ADF who has this theory that if something feels right you probably shouldn't use it. He says most of us have been raised in a Judeo-Christian society and what feels right is probably not what we should be doing. I think sometimes that's true.

Nah. Not for this one. Mary Mooncoin is so appropriate; it's the physical moon that looks like a coin and the Mother Mary.

And the silver of the moon. And what can you buy with mooncoins? Is there anything else you want to add?

I have met a lot of people who are just stuck in being 'Celtic'. I use the term 'Celtic nerds'. It's just the be-all and the end-all. I think there's a lot out there. Even if you are working from a Celtic direction you shouldn't burn all your bridges to what is happening in the world. The more I do the academic Celtic studies thing the more I am realizing that there is very little you can point at in the literary-historical records that is purely Celtic and uninfluenced by other things.

There are Norse influences from the later Middle Ages. There was inter-marriage and they dealt with each other on a daily basis. There is a lot of Latin influence in what we have preserved in the manuscripts. I'm getting ready to do a thesis now and I'm trying to train myself to a point where I am as familiar with the Latin culture of the Middle Ages as I am with the Celtic culture because there haven't been many people who could do both.

You tend to get Celtic Studies people who know their stuff, but who don't have the tools in the other camp to realize how much interplay and interaction there was. Celtic people tend to be able to read Latin, but Latinists don't know anything about the Celtic languages.

For you that is honoring both sides of your ancestry.

I guess it's the bridge builder thing. Within the academic world I'm trying to get beyond the compartmentalized approach. I don't feel it's putting down the Celtic heritage to acknowledge the fact that they were seeking and they didn't have all the answers.

For years, especially in Ireland, the ways Celtic Studies was going, it was tied up with the whole political movement. When Ireland became its own country and The Republic of Ireland was formed, part of the revival was the idea that the scholarly stuff was pure Irish going back to the dawn of time. There's a big counter-reaction to that now in the Celtic Studies field. Now people are saying that almost everything comes from the Church and has been mutated, that Irish monks took what they learned from the Latin literature and 'Irished' it a bit. And that's too far in the other direction. Somewhere between those two extremes is where the truth lies.

That's a very Druidic way of looking at things. That's one reason why we always think in threes – you have one statement then you have the opposite statement and the job of the Druid is to find the harmony between the two. Just like the harp is built in three parts – that's why the harp is the symbol. You have the female part which is the soundbox and you have the male part which fits into the box and then you have the bridge on top, between the male and the female, between the intuitive and the rational, the active and the contemplative.

I think it's important to realize that. We have a lot of extremists out there. When I first started I had this great romantic notion of what Celtic Studies would be like, most of which was based on equal doses of The Incredible String Band, Jethro Tull and Dafydd ap Gwilym, who was a Medieval Welsh poet best known for writing love songs. He wrote love songs that sounded like Jethro Tull songs. That's what I felt the Middle Ages should be like – rowdy and drinking beer with wenches.

Then I actually got into it and I realized there is very little stuff like that, it's mostly dry material which I have learned to love, like the praise-poetry. There are acres and acres of place name lore, which is very dry reading, but there is a lot contained there, just the fact that people would want to write thousands of words about the names of things on the land and what they mean.

A friend of mine went to visit a Scottish-Gaelic poet from the post WWII Scottish Gaelic revival, Sorley MacLean. They went for a walk; he lives on a peninsula that takes about an hour and a half to walk to. This poet, who is definitely a Bard in the old sense, had a name for every little lump of ground that was distinguishable from another one. Every little stream, a hillock, and pile of rocks. And the names all had stories. He's probably the last person who can name all that stuff in the landscape down to the little details.

I have talked to Native Americans who can find the grave of someone who died six hundred years ago because they have that kind of detail in the oral tradition.

The more I learn about Native Americans the more they remind me of the Celts. My uninformed notion was that when white people got here they came in and just conquered everybody by brute force. If you look at the history it wasn't hordes of white people coming in and conquering everyone. A small group of outsiders came in and the native peoples who were in conflict with each other looked at this and decided to use these people against their enemies. It was a tool from the outside that got way out of control.

The same thing happened in the Celtic countries. Before they knew it the outsiders were too strong. It was fifty Spaniards and a few hundred thousand disgruntled subject peoples who saw the Spanish as a way to get rid of their oppressors, the Aztecs. They didn't realize they had come to stay. They could have not let them in in the first place and maintained that for quite a while.

With the Celtic peoples in Britain it was the Germanic raiders. At first they would come in and sometimes get their plunder and sometimes not until someone decided they could use them against their enemies and before you knew it, it was out of control.

Where they are now, the minority communities in what was once their native land, endangered languages, societies breaking down, are the same. If you say that in Britain a lot of people will get offended because you are comparing them to these 'savages' running around in loincloths. You have to be careful who you say it to.

Since this has come up, and since we are living here on American soil, how do you think the native spirits figure in the Celtic revival or the Druid path here on Turtle Island, America?

Obviously Celtic people were very attached to the land. They wanted to know the history in the minutest detail. If something was called 'Malcom's Knoll' there was a story telling you why it was called that. If the original story was lost, one would be created to fill the gap.

If we are trying to make that kind of connection in America I think the Native Americans, to the extent that their traditions have managed to stay intact, know the land better than we do. I think you can deal with this land from a Celtic framework, but if you want to get to know the land then the Native Americans are the ones who can tell you the name of that knoll and what the story is.

The sad thing is that a lot of times they can't, especially here in the Northeast.

That's the thing about memory. It's supposed to keep you from having to re-invent the wheel every generation and that's been broken. What we are trying to do our ancestors spent thousands of years putting together and passing along and somewhere along the line we lost it. And now we are trying, in a short period of time, to reassemble generations of knowledge about the land and our relationship with it. And Europe is not much better.

Yes, there was this little thing called The Inquisition. A temporary pause in the thread. What would be your advice to someone who wants to go on the Bardic path?

Robin Williamson says whoever wants to be a poet must take up 'the harp, sorrow, and the open road'. I think it's probably possible to be a Bard without playing the harp. I don't want to be harpocentric.

I would say the Celtic material is a very good training ground.

Robin Williamson is my paradigm of what a modern Bard can do. He doesn't just get the song out of a book, learn the words and perform it. When he performs something it becomes his song. He can do a performance that is half traditional and half original and it's seamless. His original material is full of tradition and he puts his own voice to the traditional material. Treating traditional material as if it has to be done in a certain way just kills it. And I don't think you can project magic if you are reading the music off of a piece of paper.

The Tarot Fool is one of my totems. If you are doing things right you can close your eyes and kind of blunder forward and you'll go the right way. If you are really on the path and the power is flowing, you will do fine.

'Brahm' Stuart De Usoz

Interviewed July 25, 1996
Starwood Festival, Sherman, NY

'Brahm' Stuart De Usoz has been a performer of Celtic music for many years in the United States and in Europe. He learned to play fiddle, tin whistle, and bodhran in the Berea peninsula of Southwest Ireland and is the leader of the musical group Shaman, which performs regularly for the Irish and Pagan communities.

Shaman's recordings include Feels So Good Live!, a collection of high energy Celtic-rock jigs, The Green Man, a blend of acoustic and rocked-out renditions of traditional and original music, Live! Hobbit Day '92, Elven energy that takes you to Middle Earth, Ode to Mother Earth, an all-acoustic recording of original songs, somber and ecstatic, Dans Mediterraneo, folk songs and dances from Spain, Israel, Italy and Greece, Music for a Faere Day, Celtic and English songs and dance tunes, and Flight to the Crossroads, a solo album featuring Stuart on vocals with blues-rock New Orleans rhythm and soulful electric guitar.

These days you can catch him on the YouTube channel Shaman Starseed.

Can you talk about your childhood, about how you were raised in terms of your spiritual upbringing?

I was raised in a dysfunctional family as far as divorce and alcoholism. I was raised Catholic, but it was not a very religious family by any means. I grew up in New Orleans and my mother raised me pretty much. She had a very strong, firm belief in God and in doing good. She is a deeply religious person even though she doesn't go to church. I went to a Jesuit high school for one year and I left my mother's home when I was fourteen.

I read the *Bhagavad Gita* when I was thirteen, which totally changed my life. I went into my grandfather's library looking for a book, it was like throwing darts, I just spun around and put my finger on this book, a little bitty paperback called *The Song of God*, a Mentor Classic translation by Christopher Isherwood and some Swami or Yogi guy who collaborated with him. I read this, I had just started eating acid at the time and smoking a lot of pot. Everything in this book rang clear to me as far as the psychological desire and the need to escape the wheel of Samskara. The whole nine yards just clicked with me, it enabled me to cope with my whole condition in a really distraught family.

Then I moved to Mississippi with my uncle because my mother thought I was becoming too derelict – I was skipping school and stuff like that, smoking pot. I ended up going to a private Episcopal school because my uncle is kind of rich. He had lots of kids so I was just one more.

There was a mushroom field maybe one mile away from school. Down there *Psilocybin cubensis* grow in the cow paddies, wild, after every rain in the spring and fall. So this became one of my pastimes. In fact for the rest of high school, right into college, this became a regular sacrament for me and it totally opened me up. More than any of my friends I was having religious experiences every week. I was armed with the *Bhagavad Gita*, with this idea of the Astral Plane and the Battlefield of Opposites, and the onepointedness, the need to concentrate on the light within and the soul that was looking to unfold.

I became very aware of nature. I became aware of nature spirits and I had never heard of nature spirits. I became aware of cloud spirits and tree spirits and lake spirits. The green of the grass just spoke to me in such a way that I was in bliss. I was very reverent about the whole thing, I didn't take it lightly.

I was playing guitar then, I played Neil Young songs and Bob

Dylan and I made up a lot of songs. I was a budding musician. Then I decided that I wanted to travel around so I decided to become a Merchant Marine Seaman. I wanted to go to China and India and Australia and Europe, this was my ambition. Then my uncle and aunt said I had to go to college and get a degree so I could be something in life. I said nope, I'm going to sea.

They found a college in Texas that had a Merchant Marine school; it had a mushroom field near it too. I quit college after a year and I became a street musician. I gravitated back to New Orleans where I met a bunch of street musicians who played fiddles and washboards and Appalachian music and jazz. I became a guitarist who would back them up. Every now and then they would play an Irish tune and I always thought that was kind of neat.

Then another band came through, the Skiffle Buskers and they were *really* magic. They had a dancing girl and they were all hippies, really Old World. They lived in a commune in Saskatchewan and I ended up travelling back there with them and planting trees in their tree planting camp.

Then, back at the commune, they put on a tape of The Chieftains. It was Matt Molloy on the flute and fiddles and all and I said what kind of music is *that?* And they said Irish music, real Irish music. I said, man *that* is for me. I had already played rock and blues and bluegrass and Appalachian and I realized I was into folk music more than rock music but this Irish music was something. The quickness and the energy just brought out memories of nature and the energy I felt when I was tripping and stuff. It was, like, *there.*

I gave my guitar to the leader and I went back to New Orleans to the fiddle maker I knew and I got a fiddle and I went straight to Ireland. I spent many months there. I ended up staying with some very Earth-type hippies who were very Druidic even though they didn't call themselves Druids. They read really cool out of print books from the eighteen hundreds written by so and so 'The Arch Druid'. They were into dowsing and Ley lines and standing stones and sacred trees. I hung out with them for months on the Beara peninsula in West Cork.

Where they lived was a boreen, a little road. All over Ireland there are stone walls to keep the cows together. On this boreen there was a nine foot stone wall whereas all the other stone walls I had seen were only waist high. This was to keep the deer in; the King's forest was on the other side. It had never been cut down. Even the noble English who had taken over kept it primeval because it was a hunting ground for them.

So they lived on the edge of this forest. In fact one of the walls of their house was this high stone wall along the boreen. It was very rustic with no running water. They had a stream that ran right by their house. It was pristine. They would dip the bucket in right there to get their water.

They told me stories and stories about the Fairies. They had this island there in the bay near Glen Gariff, Bantry Bay. There are three Fairy forts on the island, ring mounds and barrows. It was a sacred place and nobody would live there except maybe one keeper who had a protective, custodial job.

Exxon or Texaco, one of the oil companies, leased the island and decided to build a supertanker port there because it was one of the two places in the world where you could bring in a super tanker, right against the land without having to do anything dredge wise.

So everyone said, oh, the Fairies aren't going to like this, and sure enough within a short amount of time after they had completed this big complex, it burnt to the ground. Half the people say it was the Fairies and the other half say it was the IRA. Maybe the IRA was working for the Fairies! But at any rate Exxon left and the Fairy mounds are still there and you can see the burned out tanks on one side of the island.

This place abounded in stone circles and standing stones. They would take me on a walk and show me half a dozen in a day. There was this one peculiar spot where they had a standing stone once and the bully of the town, a hundred years ago, decided that he was going to knock it down. He had no regard for the sacredness of it and he knocked it down. And out of that very spot grew a Rowan, a Hawthorn and a Holly tree in a spiral. The trunks are wrapped around each other as if somebody had trained them. There was *unbelievable* energy coming out of this spot. They say that when dowsers go there the dowsing rods just go crazy.

I stayed there, playing my fiddle and practicing. I had just come from Willy Clancy Week, which is in Milltown Malbay in County Clare.

This is probably one of the best festivals to get traditional music. It takes place the first week in July. I was there for the whole week, absorbing the music, and then I went to West Cork. They played penny whistle and bodhran so we played and played. I was totally immersed in it.

Before long I was entranced. I'd be playing a tune and all of a sudden I'd feel Celtic knotwork going through me. I was having visions as I was feeling the tunes.

The dance is the same; Ceilidh dancing makes the knotwork too.

Right. I was feeling it and it was coming through my feet, through my solar plexus, through my heart, echoing from my throat, out of my hands and my fiddle. My third eye would connect to it outside somewhere and I became a Celtic musician. I was transformed.

It wasn't anything that anybody taught me or any beliefs that I had, it was just a visual thing and my connection with nature. I realized there was some message in the knotwork, some deep message that spoke of the wind going through the trees and the goats running up the hill and a lady milking a cow and all the pictures of life and nature unfolding. Dying and unfolding and dying and unfolding. It was all wrapped into this music, in tone poems.

I used to go up to this standing stone that was very close to their house. It was on one of the keeper's properties. He was this old man who only spoke Gaelic. Every now and then you'd be walking around and the hair would bristle on the back of your neck and you'd look up and he'd be standing there.

I asked him once why he kept pieces of iron on the standing stone and he more or less told me I shouldn't be asking questions about things I don't know about. My friends told me it was to keep the Fairies down.

Because they don't like iron.

Right. My friends told me that certain families owned certain bits of land and that certain people in the family end up inheriting the job of keeping the Fairies down, under the ground, or out of mischief. They take this very seriously. Sometimes I'd go there and there would be these iron nails and I'd look up and he'd be looking at me.

One time I was standing there and I was playing this tune that really touched my soul. And I looked up and there was a Deva looking at me. It was as tall as me. And my eyes were changing as I was playing this music. The eyes of the Deva were so beautiful, they were a little bit slanted and pointy at the ends and there was so much wisdom in them. They were almost snake-like, but warm. The face was just like you would think – pure, beauteous, pointy, and my eyes went like his. They disappeared.

My eyes became his eyes. I can't describe it. I don't know what happened. The way that his eyes looked, I looked like that. The way that I held my eyes became different, the muscles or something in my eyes changed. His eyes became my eyes. That was a mystical experience.

I know what I saw, and I believed it. And I know that he was a guardian spirit and that he liked me because I was so imbibed with the energy of the Celtic music. It was the same thing he was doing as an overlord of the nature spirits who were unfolding the flowers and unfurling the buds in the trees. He knew that there was a kindredness here.

The overwhelmingness came over me and then it was gone, and I never saw it again, but it stayed with me. I'll be playing and it's there with me. I knew that he was a local guardian spirit and now it's in the way I see the trees.

All the trees have eyes don't they?

Yes, I see them... I'm not saying this was Pan or anything. I'm almost sure that he was a local guardian spirit. He was just checking me out, and lending a bit of his energy my way.

Now I know that in the English language we 'play' music and we also 'play' soccer and 'play' football and 'play' cards. It's a divertissement so to speak, of our mind, away from what's important. My point is that I think I 'touch' music. I 'invoke' it. In Spanish it's 'tocar'. 'Tocar musica' and 'jugar football'. To me that says 'touch'. It's not a game. It's something very serious. Music is actually descriptive of what goes on in the etheric worlds and beyond, beyond the visible worlds. What is music? What is a melody? I've thought and thought about that.

I have realized that a melody is a collection of tones put into a certain rhythm, usually with a beginning and an end. And certain tones are used to put a melody in a certain key. In e minor you use the e minor scale. In e Dorian, the minor modal scale of the Celts, you use that scale. The different scales invoke different psychological or different emotive qualities.

Celtic music basically uses four scales, major, minor, Dorian and

Mixolydian. Celtic music is predominately melodic music. The only harmony they had, going back a hundred and fifty years, was the drone of the bag-pipe, with the notable exception of harp music. I liken that to the drone of the bees and the drone of the forest.

Stuart breaks into song:

In the forest of my dreams

There are trees so brilliant, greens so bright,
The grass so soft it seems that I could walk all day and dance
all night
The air so fresh and clean
I could breathe so deep and fill my body
With the vibrant splendor
of that magic forest light.

In the forest of my dreams
there are birds of many colors
In the branches of the trees
Softly singing sounds that mingle
With the buzzing of the bees
As the crickets drone the undertones
The voice of Mother Nature
In the forest of my dreams.

In the forest of my dreams
there is music every morning
as a fair Elven Queen
comes a singing followed by her band
Of Elven minstrels keen
Playing lutes and strings their music rings
And floods with light the forest
In the forest of my dreams.

In the forest of my dreams
Only loving thoughts may enter
Through that magic leafy screen
For the watchers of the forest
Are powerful indeed
And there is no place
For those who waste
The magic of the forest

In the forest of my dreams.

In the forest of my dreams
Gurgles from the ground a flowing spring
I drink to my heart's ease
As I splash the water soothing
To my face and feel the breeze
Ah! to smell the living fragrances
And see the many flowers
In the forest of my dreams.

In the forest of my dreams
In the breathing electricity
that oozes from the leaves
There's a magnetism 'bout the place
Unearthly does it seem
Ah! The eyes of mortals rarely see the
Hidden inner beauty
In the forest of my dreams.

In the forest of my dreams
magic rays of golden power
filter down between the leaves
from the sun's pulsating fire
In the clearings can be seen
As he glides across the boundless sky
Embracing all creation
In the forest of my dreams.

In the forest of my dreams
There is always joy and laughter
There's no death nor disease
Every face is young and beautiful
Beneath those arching trees

The shade of evil hath not fallen
on this earthly paradise
The forest of my dreams.

In the forest of my dreams

Where the immortal ones they walk sometimes
Beneath those mighty trees
And to be with them and feel inside
The depths which they must see
Ah! There's so much work that must be done
Before I really realize
The forest of my dreams.

This is my heart singing. This is the Queen and the King and the Elves. This is where I am at. This is Tir Na N'Og. It's the Celticness of me. There is nothing more I can say about it than that poem.

Now, getting back to the symbolic matrix, that's what I think a melody is. A melody has a beginning and an end and it uses a scale and or a mode as the musicologists would say. All of Western music has been relegated to major and minor scales. But Celtic music and a lot of folk music uses different scales than major or minor. So we have to go into the old church modes to describe them and talk about them.

One of the most common ones is the Dorian mode or Sun Scale as I call it. It's the most balanced scale. It's also called the minor modal scale. Suffice it to say that by using different scales and collections of tones different emotions or different qualities of the Godhead in nature can be conveyed, invoked, touched, and sung to. And you can use the planets too. The Pythagoreans say that each scale has a planetary significance.

The Harmony of the Spheres.

Yes. I ascribe to a neo-Platonic Medieval chart that works for me. It ascribes the Dorian scale to the Sun, the major scale, which is Aolian, to Venus. The minor scales are the Moon and the Myxolydian scale, which is common in Celtic music, is Saturnine. That gives you the energies that are associated with the emotional qualities that can come down and convey to and mix with mankind.

But this still doesn't tell me what a melody is. What is a melody? How do you make up a melody? I have studied a lot of Celtic music and they have all these different titles from nature, The Thrush in the Strand, The Kid on the Mountain, The High Reel, The Humours of this place and that place. Humours, I believe, are place spirits. It's a very old archaic word.

Now a nature spirit, what does it do? It might flit here and there and open up flowers and coax the leaves to grow. Or it might even be a mischievous spirit that would want to go off and mingle with mankind by taunting them, knocking on their heads psychically or playing with their emotional bodies. They probably ride our emotional bodies like we go surfing, especially really passionate, fiery people. In fact, sometimes when I am in a passionate blaze of playing my fiddle I feel that they are all around me.

The Arabic people call them Djinns, Fire Beings. They feed off human energy.

Yeah. I feel them all around and having lots of fun. And I'm having fun too because I know they are there.

Music is a symbolic matrix because it is conveying what goes on in the astral and etheric planes and things that happen in nature, including humans just squabbling with each other. That's part of nature too. We are part of nature no matter what we do. No matter what the emotional sophistication of our music it is all part of nature because we are created by nature.

Celtic music has so many tunes that are tone poems to me. Like The Pigeon on the Gate. How can somebody write a tune called The Pigeon on the Gate? Some people say the fiddler looked out the window and the first thing he saw was the pigeon on the gate. Maybe that's true. But when I play The Thrush on the Strand I see a bird singing and I feel a bird singing and living and flipping his wings and being in a happy place that he is very at home in. Birds don't think in a language like me or you. Their modus operandi is birdlike. They have bird brains.

The point is that these melodies are tone poems. By touching a melody, especially the Celtic melodies, we can touch archetypal energy. I don't think we invent melodies, by the way. I think we invoke them or else we discover them. In my mind all the melodies that exist are out there somewhere in some God-like universe and the only thing that we can do is discover them. And the Celts had such an affinity with nature that they were able to discover some that were really close to the Fairy energy that underlay the current of life. When I hear The Thrush on the Strand I feel the life of the thrush on the strand.

It's not necessary that the person who made this up had any kind of esoteric knowledge. He naturally was in tune. It was just like breaking an egg for him.

There is a tune called The Flowers of Red Hill. Have you ever seen a flower in the wind? It clicks a little bit because the stem is holding it, but the wind wants to take it. The wind comes along and bends it but it snaps back. It makes a click. I feel the Flower Fairies in that tune too. They are alive for me.

By the way, in Celtic music the three is the most important thing, the number three. And the rhythm is very important too. All throughout you will hear rolls, little shamrocks they call triplets. They have little Fairy grace-notes in them. Only Irish music has this peculiar type of ornamentation.

You know how when you are dancing a reel you go; one, two, three, four, five, six, seven, then one, two, three, one, two, three, as you step? Have you thought about that one? What does the seven mean?

Of course I have thought about that. All of these are septatonic scales, seven note scales. Seven to me is the most sacred number.

There are seven colors in the rainbow and there are seven days in the week and the Seven Wonders of the World. I think that because the Celts were tuned into archetypal magic energy and because seven is innately a magic number they used it in their music.

Nobody knows anything about Druids, but the Greeks had seven planets. Some so-called Arch Druids wrote stuff down in the 1700s; my friends had some of their books. But why did they go seven, three, three? Well maybe because if they kept going they would never come back! Maybe seven steps was just the right size for their cottage, otherwise they would just keep dancing out the window! But why didn't they decide on six? Or eight?

It really saddened my heart to find out when I got to Ireland, that so many of the best musicians were drunks. All the music was in the pub and these guys were often belligerent people. Some of these guys had a real wildness about them. But it didn't matter if they were drunk because they were in a trance and they were channeling the music.

When I was in Cork I went into a pub and the pub musician was drunk. He said; 'Oh, so you are playing Irish music and you are from America?' I said; 'Yeah.' So he said; 'Let me see you play.' I played my fiddle for him. All of a sudden he changed.

'You better watch out! The Fairies are going to get you and they won't let you go! Don't go in the pubs because they won't let you away from the drink!'

He was telling me that they had chained him to this existence. He was mad. Period. He had to stay drunk all the time and I realized this guy was dead serious. He was telling me that the Irish music would get into me and it wouldn't let me go and I had better watch out. I think that some people who touch that wild energy can't handle reality any more. The music is like a psychedelic drug and the alcohol is like a grounding downer.

I was reading *The Fairy Faith in Celtic Countries* and they have a story about a piper who claims that he was taken away and taught everything by the Fairies. I think they even had his picture in the book. It just blew my mind that this guy had his picture in there. I believe him.

I have read *The Candle of Vision* by A.E. He could see the hosts of Fairies moving. The Fairies can't think for themselves, they have a group mind. The nature spirits are not intelligent in the way we are because they aren't egotistical. And he could see their movement, he described it as being undulating rhythmic motion that was beautiful to behold. To me the melodies themselves speak of this.

We humans have Fey energy in us too. Every human does, just like a tree. If a tree has to have a Fairy to open it up, what do you think we need to get our heart pumping and to get all this stuff going through our bodies? We have Fairies inside of us, Devas.

There is a book published by the Theosophical Society called *Devas and Men*. Its quotes from Blavatsky and Bailey from the Tibetan master, D.K. they were channeling. He gets into all the different kinds of Devas, Fairy energy. There is Fairy energy for the blood and for the metabolism. We can only see the cells and the material world, but behind that world, in the etheric, something else is going on. And in the astral world it is something else again and beyond that another thing. That is where the Devic beings are doing their thing. The matter that we see is only the visible result of their workings.

The most beautiful thing we have to describe a melody is the Caduceus, the Winged Staff of Mercury with the two snakes. Every melody has two parts, I am not talking about atonal music or Schoenberg, I am talking about traditional music. In traditional music you have a melody which speaks and another melody which answers. The two parts are having a conversation over an issue. The issue is the pole. It is also the resolve. There is dialogue, 'dia' means across and 'log' is the word, from 'Logos', which means God.

Dia means Goddess.

'Dia' also means across. 'Dia-logos' could mean the Goddess and the God having conversation. The resolve is the tonic of the thing, the end, and the resolution.

You hear that in Indian ragas too.

Oh absolutely, but that's much too complicated for my little mind. So my basic idea is that if you can learn, even as a non-musician, to diddle or to hum a tune, even if you can't carry a tune with your voice, but you just hum it in your mind, then you are going to incorporate that archetypal energy that the tune is invoking. And if you learn a tune it will bring something out of your unconscious. I think that we have everything somewhere inside us and this will bring things closer to the surface. This will bring the qualities into our astral and mental bodies and make them coalesce. By doing this you have just learned a mantra of sorts, a Celtic mantra. It won't give you the power to levitate or anything, but it will give you the power to come closer to nature.

What about the wonderful Celtic musicians we have today, like Eileen Ivers from New York City. They aren't thinking about larks in the morning or kids on the mountain. What are they doing when they come up with a new tune?

It's a tradition. They don't have to think about Fairies at all. When the tradition gets hold of them they don't know it, but they are conjuring Fairy energy. But believe me, Eileen Ivers knows it. Davey Spillane knows it. A lot of them know it. Even if they don't believe one bit of what I am saying about conjuring Fairy energy they were taught to do it by their parents who were taught by their parents.

You can't learn this by reading music. These masters that you are talking about were taught from when they were children. They were taught by their parent or their uncles.

Who got it directly from nature, over in Ireland.

Right. And the Fairy magic is in their bloodlines too. They are born to play music. I think that spirits come back who are involved in conjuring up this energy. I've seen eight-year-old kids in Ireland who are masters of the Uillean pipes. Their parents are standing there in awe. They say that; 'Ever since he was five he wanted the pipes and he just insisted that we go to the pub.' And the kid has a trance-like look in his eyes. I've seen this over and over.

Timmy Britton described to me how he was bitten by the Uillean pipes as a teenager. If he couldn't play the pipes he would have pipe parts with him at all times. Wherever he was, he was piping. He couldn't stop.

That's exactly what I am talking about. He's a beautiful soul. I love him, man. And he knows what I am talking about. I think the Uillean pipes are the most Fairy-like of all the instruments.

Timmy has this rap about the Vedas, about the drone, which is like the Om, which is like the background sound of the universe, the Atma, the universal sound. Then out of the Atma precipitate the different energies. The Deities come out and then the nature spirits, and then everything else and those are the melodies over the drone.

Yeah. And the melodies are in other planes that are coming out of the Atma. I see it as dice, flying through the air. Certain dice become the energy that translates into The Thrush on the Strand. On their way, as the dice are flying, is the etheric energy I am talking about. Music describes the energy before it makes its presence known. That's my point.

Bryan Perrin

Interviewed July 26, 1996

Starwood Festival, Brushwood Folklore Center, Sherman, New York

Bryan is a longtime member of ADF where he has served as Chronicler and editor of Druid's Progress, an occasional magazine put out by that group. He was also Senior Druid of Green Man Grove, the first successful Druid grove in the New York City area, now defunct. He is a visual artist, an award-winning set designer, and has created illustrations for Druid's Progress and many other Pagan publications including Mezlim, Enchante, Green Egg, and Metro Druid Nuz.

Ordained as a one of the first six ADF Priests in 2002, Bryan now lives on a mountainside in upstate New York with his family and celebrates the eight holidays as Ritual Officiant for Our Whole Protogrove, ADF. He is an art and environmental educator. You can visit his website at www.bryanperrinstudio .com or read his Druid rants on his blog www.themadtrad.blog spot.com.

Can you talk a bit about your religious upbringing as a child?

My parents and my grandparents were not affiliated with any church so I wasn't raised in any particular religious community.

They were into a lot of different things and there was a strong sense of personal spiritual integrity. I was exposed to a number of different things on the outside but not on the inside. Everybody was pretty much an independent Protestant.

The fact that my younger brother died in an accident at a young age on my grandparents' land, helped establish associations in my head and heart of family and place and the dead and communication and connection. My dad's side of the family was very folksy and actually I could claim all kinds of lineage about that but I don't want to.

As in Celtic lineage?

Not specifically Celtic, but I have a family tradition that is passed on, particularly storytelling, which is similar to seanchaidh and stuff like that. I grew up in this funky place near Toledo, Ohio. That was where the family was from, but I wasn't from there because my father was in the Navy. I was bounced around from San Diego to Rhode Island and I had to fight with the local kids. When I hit puberty age I was back in Toledo and later I went to and graduated from Ohio University. Moving around gave me a sense of reverence for locale and place and an understanding of feeling like an outsider.

I was exposed to Pagans (who generally referred to themselves as 'witches') at around the same time I was reading Tolkien and stuff like that, about age nine or ten. My dad's second marriage several years later was a big art event attended by many local witches who were in Lady Circe's coven and other folks in this progressive alternative culture spirituality. There was this weird stuff with my family and what would be the Pagan lineage. As a teen, I was exposed to some people that were calling themselves witches and all the cool books (one of my favorite being *Faeries* by Brian Froud and Alan Lee), whether occult or spiritual or herbalist or magick and also to all that 'green' hippie stuff. My father's grandfather was involved with the historical society; we come from an old antiquarian, eccentric family.

There are Indians on my mother's father's side of the family, I don't know what tribe because they were 'colored' and you weren't supposed to talk about it. You couldn't talk about that stuff until the 70s. That was when you could say you believed in spirits, things like that.

I went through my little Christian phase in high school when the evangelistic Christians came around and said; 'Don't you believe in God?' and of course everybody said yes. So I hung out with them for a year and read the Bible. They would have different ministers show up; they wanted us to speak in tongues. I choked up at that point. For me the religion was about integrity and I believed that Jesus 'saved my soul', but I didn't want to feel prompted for a disingenuous performance just because there was a new minister in town. I do believe that spirit comes in and influences us. It was years later, post-graduate, that I began thinking about nature religions and Druids.

Where did you actually first run into Druids?

I ran into people that called themselves Druids in college. They called me 'Druid' in college and I ran into anybody there that was Druid-like in whatever weird way they associated with that. Whether it had to do with Celtic stuff or trees or Tim the Enchanter from Monty Python's Holy Grail, chances were I knew more than they did about it.

Post-college, it really was book stores in NYC that supplied me with information, either it was cultural folklore information or magical information. I first became associated with a group of Druids by answering a classified ad from ADF in the back of the Pagan Magazine Green Egg that I had purchased from my favorite local Pagan shop, the Magical Childe.

So how do you define Druidism? What is a Druid?

A Druid is somebody who is hip to the aesthetics of what past Druids have been. Anybody that is calling themselves a Druid has to understand where other people who have called themselves Druid are coming from, from the 17th century on. It has to do with an aesthetic that has to do with romanticism; it has to do with the landscape, with the person, the place, transience, and patterns and cycles. It has to do with the understanding of where you are in that cycle and I have come to understand it in the Vedic sense in terms of sacrifice.

The basic understanding is that the world is wonderful and great, but everything is about sacrifice. A Druid's core responsibility or function is overseeing of sacrifice. The reason we are here is to enjoy and what we enjoy is a gift and what we have to give back to the world is a sacrifice. We are here to experience and then we transfer that experience by giving back to the world in a beneficial way.

As Druids we try to give back to the world in a way where we go beyond this regular world. We want to drop our Magic offering into the fountain and we want it to make things different. We want it to go into that Otherworld. We hope that our Magic offering will make a difference to Them somehow and that if in Their world They think we are cool They will drip something into our world that will make a big difference to us. We become a kind of intermediary between this world and another world. I think there is something intrinsic in the Druidic process and in the Celtic process that has to do with the creative inspiration as a special way of leading into that Otherworld as opposed to how Zen awareness or something like that that leads you into yourself.

We have the heroic aspect and we have the creative aspect. We are searching for a way to relate to this beautiful nature that we are all a part of and we are also looking for how we can express that back out to the group and how we can all grow better from the experience. It's a part of getting in touch with that Otherworld experience through the creative process that I think is unique to Druidism or to the Celtic way of thought.

Anybody, whether a 17th century monotheist, someone of other spiritual practices, whatever, is still attuning to a certain resonance that is there. People are aspiring to understand that oneness that everybody is looking for in religion. Even though I don't think Druidism is just about oneness we still find that encoded in the Druid frequencies of understanding.

We are at a point right now where the rest of the world is catching up with us. They are starting to see that it is cruel to be brutal to other cultures and it's cruel to take advantage of the Earth. But they haven't quite caught up with the fact that it's cruel to be cruel to other people and that religion is still a people business, even if it's a nature religion.

My personal experience has drawn from my relationship with and reverence for nature. The problem I have is that I didn't realize that getting involved with an organized religion, even an alternative one, would mean so many people problems.

I think you find that in every religion, not just Druidism.

Absolutely in every religion, and in every group too; but I think people going into Neo-Paganism get that heady mindset of; 'Oh wow, isn't this great that there are other people who feel the same way I do.' And then they find out they are still dealing with people so they have people problems, even though we have all come to this heady realization that nature is wonderful and the Earth is wonderful.

I am totally happy with this Earth, until I die. That is the way I am as a good Pagan Druid as I see it. I don't need a community or a spiritual group or a label or human comrades or the fellowship or the songs to practice my religion, even though it's nice when they are there. But human skills are required if we want to take our nature religion out into the real world.

You are a visual artist, a graphic artist, a painter and a sculptor. You make objects that represent your philosophy and which symbolize your religion. Can you talk about what it means to be a Druid and an artist?

I think it's vital in terms of the core essence, in terms of the truly personal spiritual effort of trying to make manifest out of nature a reflection of what you get from it. I feel as a Druid it is my duty to be able to say thank you nature, thank you world for all of this you are giving me. And also to go out of my way to say this is what I have to give back to you. Not only have you given me all of these wonderful things but you also gave me this talent and it isn't for me to waste. That's been a big part of my religious experience in terms of feeling good about myself.

It's something that may have made me seem more prominent than other people, I guess, because I have something to show, some weird material artifact, something that people can see. In some way that is a burden upon me, even though often people may not associate that thing with me. The whole Pagan artist sacrifice concept is an issue I am exploring. I think that sacrifice as art or art as sacrifice is a vital issue of Neo-Paganism.

I'm involved with different publishers who need art, black and white graphics. This art that I was doing that was inspired by mythology and such is my attempt to get to know and to get closer to these other worlds, these other beings. It is an attempted communication or prayer if you like.

One thing I did was to develop the Nemeton[25] here at Brushwood. It's a ten-hour drive for me; I'm in New York City. I get here a couple times of year, tops. All of a sudden a time came when I couldn't work on the site because now they are using it as a workshop space.

That's a little weird isn't it?

Oh yeah, politics beyond compare. So it turns into this thing of how do you avoid the politics and at the same time maintain the integrity of your sacrifice with the land? And so it turns into personal politics and how do you deal with this weird wonderful personal spiritual relationship you have with the nature spirits and the world and how do you groove that in with all these intruders who are also Earthling people who are calling themselves Druids or other Pagans?

Can you talk about your painting and your sculpture?

Most of what I have done was stuff inspired directly by the Pagan community and by ancient sources. My sources are the *La Tene* Celtic style and Romanian stuff, a lot of cross-cultural things. I tend to use certain symbols, iconography, like what you find in Marija Gimbutas' books. If you wear your Goddess-goggles then everything is a symbol of the Goddess.

That is Art History. Who knows what those symbols really mean mythologically? Sometimes they don't mean a thing, but they still mean cultural comparisons, which us history nuts are into. So we get into cross reasoning in terms of what people's interests are. In the Pagan market people's interests are not necessarily what is historical truth or fact.

My gig is that I am coming out of historical, Northern European Art History and the way they represented Gods, Deities and spirits in their wood-working and metallurgy and re-creating that and trying to convey the attitudes these people had about the Otherworld. And no, they weren't comic book heroes. Sometimes it was the household shovel or the household knife which had a little face on it. It all got blurred, whether it was a God or a spirit or an ancestor.

In Art History terms all they care about are lines and curves and styles of representation. I can see things representationally and I can see by the lines when the Romans hit the Celtic lands. I can see when they start representing that. And I can tell the work of Thracian slaves for Danish Lords. It's what I do for a living. Here I am thousands of years later.

So in a way what you are doing is Celtic Reconstructionism in the way some people are doing it through scholarship and liturgy and through Bardic work. You are doing it through visual arts.

Yes, that's what I am attempting to do, though it is not my intent to revive all of the Ancients' beliefs and how it all went down. A lot of people are pushing the gimmickry of the Celtic knotwork, but there is something underlying that. Personally, as a visual artist, I think it's impossible to read Celtic mythology and not be influenced by it. There is something essential about the nature of this old material that has been passed on. It has an effect upon people and it affects our understanding of how we deal with the world and it becomes religious and it becomes Druidic. It doesn't matter if people agree exactly with the Ps and Qs of dogma of religion. A lot of it has to do with passion, especially the Celtic stuff. Passion is intrinsic to it.

Is there anything you would like to add about Druidism in general?

The big thing is not to get too disappointed by dealing with people problems. Just keep on going. I truly, zealously, believe we have a wonderful religion. I just don't want to bang people over the head and tell them about it all the time. It isn't about marketing and group identity or getting it 'right'. It is about personal relationships between your innermost person and all these spiritual connections that we have with other beings. It is about gratitude.

Searles O'Dubhain

Interviewed September 21, 1996
Via internet

Searles is a working electrical engineer, a teacher of computer programming languages and of Celtic traditions, and plays banjo, bodhran and guitar. He has been published in a variety of Pagan journals and magazines including Keltria: Journal of Druidism and Celtic Magic and HearthFire. He is currently writing a book on Ogham divination. He has lectured before many Celtic and Druidic groups, was at one time a lay reader of the Anglican Communion, a vestryman of the Episcopal Church, and a church school administrator. He is a sponsoring member of the Association for Research and Enlightenment (ARE) founded by Edgar Cayce and co-founder of The Summerlands, a Druid online community.

Searles traces his lineage back to the O'Dubhains that were lords of Slane and Cnogba, circa 1000 CE. In the Metrical Dindshenchas his family name is also listed as Duban, who was said to have constructed the passage mound at Dowth some 4,000 years earlier. He said:

> If Irish culture had not been destroyed during the 17th century, perhaps I could have also claimed an unbroken family tradition from those times. As it is I'll have to sleep on the graves of my ancestors to have any chance of regaining their ways and wisdom.

Beyond all of that he has chased a deer; caught a fish; talked to a tree; been watched by a house, as well as falling off one. He has looked down both ends of a rifle; travelled at 128mph backwards; seen the moon turn blood-red and has spent the night in a cloud on the highest mountain east of the Mississippi. He added; 'In many ways I have seen that what we sometimes call reality, may well be a dream.'

Can you describe your religious upbringing as a child?

To separate my religious upbringing from the rest of my childhood is really not possible, because in my experience, within my family life, and within my community, religion was not differentiated from the rest of life. I was born and raised in a small Southern US town during the late 1940s and early 50s. As such, you could say that I was born into a community that had seen very little change in its ways and customs for hundreds of years.

The Old South was a place that lived by a code in much the same way that our Celtic ancestors also lived. Truth, honor, and hospitality were the basis of society. Violating the written law could land you in jail. Violating the 'code' was a crime punished by being outcast from society, beyond nine waves and never to make amends.

My religious upbringing was threefold. I learned my first lessons from my family. We were very close-knit, as my uncle and aunt lived in the upstairs part of our house and my grandparents lived next door. The farm of my great-great-great-grandfather was only ten miles away and my other relatives mostly lived in the same town as I. The town had then, and even now, only about two thousand people living within it, and my father seemed to know every one of them on a first name basis.

My grandmother could have told you how we were related to each of them, being the family genealogist. I learned my connection to family from her, as well as many a tale regarding the 'faeries' and 'things that walk in the night'. Within her flower garden, faeries were constantly chased as I endeavored to catch them, butterflies being faeries in disguise. From my grandfather and my father, I learned of our connection to the Land and the animals around us.

Many days I would walk with my grandfather as he ploughed the fields, sometimes walking behind a mule and sometimes pushing a hand plough on his own. My father would take my brothers and I into the woods to check out a new rifle. Sometimes we would go to the river for swimming and fishing. My mother taught me the value of truth. If ever there was a person worthy of being a Brehon, it is her. In general, my family taught me to love the Land, to respect the Truth, and to always be a part of family and community. These three ways are the foundation of Celtic religion and tradition.

The second part of my religious upbringing as a child saw me attending a variety of Southern Baptist and Methodist churches. My major impression of these churches was that they were very clean, with a lot of sharp edges. They abounded in pictures of the Risen Christ, with hardly any emphasis being placed upon his crucifixion. When Easter came, it was a time to rejoice in Jesus' victory over death. We did not celebrate Lent, nor did we closely embrace the concept of 'Original Sin'. Adam and Eve were relatives that had behaved badly, were cast out of Eden, and now we were making a new life for ourselves by toiling in this world. We studied the Bible and we learned our hymns and psalms.

The churches of my youth were places where children were 'seen but not heard'. They were places created by mankind to glorify God, seeming to me to be very artificial and removed from the rest of our religion. As I grew older, I sought religion on my own, being baptized by immersion at the age of fourteen in a Baptist church. The duality and hypocrisy of life inside of these churches, as contrasted to the actual religion of life outside of the churches, was what led me to look elsewhere.

This quest for religion and connection of spirit had its roots within the tales that were told at night on the front porch of my grandparents' house. I was frequently swept away as their words conjured images from the darkness. My brother and I would lay abed scaring and thrilling one another as we conjured our own shapes from the darkness. We frequently discussed our dreams and developed our dream talents to the point of being able to dream lucidly. In our dreams, we were the ones controlling the reality. We were able to fly, to die and be reborn, to face the Gods and our inner fears.

To this ability to lucidly dream, I eventually coupled the ability to meditate and to control my breathing, as well as regulating my heartbeat. At the age of sixteen, as I lay struggling with questions of religious philosophy and the pitfalls of circular arguments, I was 'taken'. I was called forth and I passed through the doorway that opened into a world apart from this one. I was aided in this passage by a being of sparkling golden light who embraced me with an overwhelming ecstasy. Our thoughts passed from being to being. No words were necessary. Between us there was only Truth. In that place between places, we could see anywhere, be anywhere, know anything and create anything, yet we also had the knowledge that we really had little to actually change. Creation is generally as it should be, in spite of our individual perspectives.

This Otherworldly experience showed me many things and many wonders. Most of these experiences were non-physical and have little relationship to this world. What I did see about our physical world, were the many ways in which it is contained within a greater reality, and how each part of it interconnects with every other part of it. Leaving that No-Place and the golden Being of Truth to return to my body, was a difficult decision. My decision to return to this life was based upon the certain knowledge that there are many things yet to be accomplished within this world. We each have our work to do and our choices to make. This mystical experience reinforced my connection to the Otherworld, clearly showing me a life beyond this life, as well as a joy and purpose within all of being.

Upon my return to my body, I immediately began to read and study everything that I could find about philosophy, psychology, physics, religion, and the occult. I studied the writings of Edgar Cayce.

I took classes in world religions and philosophy. I immersed myself in the physical sciences and engineering. This study, coupled with my quest for my roots, eventually led me to discover a path called Draiocht and a people that followed the Ways of the Wise.

How did you first hear about Druids?

My first knowledge of Druids came from reading about King Arthur and the Knights of the Round Table, as well as their quest for the Holy Grail. After that, I read everything that I could find about the Celts and Druids. I'm still reading and it has been over twenty years.

What caused you to become involved, what drew you into that path?

Two things got me involved with Draiocht: First, my quest for the Truth and second, my search for my roots.

How do you define Druidism?

Druidism is a search for the Truth that exists throughout all of Creation. In its most basic form, it is living that Truth within the Three Worlds of Land, Sea, and Sky. It is a stewardship of the Nine Harmonies that should exist in the Three Worlds. These Harmonies have many names and guardians. They include the concepts of: foundation, substance, form, life, growth, intuition, awareness, inspiration, and authority. Druidism is the power to tune such harp strings of Creation so that their Music might be brought to Life. This act of creation can often be done by working within the No-Place, the realm of the 'in between'.

Druidism is Draiocht. It is both Old and New. It is both Now and Then. It is the ability to bring the Truth from one world to the next. It is literally upholding the Truth of Creation, 'the Truth against the World'.

How were you trained?

I was guided by my Otherworldly teachers and my own personal thirst for Truth. I might add that my backside has been paddled many times whenever I've strayed from the pathway that was mapped out for me. I guess one could say that I was trained by 'trial and error' and by following the Truth.

Do you belong to any groups? A Grove?

I am a member of The Henge of Keltria. It is the neo-Druidic group that most closely parallels my own beliefs while it also broadens my perspectives regarding worship, ritual and Druidic thought. ADF is another group that is clearly walking the same pathways and I have great respect for their efforts. I also have a connection to a group of thirteen people for Magical workings. In addition to that, I have a strong connection to my family, my ancestors, my children and my wife, Deborah. In much that I do, I work alone or in concert with Deborah. The wellspring of my Ancestors is always there to lend me its strength and guide me with their wisdom.

You seem to be something of a poet can you talk about the role of poetry, of Imbas in the Druid path?

The world came into being through Poetry. It was the First Song that was sung and it was itself carved within the Being of the First Tree. Einstein said that energy and matter were related by the speed of light acting upon itself. The fabric of being is determined in much the same way. Form and poetry are resonated within the First Song (Itself being a Tree). Poetry is rhythm and interaction. It is a light that illuminates existence within each of its living words. Its Music plays upon our Spirit, shows us many shades of Light and Shadow. Poetry is the Song of Being. It is the Breath of Creation. It is as complex as a leaf or as simple as the Universe.

Imbas is the sudden Light of Inspiration that can sometimes spontaneously flow out of our resonance with the Song. If we clear our thoughts and thin our own mundane barriers, we can be filled by its Light. Achieving this state of resonance, requires that a Poet separate him/herself from the influences of the mundane. In olden times, this was usually accomplished in a place called the 'Bed of the Poets'. Nowadays, we might use an isolation chamber or some other equally shielded and protected place to discover our Imbas.

There are three forms of Imbas: that which comes from the Inner Light, which is called Imbas Forosnai; that which comes from touching an object (as well as its interaction with the Poet's connection to Harmony), this is called Teinm Laeda; finally, there is the Imbas that comes from association and symbiosis, which is called Dichetal Do Chenaib. One form of Imbas comes from the 'fire in the head'. Another form comes from the mixture of songs: the Poet's inner harmony and the song of an object's existence. The third form of Imbas comes from breaking things into their component parts; discovering how they truly work (discarding falsehoods and removing distortions). Here is a song that I heard as I watched our Ancestors journey within the flames of Imbas Forosnai:

Children of the Land

Warriors of Fal,
Children of Light,
Gael of Destiny,
Gael of Sure Fate.
Eagles of Opportunity, Ploughman's delight.

Grian's spearmen,
Hunters and Hounds,
Manannan's wave runners,
Ogma's sharp strokes,
Save us and defend us,
Until the Morrigan's call sounds.

Until World's end and darkest of days,
Beyond Life's ending is our true fate.
Until stars shift and Sky falls,
Land shakes and Sea swells.
We are Warriors of Fal always.

Bright Blessings of Danu,
Anu's Lush Embrace,
Hearthfires of Brighid,
The Daghda's Red Knowing,
Give home to the Sun's Brugh.

It is Ireland Forever!
For we are the Gael!
We call to you Banba! Fodla! Eriu!
We are the Gael!
It is Ireland Forever!'
Copyright by Searles O'Dubhain (Samradh, 1995)

As I contemplated the Song of the Trees and the Wheel of the Year, I placed my hand upon an Ogham fidh representing the diphthong 'OI', which is known in Irish as Oir (Spindle Tree). This is an example of Teinm Laeda:

Pathways

A mouth of fire opened,
Calling me forward.
Swallowed alive,
Devoted to Life.

Who is the Devoted One?
Who eats the cake?
Who Builds the Fires ?
Who Makes the Leap?

Wishing at the Well, Sneaking a peek,
Wordwaves of Nine Realms, Songs of Many Voices.

We are the Roots of Doing.
We are the Purpose of Connection.
We are the Joining that Grows.
We are the Making of Health.
We are the Healing of Spirit.
We are the Chanting of Dreams.
We are the Wishing of Stars.
We are the Delight of Sun.
We are the Pleasure of Power.

Bannocks of Barleycorn,
Fires of Bíle,
Fertility of Anu,
Eye of Fire.

Daughters of Dancing,
Sons of Sacrifice,
Turnings of Spindles, Wheels of Life.

Who is the Devoted One? Where is the Bed?
What is the Marriage Price? Throbbing of Pulse!

A mouth of fire opened,
Calling me forward.
Swallowed alive,
Devoted to Life.
Copyright by Searles O'Dubhain (Bealtaine, 1996)

*You are involved in several interesting Internet projects and I know
you participate in various online discussion groups, can you talk about
them?*

Currently, Deborah and I are developing a World Wide Web-based forum called The Summerlands. Using the latest Microsoft products, we are offering a safe haven within cyber space for Pagans, Witches, and Druids to meet, exchange ideas, sell products and hold rituals. What sets The Summerlands apart is the interactive nature of its software. People will be able to use both audio and video to make presentations, as well as to market their wares and services. Online rituals can contain chanting, music, and drumming. There is a space provided for interactively placing offerings and making readings. A person in California could perform an interactive Tarot reading for a customer in New York or Sydney using one of our private conference rooms. We are also implementing a 'Hall of Remembrances' to honor those who were so cruelly tortured and murdered during the Witch hunts of the Middle Ages. In addition, we have a Bards' Hall and a place for Poets, as well as an Inn for Kitchen Witches.

The best way I can describe the project is that it will contain elements of cyber-reality that are similar to the worlds found within the latest CDROM-based games (such as Myst). We are going beyond the features offered in such games at The Summerlands, by providing a multiple user and an interactive environment. The Summerlands will be a place to live, worship, relax and learn. Deborah and I are very excited about its capabilities and the possibilities, especially the potential to allow Pagan folk to interact over great distances. I plan to teach Celtic Workshops online as only one of a group of like-minded scholars and Druids.

We hope that many a Bard will sing in our hall and that every Pagan author will discover new opportunities to contact the worldwide Pagan community within our space. There are currently over twenty different esoteric groups sharing the Tech-Gnosis umbrella with The Summerlands. Each of them shares our goal of providing a more universal meeting place for those who walk the Ways of the Wise.

In addition to The Summerlands, I am also involved in three unique internet discussion groups that are each attempting to re-discover and share the Old Ways of our Celtic and Druidic ancestors. These are Nemeton-L, Imbas-L, and the Order of the WhiteOak. Nemeton-L is the senior group of the three and was established by Erynn Darkstar and Lorax. This list offers an excellent 'Hedge School', as well as outstanding Celtic scholarship. The list focuses on the ways of the Filidh, as well as those of Druids.

The Imbas-L list was created by Danielle Ní Dhighe to provide a place for the establishment of a Cyber Tuatha[26] of Celtic Reconstructionists. Imbas-L is in the process of becoming a chartered, not-for-profit corporation. The folks at Imbas-L have an excellent website.

The Order of the WhiteOak is the third Celtic group in which I participate. It was established by yourself as a forum that would provide the means for re-establishing a Druidic Order of law, based upon honor and the old traditions. My impression of this list and its mission is that we have our work cut out for us, since modern society is so unlike the ancient Celtic society. Adapting the Brehon Laws of the Celts and inventing new laws or making judgments is difficult at best. If we are to establish a new code that is fair for all, it will take many years of effort and much hard work by everyone in the Pagan community.

A way of life and a code of behavior is not the work of the few. It is the work of everyone. We Druids have long recognized the need for such a group. I'd like to take this opportunity to thank you for your insight and character in embracing such an arduous task. May I also ask you for your views and thoughts on the Order and its direction?

Well, thank you. The Order consists of the individuals who frequent the WhiteOak discussion group in cyber space and we do attempt to have 'live' meetings from time to time. Mostly I am concerned that Pagans and Druids be aware that there is a rich body of law and tradition attached to our religion. This is not an 'anything goes' kind of path, though many would like to steer it in that direction.

The people who make up the list analyze stories for ancient ethical values and quote Brehon Law when someone posts a problem. The best way to understand the group is to get on the list as the discussions cover a wide range of topics and responses and conclusions vary from individual to individual.

But back to you now! Are there any issues of particular importance to you within Druidism today? Are there any problems you are aware of in the Druid religion?

The major focus of my own Draiocht is in finding, understanding, and embracing the Old Ways of the Ancient Ones. There is a real need to understand the Truth of Creation, as well as the ways that we can serve that Truth. Much has been written in the past several hundred years, but little of it is unified or unblemished. We need to get back to basics in our research, as well as our spirituality.

The problems facing Druidism today are threefold: the fundamentals of the traditions are not well defined; a lack of focus exists in today's Druidism that seems to exist across the board, from the individual to the organizational level; not enough work is being done on a spiritual and personal level. These three problems are the woods that feed the fires of dissension and division within our ranks. Too often, Druidic energy is channeled into politics and ego, rather than developing into Truth and Harmony.

Druids must be able to stand apart from the mundane in order to see, to judge, and to do. This work begins within the quietness of each of us. How can we present the Truth to the World, if we do not first possess it ourselves? How can we recognize Truth if we are filled with personal bias and intrigue? Are we not Druids?

Where do you think the religion as a whole is headed and where would you like to see it go in future?

I see an increasing of interest in our ways. I sense an

impending crisis of the spirit within our society and our world. I also detect that our religion is tending to polarize itself in much the same manner that other religions are polarizing. We have our purists and our homogenizers. Many come to this path to 'belong', while few seem to actually 'be'. It is my belief that Druids must possess both of these abilities at the same time. We must have dual vision and a dual existence. As stewards of Truth, we must represent the interests of this World, as well as the Otherworld.

I would like to see more Druids becoming active within public affairs. I'd like us to become more involved in helping society address the tough issues like: over-population, hunger, pollution, and the quality of life. I'd also like to see the Druidic schools re-established publicly and with adequate funding. If we are to have a future, we must have Druids to create it. Our connection to the Land is dying. Who will make another connection for us if we do not heal ourselves? Will we all become sons and daughters without parents? Without family? Without a Land?

Anything else you wish to address?

I'd like to ask the archaeologists and the governments of this world to be more sensitive to esoteric and spiritual matters when they undertake excavations in the burial grounds of the Ancestors. Who knows what damage is being done to the World when we dig at these sites? Have none of them seen the tale of Bóann and the Well of Segais? Where is their respect in removing and displaying the ancient bones? Are we slowly detuning and dismantling our gateways to the Otherworld? When I need to sleep among the bones of the Ancient Ones, will I find them locked away in glass cases in some museum or will the womb of the Earth embrace our connection?

May there still be time for wisdom to prevail before the last stone is turned.

Ann Heymann
Interviewed via internet
November, 1996

Ann Heymann has an international reputation as the foremost performer and authority on the *clairseach* (wire-strung harp). She has reconstructed and recreated techniques for the instrument that greatly contribute to an authentic playing style for ancient music.

She has authored a tutor for the wire-strung harp based upon the first tunes taught to student harpers in the 17th and 18th centuries. Ann's recordings include Queen of Harps (Temple Records, 1995), Christmas in the King's Court (Silver Bells Music, 1992), On Tour (Clairseach Records, 1989), The Harper's Land (Temple Records, 1983), Ann's Harp (Clairseach Records, 1981) and Let Erin Remember (Clairseach Records, 1970).

Her books include *Secrets of the Gaelic Harp* (1989), *Off the Record* (1990), and *Legacy of the 1792 Belfast Harp Festival* (1992) (see her website for more of her books and recordings).

Ann has appeared on more than fifty US and European radio and television shows and has served as a member of the faculty at The Historical Harp Conference, The Edinburgh Harp Festival, and The Belfast Harp Festival, as an adjudicator at The Granard Harp Festival in Ireland, and she has taught master classes for both the Scottish and Irish Harp Societies.

Ann received the PA State Arts Board Composers Grant in 1992, has been a 'Master' in the MN State Arts Board Folk Arts Apprenticeship Program since 1988, received the Minnesota Composers Forum Grant in 1984, and received two consecutive first prizes at Bun-Fhleadh Harp Competition in Granard, Ireland, in 1981 and 1982. She played with various traditional music groups before forming Clairseach with her husband Charlie in 1979.

You are a pioneer in the wire-strung harp revival. What led you to that pursuit?

When I was nineteen, two friends began touring to play Irish music professionally and left me their library, which contained Edward Bunting's 1840 publication *Ancient Music of Ireland*. Nineteen-year-old Bunting had been hired in 1792 to notate the music played by the harpers in Belfast at the last of the Irish harp festivals, and he became so taken with the instrument, its music and traditions, that he devoted the rest of his life to collecting its music and song, interviewing the harpers about the tradition, and publishing some of his collection in three volumes. Part of Bunting's writing concerns the instrument's decline throughout the 17th and 18th centuries, and his 1840 publication describes it as 'irretrievably gone'.

At that time Irish music was a hobby for me. I played tin-whistle in a local *ceili* band, so I was familiar with and enjoyed traditional music, but the challenge of resurrecting this legendary tradition combined with the inspiration of a nineteen-year-old classically-trained Belfast church organist compelled this nineteen-year-old with a keyboard background into the power of the Gaelic harp and it's there I remain.

How were you trained?

In 1971 there were virtually no players, teachers, recordings, how-to books or musical arrangements for the instrument. It was necessary that I 'go it alone', and this suited me just fine. Obtaining an instrument was difficult, and futile attempts to have a *clairseach* built finally ended successfully with my future husband Charlie locating an early 'Castle Otway' copy made by the 'father' of modern *clairseach*, master builder Jay Witcher. I decided I wanted to emulate the old Gaelic harpers, who held the harp on their left shoulder, using their left hands on the treble strings and their right hands primarily in the bass. They also used long fingernails to sound the strings and employed special techniques for damping strings that they didn't want ringing. All of this contrasts with the current practice of positioning the harp on the right shoulder, right hand in the treble and left in the bass, plucking the strings with the pads of the fingers. And gut/nylon strings don't sustain like brass strings do, greatly reducing the requirement for damping. It was easy to understand the need for nails on brass wire, and my ear made obvious the need to damp certain long-ringing strings, but it was hard to see the relevance of playing on the left shoulder. Perhaps fortuitously, I decided to go that route anyway, which made things initially inconvenient for a right-handed ex-keyboardist.

Soon I found that despite there being no person to teach me, I had the best teacher I could possibly have wanted – a good instrument. When my efforts were in the right direction, its voice was clear and bore a striking beauty. When I erred, the instrument would respond with screeching or unintelligible confusion.

How do you define Celtic spirituality and what caused you to follow that path?

First let me relate a few anecdotes. When I was five years old, I had a dream. I was in a cold, dank, windowless stone room (a dungeon?), naked and lying on my back, strapped with chains atop a wooden box (a coffin?). An older man, hairless and chubby with a brown robe and cowl tied at the waist (a monk?) came out on a balcony, dimly lit by a wall torch. The man mocked me and defamed everything I loved and held dear. I have no memory of exact words, but the sound of his voice and hideous laughter are with me forever. I felt an unbearable sense of loss of my world. To my dismay, during my waking hours this voice became a frequent unwelcome visitor. Initially I viewed the voice as being evil, and as a young teen I considered the possibility that I was experiencing schizophrenic symptoms. When I eventually 'found' the harp (or it found me) as a young adult, the voice never returned.

Secondly, when Robin Morton of Temple Records, Edinburgh, heard me play the MacDonald clan march, he asked me to record with Alison Kinnaird, Scotland's premier traditional harper. This resulted in the 1983 release The Harper's Land. And third, several years ago Scottish scholar Keith Sanger sent us an article he'd published about the MacShennog [McShannon] family of Kintyre, Scotland, hereditary harpers' to the MacDonalds since the 1400s. Keith discovered that when a Neil MacShennog died in 1731, he willed his portion of the harpers lands that had been granted his family two centuries earlier to his widow – Ann Heymann! We were astounded to find the German surname Heymann in Scotland at such an early date and, especially, to find an Ann Heymann directly associated with a Gaelic harping family!

Was it coincidence that my playing the clan march of the MacDonalds, patrons of the MacShennog harpers, led to my collaboration with Alison? Was it coincidence that the name The Harper's Land was chosen by Temple Records for that recording, years before Keith Sanger's 'Ann Heymann' information came to light?

Keith also identified an 'Annie Heyman,' named in 17th century Scottish witch hunt testimony, whom he thinks may well be the other Ann Heymann's mother. Might her experience have an association with my early dream? Mightn't she have been subjected to ridicule and imprisonment?

I don't think 'spirituality' needs a definition, but as the term 'Celtic' has become fashionable nowadays, especially as a marketing term, I would like to emphasize that it literally refers to a group of languages and has only relatively recently been used to embrace any and all qualities of any people whose current or past languages belong to that group. I presume we are now using it in that context. I consider it a 'Celtic' trait to see all things as dynamic entities. All of these coincidences in my life might be seen as relevant signs. They give me courage when I question my life's direction. I accept the role I play as fate – that through the coupling of my given name Ann to Charlie's surname Heymann, the 'wheels' were set into motion. Our marriage and subsequent partnership are simply a proper reflection of a Gaelic tripartite cosmology symbolized in their harp. This cosmology is discussed at length in Cláirseach: The Lore of the Irish Harp, *Eire-Ireland* 26:3 (1991) pps. 82–95 and in *The Companion to Traditional Irish Music* (Cork University Press, 1999), pps. 175–181, but for the sake of convenience I'll try to put it here in a nutshell.

The clairseach not only played music connected with ceremony and ritual; it was also a symbol itself – its sound box, pillar and neck reflected a tripartite cosmology of the universe made up respectively of female, male and spiritual components. The sound box was female, the fore pillar male, and the harmonic curve was spiritual and androgynous or hermaphroditic. These genders are shown in numerous ways, including the parts' construction, structural use, nomenclature and animal symbolism. The sound box was formed with a female mortise or 'socket' at each end; the pillar had a male tenon or 'plug' at each end; and the harmonic curve had one of each. Each tenon fit into the appropriate mortise, and string tension alone kept the parts together. The 'female' role of the sound box is to bring forth the harp's voice. The pillar's 'male' strength allows sufficient tension to generate a proper character for the instrument's voice. And the 'spiritual' harmonic curve regulates the proper and accurate tuning of this voice. The Gaelic name for the sound box is the feminine noun *coim*, meaning 'belly' or 'womb'. The pillar carried the masculine name *lamhchrann* or 'hand pillar'. There are three possible spellings, and therefore meanings, for the harmonic curve: *corr* (feminine) or a white long-necked water bird such as the crane; *cor* (masculine) or the act of establishment; and *coir* (neuter) meaning propriety. All three may be considered collectively under the 'spiritual' heading as allegories for the harp's neck, and, indeed, for the entire instrument, being a bridge between the Otherworld and the earthly realm. Finally, the symbol animal of the sound box was the 'feminine' bee; that of the pillar was the 'masculine' eel (Ireland's serpent); and that of the harmonic curve was the crane, a 'spiritual' bird carrying ancient and apparently universal associations with stringed instruments. A host of other triads may also be interpreted in the light of this cosmological harp mandala.

Do you see any problems with current Celtic spirituality?

I have no problems with true spirituality of any sort, but I am not knowledgeable enough on the subject to know how Celtic spirituality differs in essence from Native American or other established ancient spiritual traditions. I am concerned, though, with how individuals and businesses have adopted the catchword 'Celtic' as a marketing aid and use it to peddle all manner of commodities.

What is the place of magic in your music?

The Gaels saw the clairseach as a bridge between the Otherworld and ours and, when it is played today in a manner sympathetic to its idiosyncrasies, both player and audience can bear witness to a powerful potential in its voice. All aspects of Gaelic harp tradition stress the dynamic unity of a three-part whole, and I believe that magic exists whenever there is intercourse between the basic universal principles of 'female', 'male' and 'spirit', whatever form that may take.

I've discussed the harp form mandala, and this is only the beginning. Gaelic harp tuning created 'male' and 'female' voices within the instrument's gamut that combined to create a unified voice of the spirit or Otherworld. That's the reason for playing on the left shoulder – so the female and male hands could sound their corresponding voices. I believe in the two hands working together equally and not separately as 'melody' and 'accompaniment'. I call this approach 'coupled hands'.

The Gaelic harp's strong character naturally directs the course of its music. The tones that have been sounded greatly determine both those yet to be sounded and those to be damped. At this intersection of past and future dwells the magic of the now and present.

In performance the wire-strung harp is an aural mirror of the listener's spirit, helping people recognize the shapes of their feelings and the vibrations of their souls. Within the Gaelic harp and its music is encoded an elemental and most perfect balance of imbalance, a sort of philosophical gyroscope corresponding to the universe in its true harmony.

Can you describe your personal relationship with your harp?

I am the tool for expressing the instrument's message. It is the harp that soothes, excites or caresses the soul, and not I. The wire-strung harp has a very strong character and directs all proceedings; she is queen. So actually, when I compose or arrange, I simply follow her dictates and 'find' the music. Interviewers invariably want to know about me, but actually I consider myself meaningless next to the harp. I see myself not as an artist, but rather as a devotee or servant of the real artist – the *clairseach*. The music is all hers.

What is your vision for the future of Celtic music? Where is it headed now, and where would you like to see it go in the future?

'Celtic music' is such a broad term, but I think it is safe to say that it was once the aurally transmitted expression of a primarily rural pastoral/agricultural society with close ties to its natural environment. Our techno-industrial world estranges us from Mother Earth by isolating us in artificiality, so the melodies, rhythms and subtleties of earlier generations are not always appreciated today, even by many popular 'Celtic' musicians. 'Celtic music' today appears in all conceivable shapes and forms, and is headed in every direction, so I foresee no single future for it. Our children and grandchildren will determine whether or not the music survives and if so, in what form. One road to survival, outside of archives, is that of concert and mass media exposure, but commercial success along this path has all too often accompanied a musical transformation that has little in common with its source. Fortunately, there still exists music with a natural sensibility, even if it is increasingly hard to find. As I am not always against change, I hope for a move away from our human-centered materialistic world-view and towards an Earth-centered philosophical one, a move that would make us once more receptive to this fast disappearing natural music and save it from the same fate that befell the Gaelic harp two hundred years ago. Both scientific and historical evidence of music's power has been amply illustrated, so maybe the Gaelic harp can help influence just such a paradigm shift!

What new projects are you currently engaged in?

Charlie and I will continue our investigation and experimentation in the areas of performance technique and style, and I hope harp makers will put similar efforts into experiments in the area of traditional Gaelic harp construction. Harp makers prefer to build sound boxes of glued slabs rather than carving them out of a single log, as was traditional. Could there be good reason(s) behind the unified box idea? Other areas demanding investigation include the 'ceremony of the raising', which I think was a purposeful bending of the soundboard, and the design of harps that use materials described in numerous myths.

Other future projects include recordings of O'Carolan, Scottish lute music (tracks 3, 9 and 11 of www.harpofgold.net), epic poetry sung to *ceol mor* or art music of the Gaelic-speaking peoples consisting of a melodic theme and extended formalized variations as illustrated on tracks 7, 10 and 12 of *Cruit go nÓr • Harp of Gold* (www.harpofgold.net), and books illustrating my 'coupled hands' approach to harp music *Coupled Hands for Harpers.*

What advice can you give to aspiring Bards, harpers and Filidh?

Be true to your ethics. All else is subject to this.

William Shaw
Interviewed September 1996
Via US mail

William is a member of Council of the Clan Chattan Association, Inverness, Scotland. He is Seannachaidh to the Chief, Clan and name of Shaw (worldwide), Lieutenant to the Chief of Clan Shaw, and fifteenth Tanist to Clan Seumas, the Shaws of Crathienaird, Glenshee, Glenisla, and Glengairn.

The Clan Chattan Journal is distributed worldwide, An Biodag is the quarterly newsletter of the Clan Shaw Society and Clach Na Faire is a journal of the Clan Shaw. William's articles have appeared in The Clan Chattan Journal, An Biodag, Clach na Faire and in Pawprints, the newsletter of the Clan Chattan U.S.

Please describe your early religious upbringing. What was it like at home?

Where I grew up was an integral factor of what I am spiritually. A fourth generation Pacific Northwest native, most of my family had a hardy love of the woods, beaches, waters, and mountains of Western and Central Washington. My young adult years (since age eleven) were spent living near still wild forest – with scattered patches of old growth. As a boy and young man I have felt the breath and rhythm of God/Goddess in its deep green, grey and brown isles. That was my church. I understood the reverence of ancient man towards the moist tendrils of power that are in each plashing brook, the earthly harmony that rings out from each hill.

When I was seventeen I was sunbathing sky clad in a tiny private meadow when along came some hesitant yet lordly deer. Standing stack-still as long as possible I leapt forward – chasing but running with them over logs, brown earth and warm mud. Nearly touching one I held up and let them go, vanishing into the woods. Naturally a 'regular' church was a pale, cold, sterile and joyless thing after that.

I grew up with lots of Bible stories. My mother was raised old pre-Vatican II Catholic, my father rarely discussed religion. Even as a young kid I found God in nature and in the woods – not in a church and man-made rules. I found more spirituality in The Piper at the Gates of Dawn chapter in *The Wind in the Willows* than most 'Young Life' or 'Campus Crusade' type religious organizations geared towards high school age kids in mainstream America.

At eighteen or younger I studied the Oxford edition of the Bible, then at University I took a few Bible-as-literature courses from a Talmudic scholar. I then went to Britain, staying with a great-great aunt who lived in Bucks at a convent. She had been my confidant and advisor since I was fifteen. She was in her eighties and was a Mother Superior until her seventies. She was Highland Scot well versed in Celtic history, our clan history and Celtic/Culdee Christianity.

Her simple, joyous, humorous, and quite simple monastic way of life coupled with a deep love of nature; 'Billy, the land *is also* my Bible,' dove-tailed with what I felt. She was a strong Catholic, but her naturalness would have been at home in any Druidic College.

It was there at her convent that I took my first 'Communion' – at an ancient 9th century Saxon church on grounds mentioned in *The Domesday Book*. We broke all the rules, no classes, no schooling, but did so joyfully.

So how did you first find out about Druidism?

After my communion my studies in Celtic history also included Culdee or Celtic Christianity and its gentle evolvement from Druidry. I found a natural place for my heart to sing – in a Grove of my own making, this was in 1980 or so. When I was fourteen I had a tree-fort in a huge fir tree. It was such that I could climb over 150 feet to where the tree was three inches thick. I could see for miles.

Once as a young man in my early twenties I climbed that tree in a snowstorm at night. As the snow fell the only thing I could see were the dark sentinels around me, all covered in white. Nearly hypnotized by the silent whispering flakes, I saw woods lit by a low half-moon skidding out from the clouds, lighting a black-and-white serrated world of sharp angles. I felt that God was sharing a quiet joke with me for a minute, then all was dark and cold again. In my prayer life I always go to that tree in my mind to find peace, harmony, and the busy stillness of silence one can only find in a tree in a snowstorm (try it).

I also trained myself through my studies as a Celtic Christian.

I found many parallels in Celtic and Christian symbolism: Christ, the King Stag, dying for the collective herd, Mary the Blessed Mother in her triplicate form of Virgin/Spring Maiden, Mother, and Crone of Wisdom, Lord God Yahweh as the Sky God 'El' (to use the Hebraic) as Bel or Belennos who has sky and sun symbolism as well as that of a bull with its sacrificial connotations.

I think Christ would have made a fine Druid – he had a very strong connection to nature and the elements in his living and in his teachings... I could go on forever...name one Christian symbol or connotation that isn't spiraled into Celtic religion!

Are you a member of any Druid group or Grove?

My sister-in law is a Wiccan, sometimes a solitary, sometimes in a Coven (or Moon-group as she calls it). I know just as much (or more) than her spiritual/ritual leaders. What little, slightly hesitant contacts I had with any 'organized' Pagan or Wiccan groups were (thus far) not welcoming. I find in Covens that there are too many agendas involved so I remain a solitary with my family as my vessel. I have found Coven leaders to be a bit anti-male or uncomfortable with myself as someone with a great store of collective tribal, Druid, and Celtic-Christian lore, most of which, I do not like to say it, outstripped their own. I did not find these groups in harmony with my intertwining of male and female aspects of Celtic spirituality, Druidic or Christian, as seen through my Celtic 'sight' or 'vision'. Besides, they were just too serious.

Although half of my personal faith is intertwined with Muire, the Mother-God, The Mother Goddess, etc., I retain balance with all the male aspects of God: Yahweh/El, Jesus as the Son of Man as well as the King Stag of sacrifice/the Holly and Oak King, Cernunnos and Bellenos, etc. Were I a single male, naturally I would find myself 'drawn' to the female, sexual aspects of Covens, but as I said, many have agendas and many also are out of balance and anti-male.

However, the Pacific Northwest is a great 'home away from home' for Celtic exiles and spiritual pilgrims. The three hundred miles between Portland, Oregon and Seattle, Washington and Vancouver, British Columbia, has large and active Irish and Scottish and general Celtic communities. The Northwest is also a spiritual haven for Pagans, Celts, Wiccans, etc., by the broom-full! My negative contacts were far swept aside by the individual meetings of many singular kindred spirits, Druidic and Culdee, all moving in harmony to the same spirituality and Celtic marriage to the land and its God/dess given rhythms. In quiet, reflective conversations and Celtic garrulous yelling and joviality (depending on the person) I find happily that Celtic spirituality in all its forms is beginning to bud in the US. I will always do my best to help it along. No, Ellen, I haven't had any contact with a truly 'organized' Druidic group.

Can you describe some of your rituals or how you worship?

We have many rituals in my family, starting with the sign of the Cross/Tree of Life/Stag's Antlers; 'In the name of the Father, the Mother, the Son and the Holy Spirit,' a Celtic intertwining of all facets. My wife Mary Beth and I merely intertwine the Celtic/Druidic into the Christian as we progress through the 'Wheel of the Year'. We just accent the Celtic while joyously honoring the Christian: Samhain/All Souls, Yule/Christmas,

Imbolc, Spring Equinox/Saint Patrick's, Easter/Beltaine, Mid-Summer Solstice, Lughnasad, Autumn Equinox etc. Throw in St. Chattan's Day (17 May) and all the rest. Within my own household – under my own roof-tree as it were, we simply make it up as we go along – combining Celtic symbols, plants, God/dess aspects and historical knowledge.

How would you define Druidism or the Celtic spiritual path?

The Celtic spiritual path, whether it is Culdee/Christian or Druidic, finds physical and spiritual harmony in intertwining itself with the pulse, heart and rhythms of the planet, as read and interpreted and felt through a Celtic way of seeing beyond today's materialism into the roots of the legends of our Ancestors. Seeing into the causes and roots of the legends of the Celtic past and its spirituality entwines us in a natural, comfortable never-ending green chain of life, both spiritual and physical.

Do you think Druidism is unique from or similar to Wicca and the Pagan revival in general that we see today?

Tough question. I think that the Wiccan and Pagan trends are a natural result of the oppressive religiosity of the past three hundred years as well as a natural outlet of the modern world where most people are divorced from the Earth and nature's rhythms. Some of the current trend is caught up in today's marketing trends – I find some quantity of 'bogus' material or literature. Reaching out is one thing, mass marketing is another.

I do find the Celtic and Druid path similar to the Pagan and Wiccan in many ways – there are many parallels with Native American spirituality as well, not to mention Australian aboriginal religion also.

These questions are not easy for me to answer as I have been on my own meandering pilgrimage of Celtic spirituality – teaching people here and there and hopefully, quietly inspiring. I haven't looked at the 'movement' as a whole – the collective, cohesive, orchestration is historically alien to Celtic culture... I would like to know more.

Can you please talk about the role of the Seannachaidh, the story-teller, in ancient and modern Druidry?

The Seannachaidh was also a poet, using words to 'shepherd' the clan towards great deeds; cattle-raids, midnight forays on a late summer night down in the lowlands, doing a bit of good-natured roof-burning against any neighboring clans who were encroaching on the ancient tribal lands, and to share with the tribe tasks of seasonal rhythm such as harvest, sowing, plowing, driving cattle to and from summer pastures, etc. Binding the everyday chores of communal necessity with the rhythms of the land and seasons. He was a living reminder that all life, mundane and glorious, was a story: each life of each clansperson was intertwined with the past and the present and each other.

Since my great-great-great-grandfather was a Seannachaidh of Clan Shaw (1860-1871) I seem to have inherited his and his father's gift of storytelling. Starting with the basics of Clan Shaw history when I was fifteen or sixteen I quickly learned more of our history with its branches and septs: some grand, some poor, all war-like, Celtically gaudy, and 'much trouble to their neighbors'. Our collective and segmented history is enfolded into the spiraling movement that was Highland tribal geopolitics and Scottish general history. Overlay on top of that a strong sense of Celtic cultural determination: my goal is to keep the Celtic history, culture, tribalism and spirituality ancient yet evergreen. In my own way I try to keep the fire of Celtic ways burning.

The role of the Seannachaidh in the modern clan has many facets; as a historian, a storyteller, and a bridge or custodian of a tribal path, bridging past, present and future. In doing so, its collective role is just as important as the Chief's. My dual function also is to act as a 'guide' to linking people with our clan/tribal lands of old, to act as a matchmaker of each individual's relationship and/or renewal with the land and it's ancient rhythms.

In the Court of the Lord Lyon, today's Ard Seannachaidh of Scotland, the Seannachaidh of the clan also legally instates the next Chief's succession (wearing a black robe). In ancient days and today the station of the Seannachaidh is above that of a Bard, seated next to the Chief and Chieftains of each house. I personally am also heavily knowledged in herb-lore both medicinal and culinary, as well as being a gardener of flowers.

In the Celtic West, each tribal culture cherished strong traditions of reverence towards certain sacred places or natural objects. Intertwined throughout our collective Scottish history over the past three thousand years there has always been a respect for certain 'special' hills, Groves, lochs, pools, crags, or singular or arranged stones. Each place or stone was felt to be a conduit or focus of positive Earth energy or of the Gods-given life force, bringing rejuvenation, spiritual enhancement, fertility or just plain luck. Many stones were also used in sacred ceremonies of initiation, both Druidic and Celtic Christian – be they rites of baptism, hand fasting, oaths of allegiance, harvest and sowing or funerals. They were also used as touchstones in the coronation ceremonies of Clan Chiefs, the local kings or 'Sub-Regulus' and even the Ard Righ or High King of Scots and Picts. Countless significant ancient sites both large and complex or simple and small remain with us today – their stones still quietly aligned in harmony to various solar or lunar events...a testimony to the Earth-centeredness of our past clans folk. Still held in esteem by many, they bridge the opposing yet intertwined aspects of the female Earth with the male-oriented sun and sky. They sing to our hearts and minds still.

In days of old the Seannachaidh had the 'Silver Branch' – an ash wand with nine silver bells. The tinkling bells were to quiet the clan round the fire when it was story-time. The nine bells, three times three: a sacred number, also acted as a signal, indicating a small mini-Shamanic 'rift' between past and present, natural and supernatural boundaries. In days of old the

Seannachaidh also acted as a healer with the Wise-women of the tribe, as a soothsayer, and at times a Taliesianic shape-shifter.

On my family arms there are many totemic devices: the tree, symbolizing Rothiemurchus Forest, the oldest pine forest in the UK, which was our original tribal country, the lion rampant, the heraldic/totemic beast of the Kings of Dal Riada (based on our descent from the kings of Fife and Moray), the plunging dagger, symbolizing the wild ambush of the Comyns of Altyre (who usurped Rothiemurchus from us in 1411, we killed their Chief at Lag na Cuimeanach in Strathspey with a final, frenzied, desperate dagger thrust), and the white wolf, a Robertson device, because we married into Robertson women and land in the 1750s. My clan plant badge is the Red Whortleberry, clans of old wore significant plants in their bonnet – the plants that retained the tribal 'lucky spirit'.

Long before tartans gained any significance as an indicator of which clan, sept or tribe you belonged to, the plant badge was usually worn in the bonnet or affixed to the cloghaid, a conical helmet loved by Celts in Scotland and Ireland until the 1500s. Said plant badge is an ancient link to our primitive late Bronze Age forebears who held that certain plants contained a stronger essence or 'lucky spirit'. Strongly connected with their natural environment in heart, mind, body and spirit, the ancient Celts believed that the tribal spirit was enhanced by near worship of the sacred or lucky plant or tree.

This adherence continued strongly well after the Christian era into the Middle Ages, Renaissance, and until the end of the highland clan system in 1746 and is still used today. Some tribal badges include a sprig of yew, mistletoe, pine, heather, holly, oak, boxwood, cranberry, or even cat-tail. It was also considered lucky to plant these plants or trees near your home.

Another aspect of our Gaelic culture that has survived centuries of cultural and economic pressure from the English government is the tartan, or in our own language: 'breacan' or 'mottled'. Ancient Classical Greek and Roman chronicles and annals told of the fantastic, fearsome appearance of the mounted Celtic warrior, his long hair and moustaches stiffened by lime, his deep love of horses and elegant, yet deadly, efficient swords, knives and spears and the age-old Celtic detestation of the 'unmanly' scale, chain or plate armor that protected Greek, Roman, and later Norse, soldiers. Another aspect of the Celt remained constant whether he was a tribesman from Austria, Ireland, Gaul, or Spain – the deep love of colored cloth.

From the primitive tunic of contrasting tan and black squares of the simple herdsman to the vibrant multi-hued cheques and crossstriped cloak and trews of the golden torqued, chariot driving Chief or local King – tartan was a constant throughout Celtic society and continues to be important today.

In the grave slabs over tombs of ancient Scottish Kings and Chiefs (Kenneth Mac Alpin, High King of Alba who united the Pictish and Scottish thrones circa 860 AD) we find carved reliefs of them wearing great saffron colored linen and/or wool tunics, most times pleated to the knee and with long, flowing sleeves. Over this was worn a large tartan mantle, fringed so as to aid in the run-off of the ever-present rain and mist. This great mantle could be broached, gathered, or belted in many ways to fit the need and style of the wearer.

By the 1600s the ancient tartan mantle, usually belted, had developed into the great breacan phille, or belted plaid. The ancient saffron tunic was a simple shirt of wool or linen, still usually yellow or brown. At this time the great nobles, chiefs, and chieftains usually went about mounted and wore a large tartan 'shoulder plaid over a short Highland coat' and tartan trews, which were a close-fitting breek and hose combination.

Colors of tartan depended firstly on the ease (or difficulty) in getting certain vegetable and herbal dyes. Over the centuries local areas developed a preference for the only means of gathering certain colors and developed rough, home-made patterns, but distinct tartans were not consistently worn. The earliest noted use of an actual 'clan' tartan was in the 1630s when the MacLeans had rent payable in ells of 'black, white and green cloth' (their tartan today). By the late 1600s and early 1700s some more affluent Chiefs and Chieftains preferred that when armed and mustered for war, (or visiting another Chief) that their tribe (or tail) would dress in the same tartan. Also by the 1700s the phillibeg or 'little kilt' emerged, it being a halved version of the belted plaid with a separate pleated kilt and shoulder plaid that we wear today.

After the disaster at Culloden and the resultant cultural repression afterwards by the Hanoverian government, Lowland Scots, and certain Protestant clans of the Southwest, it was punishable by death or imprisonment to wear the tartan, kilt, plaid, or hose. This brutal enactment was so well carried out that what Clan, family or district tartans there were, were soon lost. Most of the old 'sett-sticks' containing thread count and colors of tartan warp and weft were gone, the colors of the so-called clan tartans were left to the memories of a few middle-aged folk by the time the tartan proscription was repealed. During the 'tartan-revival' of the late 1700s and early 1800s, the only tartans remaining were of the Government Tartan, or Black Watch. Many Chiefs, having no idea what their grandfathers' parents wore, used the Black Watch tartan as their base, adding crossstripes and colors. The weaving firm of Wilson's of Bannochburn, in its marketing strategy, cannily made up all sorts of semiauthentic and mostly imaginary tartans, selling them to all comers. Many of today's 'ancient clan tartans' are from Wilson's own designs.

Where would you like to see the Celtic spiritual path develop in future and where do you think it is headed now?

My vision is that I would hope other 'regular' faiths could see how the Earth-centeredness of human-kind is dangerously adrift and that we need a bridge back to the life-giving Earth that God/Goddess created, bridging body, spirit and existence.

Are there any problems that you have noticed in the Pagan and Druid communities of today?

Yes. In my thus-far narrow acquaintance I find that some in the Pagan and Druidic community take themselves too seriously. I personally find more affinity with a more open, joyous, celebratory method of sharing the great marriage with the land and its rhythms. Some forget that Druids and early Celtic Christians, most of whom were Druidically trained, continually expressed a multifaceted ode to joy in song, laughter, and a continuous affirmation of life. Every deed, however spontaneous, was a step in the dance of life, a harmony in the song of the earth, a note in the chorus of the never-ending concert of life. That is what a Druid was and should be.

There are some native-born Celts who have come to this country and now claim that it is impossible to practice a Celtic spiritual path here because the connection to the land, in Europe, has been lost. Do you think that is true? And I have had Druids here in the US tell me they 'only feel spiritual in Scotland'. What do you make of that?

I would urge them to undertake a re-marriage to their new land. My heart and soul long for Rothiemurchus forest, and lovely Glenshee and to stand under the stars at Clach na Faire, or to rebaptize my soul with water from the Dunlichity Baptismal stone in Strathnairn. However, this land is good and holy too: it is and was such for the Native Americans, the Snoqualmie, the Yakima Nation, the Snohomish and Muckleshoot. Yes, I would prefer to harmonize my soul back home in Scotland, but I use my Celtic spirituality as a 'tool of communion' here until I do.

Further Information about the Contributors to this Book

Ann Heymann http://www.annheymann.com/biography.htm
http://www.clairseach.com/shop/books.htm
Ár nDraíocht Féin: A Druid Fellowship https://www.adf.org/
'Brahm' Stuart De Usoz - http://www.soundclick.com/bands/
    page_songInfo.cfm?bandID=1065037&songID=9098258
Brigit's Sparkling Flame http://brigitssparklingflame.blog
    spot.com
Bryan Perrin www.bryanperrinstudio.com www.themadtrad.bl
    ogspot.com
'Cathbad' (Brendan Myers) http://www.brendanmyers.net/wi
    ckedrabbit/
Ceisiwir Serith http://www.ceisiwrserith.com/
Council of British Druid Orders http://www.cobdo.org.uk/
Daughters of the Flame http://www.obsidianmagazine.com/
    DaughtersoftheFlame/
Dr. Patrick MacManaway http://patrickmacmanaway.com/
Ellen Evert Hopman http://www.elleneverthopman.com
Erynn Rowan Laurie http://searchingforimbas.blogspot.com/
Glastonbury Order of Druids http://www.glastonburyorderof-
    druids.com/
Hasidic Druidism http://smartsheep.org/druish-books-of-the-
    hasidic-druids-of-north-america-index-22
Imbas http://www.imbas.org/imbas/
Isaac Bonewits http://www.neopagan.net/
John Matthews http://www.hallowquest.org.uk/
Kaledon Naddair http://www.keltia-publications.com/lectures/
Liz and Colin Murray http://asphodel-long.com/html/ colin_
    murray.html
Mael Brighde Brigit's Sparkling Flame http://brigitsspark
    lingflame.blogspot.com

http://www.obsidianmagazine.com/DaughtersoftheFlame/index.
htm

Mara Freeman www.chalicecentre.net and www.celticspirit
journeys.com.

Michel-Gerald Boutet http://www.midwesternepigraphic.org/
ogam.html

Philip Carr-Gomm http://www.philipcarr-gomm.com/

Prydwyn Olvardil Piper http://www.allmusic.com/album/release
/at-the-feet-of-mary-mooncoin-mr0001901780/credits

Reformed Druids of North America http://rdna.info/

Ronald Hutton http://en.wikipedia.org/wiki/Ronald_Hutton

Steve Wilson http://www.fellowshipofisiscentral.com/druid-clan-
of-dana---cobdo-and-stonehenge

Susan Henssler http://obod.bandcamp.com/track/thunder-perf
ect-mind-susan-henssler-and-youth

The Ancient Order of Druids http://www.aod-uk.org.uk/home
.htm

The Ancient Order of Druids in America http://www.aoda.org/

The Association for Consciousness Exploration http://www.rosen
comet.com/about.html

The British Druid Order http://www.druidry.co.uk/

The Breton Gorsedd http://www.gorsedd.fr/?lang=en

The Carleton College International Druid Archives http://apps.
carleton.edu/student/orgs/druids/archives/

The Druid Clan of Dana http://www.fellowshipofisis.com/druid-
clanofdana.html

The Druid Chronicles http://orgs.carleton.edu/Druids/ARDA/

The Druid Network http://druidnetwork.org/

The Fellowship of ISIS http://www.fellowshipofisis.com/

The Gorsedd of Bards of Caer Abiri http://www.druidry
.co.uk/getting-involved/the-gorsedd-of-bards-of-caer-abiri/

The Henge of Keltria http://www.keltria.org/

The Insular Order of Druids http://www.lugodoc.demon
.co.uk/Druids/IOD.htm

The Loyal Arthurian Warband http://www.warband.org.uk/

The Order of Bards Ovates and Druids http://www.druidry.org/

The Order of WhiteOak (Ord na Darach Gile) www.whiteoak-druids.org

The Secular Order of Druids http://pagan.wikia.com/wiki/Secular_Order_of_Druids

The Summerlands http://www.summerlands.com/

Topazowl http://www.keltria.org/biographies/topazowl.htm

Tribe of the Oak www.tribeoftheoak.com

William Shaw of Clan Shaw http://www.theclanshaw.org/page19.html

Druidic and Celtic Bibliography

Bord, Janet and Colin, *Earth Rites: Fertility Practices in Pre-Industrial Britain*, Granada Publishing, London, 1982

Boutet, Michel-Gerald, *The Celtic Connection*, Stonehenge Viewpoint, 800 Palermo Drive, Santa Barbara, CA 1996

Breatnach, Liam ed., Uraicecht *Na Riar* – *The Poetic Grades in Early Irish Law*, Dublin Institute For Advanced Studies, 1987

Brennan, J.H., *A Guide to Megalithic Ireland*, Aquarian Press, San Francisco, 1994

Brennan, Martin, *The Stones of Time, Calendars, Sundials, and Stone Chambers of Ancient Ireland*, Inner Traditions International, Rochester, VT, 1994

Briggs, Katherine, *An Encyclopedia of Fairies, Hobgoblins, Brownies, Bogies, and Other Supernatural Creatures*, Pantheon Books, NY, 1976

Brunaux, Jean Louis, *The Celtic Gauls: Gods, Rites and Sanctuaries*, B.A. Seaby Ltd., London, 1988

Carmichael, Alexander, *Carmina Gadelica, Hymns and Incantations Collected in the Highlands and Islands of Scotland in the Last Century*, Floris Books, Edinburgh, 1992

Caldecott, Moyra, *Women in Celtic Myth*, Destiny Books, Rochester, VT 1992

Carr-Gomm, Philip, *The Elements of the Druid Tradition*, Element Books 1991.

Carr-Gomm, Philip, *The Druid Animal Oracle*, with Stephanie Carr-Gomm, Simon & Schuster, 1994.

Carr-Gomm, Philip, *The Druid Renaissance*, ed., Thorsons, HarperCollins, 1996. (Re-issued as *The Rebirth of Druidry – Ancient Earth Wisdom for Today*, 2003)

Carr-Gomm, Philip, *In the Grove of the Druids: The Druid Teachings of Ross Nichols*, Watkins Books, 2002

Carr-Gomm, Philip, *Druid Mysteries: Ancient Wisdom for the 21st*

Century, Rider, 2002

Carr-Gomm, Philip, *The DruidCraft Tarot*, with Stephanie Carr-Gomm, St. Martin's Press, 2004

Carr-Gomm, Philip, *What do Druids Believe?* Granta, 2005

Carr-Gomm, Philip, *The Druid Way*, Thoth Publications 2006

Carr-Gomm, Philip, *The Druid Plant Oracle*, with Stephanie Carr-Gomm, St. Martin's Press, 2008

Carr-Gomm, Philip, *Journeys of the Soul: The Life and Legacy of a Druid Chief*, Oak Tree Press, 2010

Carr-Gomm, Philip, *Druidcraft: The Magic of Wicca & Druidry*, The Oak Tree Press, 2013

Caesar, Julius, *The Battle For Gaul*, David R. Godine, Boston, 1980

Chadwick, Nora, *The Celts*, Penguin, Middlesex, 1985

Chetan, Anand and Diana Brueton, *The Sacred Yew, Rediscovering the Ancient Tree of Life Through the Work of Allen Meredith*, Arkana Books, NY, 1994

Condren, Mary, *The Serpent and the Goddess*, Harper Collins, San Francisco, 1989

Coghlan, Ronan, *The Encyclopedia of Arthurian Legends*, Element Books, Rockport, MA, 1991

Cross, Tomm Peete and Clark Harris Slover, *Ancient Irish Tales*, Barnes and Noble, Totowa, NJ, 1988 (reprint of the 1936 edition)

Cunliffe, Barry, *The Celtic World: An Illustrated History of the Celtic Race, Their Culture, Customs and Legends*, Greenwich House, NY, 1986

Cunliffe, Barry, *Greeks, Romans and Barbarians, Spheres of Interaction*, B.T. Batsford, London, 1988

Dames, Michael, *Mythic Ireland*, Thames and Hudson, NY, 1992

Dames, Michael, *The Avebury Cycle*, Thames and Hudson, London, 1996

Dames, Michael, *The Silbury Treasure, The Great Goddess Rediscovered*, Thames and Hudson, London 1976 (reprinted 1992)

Davidson, Hilda Ellis, *Gods and Myths of Northern Europe*, Penguin Books, NY, 1990

Davidson, Hilda Ellis, *Myths and Symbols in Pagan Europe: Early Scandinavian and Celtic Religions*, Syracuse University Press, Syracuse, 1988

Dillon, Myles, *Early Irish Literature*, University of Chicago Press, Chicago, 1948

Durning, William and Mary, *A Guide To Irish Roots Including Celts, Vikings, Normans*, Kings, Queens, and Commoners Irish Family Names Society, La Mesa, CA, 1986

Ellis, Peter Berresford, *Celtic Inheritance*, Dorset Press, NY, 1992

Ellis, Peter Berresford, *A Dictionary of Celtic Mythology*, Oxford University Press, NY, 1992

Ellis, Peter Berresford, *A Dictionary of Irish Mythology*, Oxford University Press, NY, 1987

Ellis, Peter Berresford, *The Druids*, Wm. Eerdmans Publishing, Grand Rapids, 1994

Evans-Wentz, W. Y., *The Fairy Faith in Celtic Countries*, Citadel Press, NY, 1990

Ford, Patrick K., *The Mabinogi and Other Welsh Medieval Tales*, University of California Press, Berkeley, 1977

Gantz, Jeffrey, *Early Irish Myths and Sagas*, Penguin, NY, 1981

Gantz, Jeffrey, *The Mabinogion*, Penguin Books, NY, 1976

Gray, Elizabeth A. ed., *Cath Maige Tuired: The Second Battle of Mag Tuired*, Irish Texts Society, Vol LIV, Leinster, 1992

Green, Miranda, *Celtic Goddesses*, George Brazillier Inc., NY, 1996

Green, Miranda, *The Gods of Roman Britain*, Shire Publications Ltd., Aylesbury, Bucks, England, 1983

Green, Miranda, *The Gods of the Celts*, Barnes and Noble, Totowa, NJ, 1986

Green, Miranda, *The Sun-Gods of Ancient Europe*, B.T. Batsford, London 1991

Green, Miranda, *Symbol and Image in Celtic Religious Art*, Routledge, NY, 1992

Gregory, Lady, *Gods and Fighting Men*, Colin Smythe Ltd., Gerrards Cross, Buckinghamshire, 1993

Gregory, Lady and William Butler Yeats, *A Treasury of Irish Myth, Legend and Folklore*, Gramercy Books, NY, 1986

Gwyn, Edward, *The Metrical Dindshenchas (Vol 1-5)*, School of Celtic Studies, Dublin Institute for Advanced Studies, 1991

Harbison, Peter, *Pre-Christian Ireland, From the Early Settlers to the Early Celts*, Thames and Hudson, London, 1988

Hawkins, Gerald, *Stonehenge Decoded, An Astronomer Examines One of the Greatest Puzzles of the Ancient World*, Barnes and Noble Books, NY, 1986

Herm, Gerhard, *The Celts*, St. Martin's Press, NY, 1976

Hopman, Ellen Evert, *A Druid's Herbal for the Sacred Earth Year*, Destiny Books, VT, 1994

Hopman, Ellen Evert, *A Druid's Herbal of Sacred Tree Medicine*, Destiny Books, VT, 2008

Hopman, Ellen Evert, *Being a Pagan: Druids, Wiccans, and Witches Today*, Destiny Books, VT, 2001

Hopman, Ellen Evert, *People of the Earth: The New Pagans Speak Out*, Inner Traditions, VT, 1995

Hopman, Ellen Evert, *Priestess of the Fire Temple: A Druid's Tale*, Llewellyn Worldwide, MN, 2012

Hopman, Ellen Evert, *Priestess of the Forest: A Druid Journey*, Llewellyn Worldwide, MN, 2008

Hopman, Ellen Evert, *The Druid Isle*, Llewellyn Worldwide, MN, 2010

Hopman, Ellen Evert, *Scottish Herbs and Fairy Lore*, Pendraig Publishing, CA, 2011

Hopman, Ellen Evert, *Secret Medicines of Your Garden*, Inner Traditions Bear & Co, Healing Arts Press, VT, 2016

Hopman, Ellen Evert, *The Secret Medicines of Your Kitchen*, mPowr Ltd., London, 2012

Hopman, Ellen Evert, *Tree Medicine-Tree Magic*, Phoenix Publishing, Inc., WA, 1992

Hopman, Ellen Evert, *Walking the World in Wonder – A Children's Herbal*, Healing Arts Press, VT, 2000

Hutton, Ronald, *The Pagan Religions of the Ancient British Isles: Their Nature and Legacy*, Blackwell, Oxford, 1991

Hutton, Ronald, *The Rise and Fall of Merry England*, Oxford University Press,1994

Hutton, Ronald, *Stations of the Sun: A History of the Ritual Year in Britain*, Oxford University Press, 1996

Jackson, Kenneth Hurlstone, *A Celtic Miscellany*, Penguin Books, NY, 1971

James, Simon, *The World of the Celts*, Thames and Hudson, London, 1993

Joyce, P.W., *A Social History of Ancient Ireland*, 2 Vols, M.H. Gill & Son, Dublin, 1903

Kelly, Fergus, *A Guide to Early Irish Law*, Dublin Institute For Advanced Studies, Dublin, 1991

Kinsella, Thomas, *The Tain*, University of Pennsylvania Press, NY, 1988

Kraig, Bruce and Leon E. Stover, *Stonehenge, The Indo-European Heritage*, Nelson Hall, Chicago, 1978

Kruta, V., Frey, O.H., Rafferty, B., Szabo, M. editors, *The Celts*, (translated from Italian, *'I Celti'*) Rizzoli International Publications, New York, 1991

Larson, Robert and Isaac Bonewits ed., *The Druid Chronicles (Evolved)*, Drunemeton Press, POE 9398, Berkeley, CA 1976

Laurie, Erynn Rowan, *A Circle of Stones*, Eschaton, Chicago, 1995

Littleton, C. Scott, *The New Comparative Mythology: An Anthropological Assessment of the Theories of Georges Dumezil*, 3rd Ed, University of California Press, Berkeley, 1982

Logan, Patrick, *The Holy Wells of Ireland*, Colin Smythe, Bucks, England, 1992

MacCana, Proinsias, *Celtic Mythology*, Hamlyn, London, 1970

MacCulloch, J.A. *The Religion of the Ancient Celts*, Studio Editions, London, 1992

Mallory, J.P., *In Search of the Indo Europeans*, Thames and Hudson, NY, 1989

Markale, Jean, *King of the Celts, Arthurian Legend and Celtic Tradition*, Inner Traditions, Rochester, VT, 1994

Markale, Jean, *The Celts*, Inner Traditions, Rochester, VT, 1993

Matthews, Caitlin and John, *The Encyclopedia Of Celtic Wisdom – A Celtic Shaman's Sourcebook*, Element Books, Rockport, MA, 1994

Matthews, Caitlin, *Mabon and the Mysteries of Britain, An Exploration of the Mabinogion*, Arkana Paperbacks, London, 1987

Matthews, Caitlin, *The Celtic Book of Days, A Guide to Celtic Spirituality and Wisdom*, Destiny Books, Rochester, VT, 1995

Matthews, Caitlin, *The Celtic Book of the Dead, A Guide For Your Voyage to the Celtic Otherworld*, St. Martins Press, London, 1994

Mattews, Caitlin, *The Elements of the Celtic Tradition*, Element Books, Rockport, MA, 1989

Matthews, John, *A Celtic Reader, Selections from Celtic Scholarship and Story*, Aquarian Press, London, 1992

Matthews, John and Robert Stewart, *Celtic Warrior Chiefs*, Firebird Books, Dorset, UK, 1993

Matthews, John, *Taliesin, Shamanism and the Bardic Mysteries in Britain and Ireland*, Aquarian Press, London, 1991

Matthews, John, *The Druid Sourcebook*, London: Cassell, 1996 New York: Sterling Publishing Co., 1996

McNeill, F. Marian, *The Silver Bough*, Cannongate, Edinburgh, 1989

Merrifield, Ralph, *The Archaeology of Ritual and Magic*, New Amsterdam Books, NY, 1988

Merry, Eleanor C., *The Flaming Door, The Mission of the Celtic Folk Soul*, Floris Books, Edinburgh Scotland, 1983

Miller, Hamish and Paul Broadhurst, *The Sun and the Serpent: An Investigation into Earth Energies*, Pendragon Press, Launceston, England, 1994

Mohen, Jean-Pierre, *The World of the Megaliths*, Facts On File, NY, 1990

Murray, Liz and Colin, *The Celtic Tree Oracle, A System of Divination*, St. Martin's Press, NY, 1992

Naddair, Kaledon, *Keltic Folk and Faerie Tales*, Century Hutchinson, NY, 1987

Nagy, Joseph Falaky, *The Wisdom of the Outlaw: The Boyhood Deeds of Finn in Gaelic Narrative Tradition*, University of California Press, Berkeley, 1985

Nichols, Ross, *The Book of Druidry History, Sites and Wisdom*, Aquarian Books, San Francisco, 1992

O'Boyle, Sean, *Ogam – The Poet's Secret*, Gilbert Dalton, Dublin, 1980

O'Driscoll, Robert ed., *The Celtic Consciousness*, George Braziller, NY, 1982

O'Hogain, Daithi, Myth, *Legend and Romance: An Encyclopedia of the Irish Folk Tradition*, Prentice Hall, NY, 1991

O'Kelly, Michael J. *Newgrange*, Thames and Hudson, London, 1982

Pennick, Nigel, *Magical Alphabets, The Secrets and Significance of Ancient Scripts Including Runes, Greek, Ogham, Hebrew and Alchemical Alphabets*, Samuel Weiser Inc., York Beach, ME, 1992

Pennick, Nigel and Nigel Jackson, *The Celtic Oracle, The Ancient Art of the Druids*, Aquarian Press, London, 1991

Piggot, Stuart, *The Druids*, Thames and Hudson, NY, 1985

Quin, E.G., *Dictionary of the Irish Language, Compact Edition*, Royal Irish Academy, Dublin, 1990

Rees, Alwyn and Brinley, *Celtic Heritage: Ancient Tradition in Ireland and Wales*, Thames and Hudson, NY, 1994

Renton, R.W. and Macdonald, J.A. *Scottish Gaelic-English, English-Scottish Gaelic Dictionary*, Hippocrene Books, NY, 1994

Rolleston, T.W., *Celtic Myths and Legends*, Dover Publications Co., NY, 1990

Room, Adrian, *A Dictionary of Irish Placenames*, Appletree Press, Belfast, 1994

Ross, Anne, *Druids, Gods and Heroes from Celtic Mythology*, Peter Bedrick Books, NY, 1986

Ross, Anne and Don Robins, *The Life and Death of a Druid Prince: The Story of an Archaeological Sensation*, Random Century Group Ltd, London, 1989

Ross, Anne, *Pagan Celtic Britain, Studies in Iconography and Tradition*, Routledge & Kegan Paul, London, 1967 (reprinted 1994)

Ross, Anne, *The Pagan Celts*, Barnes and Noble, Totowa, NJ, 1986

Rutherford, Ward, *Celtic Mythology: Nature and Influence of Celtic Myth – Druidism to Arthurian Legend*, Sterling Publishing Co., NY, 1990

Sjoestedt, Marie-Louise, *Gods and Heroes of the Celts*, Turtle Island Foundation, Berkeley, 1982

Skelton, Robin and Margaret Blackwood, *Earth, Air, Fire and Water: Pre Christian and Pagan Elements in British Songs, Rhymes and Ballads*, Arkana, London, 1990

Squire, Charles, *Celtic Myth and Legend*, New Castle Publishing, London, 1975

Stewart, Robert J., *Celtic Gods and Goddesses*, Blanford, London, 1990

Toulson, Shirley, *The Celtic Year, A Month by Month Celebration of Festivals and Sites*, Element Books, Rockport, MA, 1993

Vendryes, Joseph, *Choix d'Etudes Linguistiques et Celtiques*, C. Klincksieck, Paris, 1952

Vendryes, Joseph, *Lexique Etymologique de L'Irlandais Ancient,Vol. 25*. Dublin Institute for Advanced Studies, Dublin 1959

Webster, Graham, *The British Celts and their Gods Under Rome*, B.T. Batsford Ltd., London, 1986

Williamson, Robin, *The Wise and Foolish Tongue*, Chronicle Books, San Francisco, 1991

Wood-Martin, W.G., *Traces of the Elder Faiths of Ireland: A Folklore*

Sketch: A Handbook of Irish Pre-Christian Traditions, Longmans, Green and Co, London, 1902 2 Vols.

Endnotes

1. These are migrant people who live in their cars.
2. Caer Abiri is Avebury.
3. The Celtic festival generally celebrated February 1-2.
4. She now lives in that country cottage in Wales after leaving California in 2007.
5. Note from the author – I was one of those people – Ellen.
6. Note from the author – because of his giant 'club' of course – Ellen.
7. *Imbolc, Beltaine, Lughnasad* and *Samhain*.
8. Land, Sea, and Sky.
9. *Popular Romances of the West of England* by Robert Hunt.
10. *Stonehenge: An Ancient Masonic Temple* by A. Herner.
11. Where the Summer King and the Winter King do battle at alternate seasons.
12. Mircea Eliade was a historian of religions.
13. Thornapple or *Datura stramonium* is a dangerous and possibly deadly hallucinogen and should be used with extreme caution. Please consult an herbalist before experimenting with it.
14. The Gorsedd of Caer Abiri.
15. Jack Chick is an American publisher of evangelical Christian comic books.
16. Klingons are characters in Star Trek.
17. This was more applicable to the 1990s than the second decade of the 21st century, though the 'Satanic Panic' literature, stories and purported victims are still with us.
18. Filksongs are pastiches of folksongs.
19. English translations are often published under the title *The Gallic Wars*.
20. Entitled *The Druids*.
21. Odawa, Ojibwa and Algonquin word for indigenous peoples

of North America, 'First Nations' also 'Beings Made Out of Nothing', or 'Spontaneous Beings', created by divine breath.

22. Aryans or 'free people'.
23. A festival in Western New York.
24. A festival in Massachusetts.
25. Sacred ritual space, holy ground.
26. Tribe.

MOON

BOOKS

Moon Books invites you to begin or deepen your encounter with
Paganism, in all its rich, creative, flourishing forms.